RODALE'S
SUCCESSFUL ORGANIC GARDENING™
TREES, SHRUBS AND VINES

RODALE'S
SUCCESSFUL ORGANIC GARDENING™
TREES, SHRUBS AND VINES

TEXT BY BONNIE LEE APPLETON

PLANT BY PLANT GUIDE BY ALFRED F. SCHEIDER

Rodale Press, Emmaus, Pennsylvania

Our Mission

We publish books that empower people's lives.

RODALE BOOKS

Copyright © 1993 by Weldon Russell Pty Ltd

If you have any questions or comments concerning this book, please write:

Rodale Press
Book Readers' Service
33 East Minor Street
Emmaus, PA 18098

Library of Congress Cataloging-in-Publication Data

Appleton, Bonnie Lee.
    Rodale's successful organic gardening : trees, shrubs, and vines / text by Bonnie Lee Appleton ; plant-by-plant guide by Alfred F. Scheider.
        p.   cm. — (Rodale's successful organic gardening)
    Includes index.
    ISBN 0–87596–561–X hardcover — ISBN 0–87596–562–8 paperback
    1. Ornamental woody plants. 2. Landscape gardening 3. Organic gardening. I. Rodale Press. II. Title.
    II. Title. III. Series.
    SB435.A726 1993
    635.9'7684—dc20   93–7310
                                                                    CIP

Printed by Tien Wah Press in Singapore on acid-free paper ∞

Rodale Press Staff:
    Executive Editor: Margaret Lydic Balitas
    Senior Editor: Barbara W. Ellis
    Editors: Nancy J. Ondra, Sally Roth, and Ellen Phillips
    Copy Editor: Carolyn R. Mandarano

Produced for Rodale Press by Weldon Russell Pty Ltd
107 Union Street, North Sydney NSW 2060, Australia
a member of the Weldon International Group of Companies

    Publisher: Elaine Russell
    Publishing Manager: Susan Hurley
    Senior Editor: Ariana Klepac
    Editor: Margaret Whiskin
    Editorial Assistant: Libby Frederico
    Horticultural Consultant: Cheryl Maddocks
    Copy Editor: Kirsten John
    Designer: Rowena Sheppard
    Picture Researcher: Anne Nicol
    Photographers: John Callanan, David Wallace
    Illustrators: Barbara Rodanska, Jan Smith
    Macintosh Layout Artist: Edwina Ryan
    Indexer: Michael Wyatt
    Production Manager: Dianne Leddy

A KEVIN WELDON PRODUCTION

Distributed in the book trade by St. Martin's Press

2 4 6 8 10 9 7 5 3 1 hardcover
2 4 6 8 10 9 7 5 3 1 paperback

Opposite: *Prunus* 'Tai Haku'
Half title: *Bougainvillea glabra*
Opposite title page: *Cotinus coggygria* 'Flame'
Title page: *Campsis radicans*
Opposite contents: *Platanus* x *acerifolia*
Contents page: *Magnolia grandiflora*
Back cover: *Liquidambar styraciflua* (top), *Calycanthus floridus* (middle), *Wisteria floribunda* (bottom)

CONTENTS

INTRODUCTION

Information polls tell us that the number one leisure-time activity in the United States and in many other countries around the world is gardening. It's no wonder! Gardeners know that gardening is satisfying and fun. An inviting landscape makes your living space bigger, drawing you and your family out from the house for playing or entertaining or just relaxing.

Trees, shrubs, and vines are a long-term investment in beauty, comfort, and even property value. Studies have shown that a well-designed and maintained landscape adds 5 to 20 percent or more to the value of your house. Houses that are landscaped attractively sell faster and for a higher price than those that are bare or that have unappealing landscaping.

There are many other reasons to incorporate a wide variety of trees, shrubs, and vines into your landscape. They define your outdoor rooms—separating the flower garden from the play area and from the vegetable garden, for instance—and make those outdoor rooms a pleasant place to be by buffering wind and creating shade. Evergreen trees or shrubs hide unsightly views—like your neighbor's tarpaulin-wrapped boat—year-round. Hedges offer privacy from the street and passersby, as well as muffling the noise and the smell of traffic.

Not only are these plants useful, they're beautiful, too. The white flowers of a dogwood (*Cornus* spp.) in April, the fragrance of just-picked lilacs, and the brilliant red fall color of a Virginia creeper (*Parthenocissus quinquefolia*) scrambling over wood siding are just a few of the delightful features these plants have to offer.

Whatever effects you're looking for, a tree, shrub, or vine can provide them. Nonflowering evergreens like boxwood (*Buxus* spp.) and yews (*Taxus* spp.) can provide a quiet or formal touch or accent the colors of flowers planted in front of them. Plants with winter interest, such as dangling crab apples, red holly berries, brightly colored stems, or unusual peeling bark, liven up the barren landscape, giving you good reason to stroll through the garden while it's sleeping.

Trees, shrubs, and vines are relatively permanent—much longer-lived than the annual flowers and vegetables you replant each year and even more enduring than your perennials. But don't expect your landscape to look the same forever. Your plants will grow and die, constantly altering the environment around your house and the appearance of your yard. This changeable quality is another part of the special charm of these plants. Every year will bring something new—perhaps more flowers or more shade—that you can enjoy.

Choosing specific plants for your landscape is a satisfying job that combines your needs and wants with those of your plants. The right plant in the right place is the key to a healthy, easy-care landscape. Sound organic practices keep your plants thriving, and mulch and other preventive methods help head off problems with insects and diseases. *Rodale's Successful Organic Gardening: Trees, Shrubs, and Vines* will be your guide to identifying the conditions you have available, choosing the appropriate plants, and providing the care they need to maintain a healthy, beautiful landscape.

Opposite: Some gardeners think of trees, shrubs, and vines only as backgrounds for colorful garden flowers. But keep in mind that many woody plants, like this camellia (*Camellia japonica*), have beautiful blooms of their own.

HOW TO USE THIS BOOK

Mature trees, shrubs, and vines provide an asset to your home that is hard to measure. They add undeniable dollar value, but they also add a sense of permanence and beauty. Understanding the conditions your garden has to offer and selecting plants that are well adapted to those conditions are vital to creating a landscape that will look good for years to come. *Rodale's Successful Organic Gardening: Trees, Shrubs, and Vines* will help you through the process of planning, planting, and maintaining a beautiful, functional landscape.

Begin with "Understanding Your Garden," starting on page 12, to get acquainted with the all-important factors of soil, climate, topography, and exposure. Learn to look at your home grounds with a critical eye, assessing the soil, watching how the sun crosses your property, and noting where the wind blows strongest. Even the lay of the land affects the plants that grow there. This chapter will help you understand how these basic factors interact to create the unique environment in which you live.

Use "Landscaping with Trees, Shrubs, and Vines," starting on page 20, to help you with the design process, whether you're creating a new landscape or renovating an existing one. The time you spend planning—*before* you get out your shovel—is worth it. Trees, shrubs, and vines are fairly permanent features, so it makes sense to plan their positions carefully. This chapter will get you thinking about what you need from these plants and why certain types are better than others for specific uses.

Whether you mail-order trees and shrubs or pick out plants at the garden center, how do you know if you're buying healthy, vigorous stock? You'll find out what to look for in "Choosing Your Plants," starting on page 34. You'll also find out about the four major ways plants are

"packaged"—bareroot, balled-and-burlapped, containerized, and container-grown—and how to decide which type will meet your needs.

Once you've designed your landscape and selected appropriate trees, shrubs, and vines, you'll want to get them off to a good start. Follow the advice in "Planting Your Landscape," starting on page 42, to ease the trauma of transplanting and to get your new plants growing well right from the beginning. A little extra attention to preparing the planting bed will help your new plants settle in quickly and begin new growth.

After you've planted your landscape, keep your plantings healthy and attractive by using the information covered in "Care and Maintenance," starting on page 50. Refer to this chapter to learn how to select and apply mulches to reduce watering chores and keep weeds in check. You'll also find out how to recycle kitchen scraps and garden trimmings into nutrient-rich, growth-boosting compost. You'll find instructions on how to determine when your plants need fertilizer and the best materials to use. Preventing and controlling pest and disease problems is another vital part of good maintenance that you'll learn about in this chapter.

Your trees, shrubs, and vines are the dynamic part of your home—always growing and changing—and that's why a good understanding of plant pruning is important. If you've selected the right plant for the right place, your pruning chores will be minimal. But all too often the plants have been allowed to overgrow the landscape. Then in the rush to bring their size back under control, their natural beauty is destroyed by improper pruning. This chapter's pruning section will help you prune your trees, shrubs, and vines the right way—to emphasize the natural structure of the plants and direct their growth.

If you'd like to increase the number of plants you have or if you want to save some money when starting a new landscape, try experimenting with different propagation techniques. In "Propagating Trees, Shrubs, and Vines," starting on page 70, you'll learn how to decide whether to propagate from seeds or cuttings or whether special forms of propagation such as layering and grafting would be more successful.

Plant by Plant Guide

With the many hundreds of species of trees, shrubs, and vines available for your use, how do you know which will grow best and fill the landscape you've designed? Check out the "Plant by Plant Guide," starting on page 78. For easier reference, the guide is subdivided into three different sections: one each for trees, shrubs, and vines. Within these sections, the individual plant entries are arranged alphabetically by botanical name. If you only know a certain plant by its common name, you can find its botanical name by looking up the common name in the index.

This section covers more than 125 of the best trees, shrubs, and vines for home landscapes. Use it to compare and select plants that meet your needs in shape and size as well as in cultural and maintenance requirements. The diagram below helps explain what to look for on these practical pages.

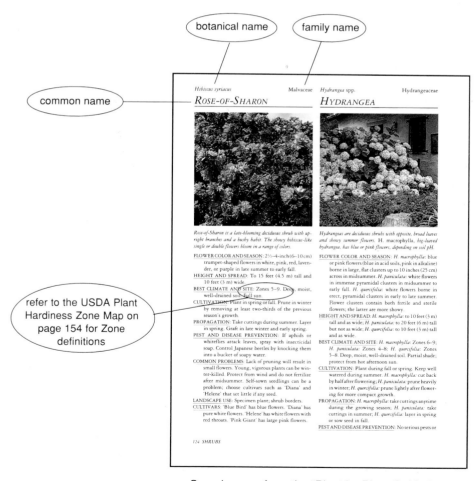

Sample page from the "Plant by Plant Guide."

UNDERSTANDING YOUR GARDEN

The key to success with trees, shrubs, and vines is putting the right plant in the right place— a place where the soil, sun, moisture, and temperature conditions match the growing requirements of the plant you've selected. If you mismatch your plants and environment, your mistake will often be evident very quickly. A camellia (*Camellia* spp.) planted in Massachusetts, for instance, quickly becomes a casualty of the first cold winter. A staghorn sumac (*Rhus typhina*) planted in waterlogged soil rapidly shows signs of distress. Even subtle influences can affect your plants. For example, the heat reflected from a white or light-colored wall can burn the foliage of trees and shrubs in the summer—and even broad-leaved evergreens in the winter. That's why it's a good idea to begin any garden plan with an in-depth look at your surroundings.

This chapter will give you the foundation for choosing plants wisely, and it will explain just what you need to look for to analyze your site and environment. Taking a close look at your soil, to gauge its texture and type, is a good place to start any site analysis. You'll also learn how climate can vary, even from one side of your yard to the other, and discover how topography affects the drainage of water and air. Finally, you'll discover how important the shifting patterns of sun and shade are to your plants.

Observations about plants that thrive in your yard will also help you learn about the soil, the climate, and the land. Determining the cultural requirements of plants that thrive naturally in your yard will give you good clues to the conditions that exist there and what other plants might be good choices. For example, if you have a spot in your yard where ferns and grasses stay lush and green even in the height of summer, there's a good chance that it has wet soil. Such a site might be ideal for a moisture-loving shrub such as summer-sweet (*Clethra alnifolia*).

One way to get good ideas about what plants grow well is to talk to your neighbors, especially those with the best gardens. Learn about the plants they are growing, and select some favorites that you'd like to try. Be sure to ask about the care and conditions the plants require to grow well, such as pruning, fertilizing, or other special cultural needs. Also ask about any diseases or insects that are problematic. That way, you can eliminate plants that require more care to look their best than you'd like to provide.

Once you've spent some time learning about your site, you'll be well on your way to selecting plants that are compatible with the conditions your garden has to offer. Plants that are growing in conditions that suit them will be more vigorous and have fewer problems than ones that must struggle to survive inappropriate conditions. Azaleas growing in a hot, sun-baked site, for instance, will never grow as well as ones planted in a spot with moist organic soil and light shade. That's why matching plant to site is the key to a successful and trouble-free garden plan.

Opposite: If you're looking for a large tree to add shade to your yard, consider a sugar maple (*Acer saccharum*). It will thrive on a sunny site with evenly moist (but not waterlogged) soil that is slightly acid.

A Soil Primer

Healthy soil is more than just the right mix of sand, clay, and silt. It's a balance of fine rock particles, air, water, and the all-important organic material that nourishes a thriving community of billions of macro- and microorganisms—the worms, bacteria, and other tiny soil animals that increase fertility, improve aeration, and protect against disease. Before you start planting anything, take some time to learn about your soil's characteristics. Once you understand what soil conditions you have available, you can choose the plants that are best adapted to your site.

Soil Texture

To really learn about your soil, you need to get your hands dirty. Start by taking a handful of loose soil, a few days after a rain, and rubbing some of it between your thumb and finger to gauge the texture. Soil texture refers to the percentages of sand, silt, and clay that make up the solid, inorganic part of your soil. Clayey soil feels slippery, sandy soil feels gritty, and silty soil feels like moist talcum powder.

Sandy soil (left) loses water and nutrients quickly; clayey soil (right) drains slowly but holds more nutrients.

Loamy soil has a balance of sand, silt, and clay particles. It is usually well drained and often quite fertile.

Contrary to popular belief, woody plants don't have long, deep taproots. Instead, trees, shrubs, and vines tend to produce extensive networks of fibrous roots, which gather nutrients and water from upper soil layers.

Squeeze the rest of the soil into a ball, then open your hand and touch the ball with a finger. If the soil crumbles very easily, the texture is light. If it takes a little pressure to make the ball crumble, the texture is well balanced. If the ball holds its shape, or if you can even roll it into a fat ribbon, your soil is heavy in clay.

Heavy soils—those high in fine clay particles—often hold too much water during heavy rains, or form surface crusts when they dry out during droughts. They are slow to drain, and can be prone to waterlogging. The roots of many plants suffocate or rot in wet soils because they can't take up the oxygen they need for growth. Earthworms and soil microorganisms also need air in the soil in order to live.

Light soils, those with a high percentage of sand, drain too quickly and hold too little water, and they lose nutrients quite rapidly. If it seems like your soil is always dry, a high percentage of sand is often the reason.

For most plants, the best type of soil is a loam. Loamy soils have a desirable blend of sand, silt, and clay. They drain moderately quickly, yet hold water without drying out too fast.

Soil Structure

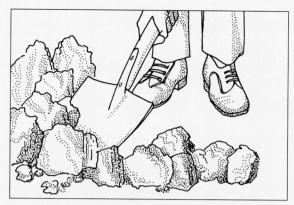

Clayey soils tend to have a tight, blocky structure. They are often hard to dig, forming hard clods.

Soils with a loose, granular structure are easy to dig. They also provide ideal conditions for good root growth.

Soil Structure

Soil structure refers to the way in which the sand, silt, and clay particles stick together, forming small clumps with pore spaces between them. Large pore spaces are usually filled with air, while small pore spaces tend to be filled with water. A soil with too many small pores drains poorly or becomes waterlogged and anaerobic (lacking oxygen). Many of the billions of microorganisms in the soil require oxygen to live, and so do plant roots. Soil with good, crumbly structure has a balanced mix of large and small pores between the solid particles.

Living with "Problem" Soils

There are some less-than-ideal soil characteristics you more or less have to live with. Soil texture, for instance, is very difficult to change. Adding a few bags of sand to a clayey soil won't do much to improve drainage. You may even make the situation worse, especially if you concentrate the sand in individual planting holes. You would have to add tons of sand—more than would be cost-effective—to make a significant drainage change. For ideas on how you can deal with poorly drained soil, see "Dealing with Problem Soils" on page 46.

You *can* improve less-than-ideal soil structure by following one basic rule: Add organic matter. Organic matter lightens a heavy soil by breaking up the clay, and it improves the water retention of sandy soils. Compost, aged manure, grass clippings, and chopped leaves will improve the soil structure and give a boost to the organisms that enrich the soil. Earthworm and micro-organism activities improve soil aeration and convert soil organic matter into forms your plants can use. For more information on adding organic matter to your soil, see "Making and Using Compost" on page 52.

Select Carefully for Success

If your landscape includes areas of water-logged clay, fast-draining sand, or other less-than-ideal soils, the easiest solution is to select trees, shrubs, and vines that are naturally suited to those conditions. Many attractive species are available for such areas. Red maple (*Acer rubrum*), for example, will do well in most average garden soils. But, being a native of swamps, this tree is also very tolerant of wet feet. If the soil in your neighbors' yards is similar to yours, take a look at the plants that are thriving for them—chances are that these plants will grow well for you, too.

Know Your Climate

To choose plants wisely, you have to know your climate. Extremes of weather such as an early frost, a violent ice storm, or an unexpected summer drought can certainly affect the trees, shrubs, and vines in your landscape. But it's the long-term picture that determines what you will and won't be able to grow.

Macro-, Micro-, and Local Climates

The same factors that comprise your weather on a day-to-day basis—temperature, precipitation, humidity, wind, and even atmospheric pressure— determine the type of climate in your area. The *macroclimate* describes the general climate of a large area (state, province, or region) in which you live. It's the average annual minimum temperature of your macroclimate that most limits what plants you can grow. To find out your average annual minimum temperature, see the USDA Plant Hardiness Zone Map on page 154.

Local climate refers to the climate of a smaller region. It may be the climate of the city in which you live, or a certain part of the land, such as a valley between two mountain ranges. Local climate is much more specific than macroclimate, and it has a strong influence upon the trees, shrubs, and vines you choose.

Your property has only one macroclimate and one local climate, but it has many *microclimates.* A site on the shady northeast side of your property, where the microclimate tends to be cooler and more humid, may be perfect for evergreen azaleas; those same azaleas may be stressed or even die on a hotter and drier southwest site. Macroclimate and local climate affect your overall plant selections, while microclimates influence where you locate the plants in your landscape.

The better you understand your climate, the easier it

Wind and Your Garden

Wind can cause different types of problems for your trees, shrubs, and vines. Strong winds blowing over the leaves of broad-leaved evergreen trees and shrubs can dry the leaves out, causing winter burn and summer scorch. Wind can rip the thin leaves of deciduous trees, shrubs, and vines to pieces or blow hail so fiercely that it will break plant stems.

You can moderate wind problems somewhat by locating susceptible plants away from prevailing winds, by planting them behind protective structures, or by building or planting wind screens. Do allow some air circulation around your trees, shrubs, and vines, however, because air movement encourages sturdier growth and lessens insect and disease problems.

will be for you to select plants that will thrive without coddling. You can't do much to change the weather, so design your landscape to include the trees, shrubs, and vines that are adapted to your particular conditions.

Precipitation Patterns

Along with average low and high temperatures, the amount of precipitation and humidity in your area will also limit some of your plant selections. Dwindling water supplies and plain common sense make it a good idea to select plants that won't make you a slave to the hose. On the other hand, if your area averages 40 inches (100 cm) of rainfall each year and has high summer humidity, then you'd want to avoid desert-adapted plants that naturally grow in areas with extremely limited rainfall and very dry air.

Even in warm climates, cold-sensitive plants—like this camellia—can still be damaged by unexpected frosts.

A sheltered spot, protected by walls and hedges, can provide a warmer microclimate for cold-tender plants.

Sun or Shade

Light is essential for plant growth, but different trees, shrubs, and vines require different light levels. As you design your landscape plan, make note of what parts of your property are sunny or shady, and at what times of day. On what side of your property does the sun rise or set? Is your land open, or surrounded by woods? Does a neighbor's garage cast a shadow over part of your landscape in the afternoons? Select plants that thrive in the amount of light your landscape provides.

Comparing Exposures

In the Northern Hemisphere, the north side of a property will be the shady side, while the south side, unless blocked by buildings or trees, will generally be the full-sun side. If you select plants needing partial shade, locate them on an eastern exposure, which will get morning sun and afternoon shade. A western exposure will also give partial shade, but for part of the afternoon the intensity of the sun may damage sensitive plants.

How Much Sun Do They Need?

Many trees, shrubs, and vines will thrive on a sunny site. As a general rule, plant deciduous shrubs in full sun, especially if grown for flowers; even partial shade may significantly reduce flowering. Most evergreen trees

Azaleas grow and flower well in the dappled shade cast by taller deciduous trees.

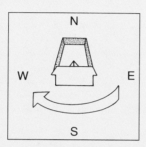

North-facing yards tend to be cool and shady year-round.

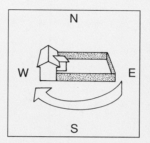

East-facing yards get cool morning sun and afternoon shade.

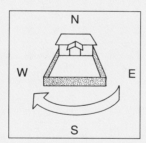

South-facing yards tend to be warm and sunny throughout the day.

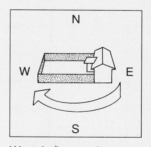

West-facing yards get morning shade and hot afternoon sun.

and most large shade trees also prefer full sun. Other sun-lovers include trees or shrubs with red or purple leaves. Species and cultivars such as red- and purple-leaved Japanese maples (*Acer palmatum*), purple-leaved plum (*Prunus cerasifera* 'Atropurpurea'), 'Crimson King' Norway maple (*Acer platanoides* 'Crimson King'), and 'Crimson Pygmy' barberry (*Berberis thunbergii* var. *atropurpurea* 'Crimson Pygmy') will begin to produce greener leaves when grown in shade.

Some shrubs and small flowering trees are understory plants. In their natural habitat, they make up the middle to upper layers of the forest, growing in the shade of larger trees. These plants, which include red-buds (*Cercis* spp.), flowering dogwoods (*Cornus florida*), and azaleas (*Rhododendron* spp.), will tolerate full sun, but they may show signs of stress such as increased susceptibility to insect and disease problems. They are healthier, though they may flower less, when planted in full or partial shade.

A good selection of attractive species prefer partial to full shade. Many broad-leaved evergreen shrubs, including most that have showy flowers, such as azaleas and rhododendrons (*Rhododendron* spp.), camellias (*Camellia* spp.), and mountain laurels (*Kalmia latifolia*), thrive in these conditions. Shade-tolerant vines include ivies (*Hedera* spp.) and climbing hydrangea (*Hydrangea anomala* subsp. *petiolaris*).

Plants in full sun often get the best fall color, like the fiery red of this Japanese maple (*Acer palmatum*).

The Ups and Downs of Topography

The way your land is shaped and the way the surrounding area is shaped—flat coastal or prairie plain, rolling hills, or mountains and valleys—has a great influence on climate and water drainage. (Mountains, for instance, can cause increased rainfall on one side and create a dry "rain shadow" on the other.) The shape of the land is called its topography. The topography of the general area and the topography of your property influence the landscape plan you design and the plants you select.

The Influence of Topography

If you live in a relatively flat, exposed area, you may need to deal with soil erosion—not by water, but by wind, which blows strongly across level, open areas. You may also find you have drainage problems after heavy rains, when the level land fails to channel away excess water. If you're near a body of water, you may have problems with flooding.

If you live in a hilly or mountainous area, your local climate depends on your particular location on the hill. Cold air settles in the lowest areas. So if you live near the top, cold air will drain downward, away from you. If you live at the bottom of a hill or in a mountain valley, however, that same cold air will settle in your area, affecting your plants. Many early-flowering trees, such as ornamental cherries and peaches, may be damaged by late-spring frosts if you plant in low areas. Plant them at higher elevations to minimize damage, or choose species and cultivars that flower later in the season.

The slope of your property is also important for water drainage. Water on a slope drains to the bottom; the

On poorly drained flat sites, a raised bed can provide ideal conditions for a wide range of colorful plants.

steeper the slope, the faster the drainage. Heavy rains can cause soil erosion on slopes and waterlogging or standing puddles at the bottom of the hill. Keep these effects in mind, and choose trees, shrubs, and vines that are tolerant of such conditions. A spreading plant that roots along its branches, such as blue rug creeping juniper (*Juniperus horizontalis* 'Wiltonii', also sold as *J. horizontalis* 'Blue Rug'), is much more suitable for an erosion-prone slope than a planting of more upright species, such as hollies. A thirsty pussy willow (*Salix discolor*) may be a good choice for the bottom of a slope, where water collects.

Dealing with Topography

As you develop your home landscape, try to work with the natural contours of your land instead of making

Cover small slopes with low-growing plants like heaths, heathers, and dwarf conifers for easy maintenance.

On steep or long slopes, a combination of terraces and mixed plantings is an attractive and effective solution.

drastic changes. Changing the grade of your landscape can be expensive. Grade changes also alter drainage patterns and disturb the layers of soil, burying topsoil and exposing the less-fertile subsoil. Modify your topography only as a last resort.

Understanding Slope Slope is measured by the amount of rise in 100 feet (30 m) of horizontal distance. A slope of 0 to 5 percent (0 to 5-foot [0 to 1.5 m] grade vertical change per 100 feet [30 m]) is considered flat land. A slope of 1 to 2 percent will generally drain lawn areas adequately, but you may need to increase the slope to 2 to 4 percent to drain water away from buildings. (The heavier your soil, the greater the slope needed for good drainage.) A slope exceeding 10 percent is considered a steep slope.

Considering Topography in Design Where possible, take advantage of your property's natural topography as you plan the layout of your yard. Flat sites are ideal for outdoor entertaining and play areas, as well as for vegetable growing and formal flower gardens.

Slopes can be more difficult to plant and maintain, but they can provide a great deal of garden interest as well. Terrace gentle slopes to provide more planting area, or plant them with a mixture of trees, shrubs, and groundcovers to hold the soil and prevent erosion. Steep slopes are difficult to plant and dangerous to navigate. If you have steep slopes, consider leaving them in the existing vegetation as a "wild garden."

Flat and sloping sites offer a wealth of planting opportunities. Plan areas for outdoor activities, like dining or playing, on flat sites. On slopes, use terraced planting beds or a mix of shrubs and groundcovers to stop soil erosion.

Regrading Sometimes terracing or regrading is necessary to make land usable. Consult professionals such as landscape architects, engineers, or surveyors if extensive grading is necessary. If you do have regrading done on your property, make sure you keep the topsoil separate from the subsoil. When you're ready to finish the job, use the reserved topsoil as the top layer—it's much better soil for your plants.

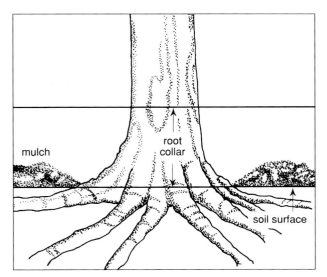

During regrading, avoid piling soil around the root collar of your tree. Keep mulch a few inches away, too.

Protecting Trees During Regrading

If you plan to have regrading done on your property, keep in mind that changing the soil level around a tree can severely damage it. If you add soil over its roots, they may die due to reduced soil oxygen or due to excess water held against them. If you remove soil, you'll actually remove much of your tree's roots, because most of the small feeder roots are within the top foot of soil. Removing roots prevents your tree from absorbing enough water and nutrients for growth and may hinder its ability to hold itself upright. One strong windstorm can easily topple a tree with damaged roots.

If you must grade around trees, build "wells" around your trees large enough to protect their roots. Use brightly colored construction tape to mark off a protected area around your trees, at least to the drip line, to keep heavy equipment from compacting or damaging roots and soil.

LANDSCAPING WITH TREES, SHRUBS, AND VINES

The design of your landscape—the inviting arrangement of trees and shrubs that draws the eye, or the scrambling clematis vine on the mailbox—is just as personal as the decorating you do inside your house. An attractive landscape, with elements combined in a way that works for function as well as eye appeal, is a pleasure every day.

The beauty of your carefully chosen plants has a practical side, too: It boosts the real estate value of your house. A nicely landscaped home will sell more quickly and for more money than an equivalent house with unattractive surroundings. Your landscape can be hardworking as well as appealing, too. Trees, shrubs, and vines can cool your house and buffer winds, reducing energy costs.

In this chapter, you'll learn all about the design process—from making a plan to using trees, shrubs, and vines effectively in your landscape. Start by taking a look around your property and deciding which areas are public or private and which are service areas. You'll have different design needs and goals for each of these areas. The public area in front of your house (and on the side if you live on a corner) is a chance for you to share your personal expression with passersby. This is the part that visitors see first, so spend some extra time making it appealing. Design the plantings to enhance the appearance of your house, and use materials and designs that complement its architecture.

The private areas, usually the side yard and backyard, are where you do your outdoor living. These areas are where you entertain guests and relax and enjoy your yard. Consider using trees, shrubs, and vines to separate or screen the private areas from the public ones.

The service areas of your landscape are those where you store your trash containers, park your boat or recreational vehicle, or hang the laundry out to dry. Trees and shrubs effectively screen these areas from view. Your landscape plan will also include the "hardscape," meaning paved areas, walks, decks, patios, fences, and other permanent structures.

Try to start thinking of your landscape as a series of rooms. Larger trees and sky suggest your outdoor ceilings; plantings of small trees or shrubs or arbors of vines are the walls; and the lawn grass, bark mulch, or decking under your feet is the floor.

Just like the rooms in your house, your outdoor rooms have their own functions: the storage room, where trash cans are kept; the playroom, where there's a flat stretch of lawn for romping. Thinking of your landscape in this way makes it easier to see where changes are needed. If your tomatoes get knocked over by the family dog who's strayed from the play area, for example, you'll need to add a "wall" between the playroom and the vegetable garden.

A well-developed plan will save you time and money. Think about how your family uses the landscape before you take shovel in hand. It's much easier to correct landscape mistakes on paper than after planting.

Opposite: Trees, shrubs, and vines don't have to be dull and boring! Choose a variety of flowering and fruiting species, and mix them with perennials and groundcovers for a season-long show.

Planning Your Landscape

Many first-time landscapers are so eager to begin planting that they give little time or thought to planning. It's tempting to try for instant results, but the time you take now to plan your design will pay off in the end. A landscape that's planted without much forethought may end up looking beautiful, but it's far more likely that you'll be moving plants around for years to come, never reaching a satisfactory design.

A tight budget is an even better reason to start with a plan. By investing in trees, shrubs, and vines at the beginning, you can establish the framework of your plan and give these slow-growing plants a head start while you fill in the gaps later.

For a formal look, include elements like straight paths, symmetrical plantings, and tightly clipped edgings.

Consider Family Needs and Wants

Make a family discussion the first step in the planning process. As each member lists needs and wants, keep the outdoor rooms concept in mind, and look for ways that an area can be used for more than one activity. With a little forethought, a single shady area could be used for wildflower gardening, reading, writing letters, and chatting with friends, for example. Remember that as the family changes, your needs and the landscape may also change. You may want to plan on transforming a sandbox into a planting bed, for example, as your children grow.

If children will use the yard, plan for wide paths, durable plantings, and easily accessible play areas.

Carefully chosen low-growing plants can provide a neat-looking foundation planting.

Rooms with a View

As you make your property map, jot down notes that describe the views out your windows and onto adjoining properties. Make notes about items you want to screen (a neighbor's messy yard, a noisy street) or accent (a pretty view of water or woods). Also check for any utility easements, required setbacks for fences, and other restrictions that will in-fluence your design. Taking special note of these features will help you incorporate them into your plan.

Without regular pruning, fast-growing species can quickly smother your house and block your paths and windows.

Informal designs include mixed plantings, curved edges, and winding paths.

Mapping the Landscape

By this time, you have a good idea of the elements you want to include in your landscape plan. Now it's time to put it on paper.

First, measure your property. A long measuring tape and a helper make the job easier. Draw the outline of your property on graph paper, using as large a scale as possible (1 inch = 10 or 20 feet [2.5 cm = 3 or 6 m]) to allow plenty of space for recording details. Mark the compass points on your map.

Next, measure the exterior of your house, locate it on your map, and draw it to scale. Within the outline of your house, label all first-floor rooms. Then mark the location of all first-floor windows, doors, and other features such as air conditioners, roof overhangs, faucets, downspouts, and utility boxes.

Draw in any existing hardscape elements, such as

A Picture Is Worth a Thousand Words

A camera is a great way to take "notes" about your landscape, and photos of your garden can be an invaluable aid in making your design. Take photos of views you'd like to accent or screen, trees or other features you'd like to highlight, or other elements you want to keep in mind as you draw your plan. Photos give a three-dimensional view to your flat drawing, and they'll refresh your memory when you sit down to draw your plan.

driveways, sidewalks, fences, and patios. Mark the location of both above- and below-ground utilities, water lines, and septic tanks. On your plan, or on a tracing-paper overlay, mark slopes, prevailing wind directions, patterns of sun and shade, and wet areas. Also draw any existing plants on the plan at their present size.

The New Design

Use your scale drawing as the base map for your design. Tape tracing-paper overlays on top of it, and mark the general areas—public, service, and private—of your landscape. Then sketch the series of outdoor rooms you envisioned into the design, arranging and rearranging until you have a plan that suits you.

When your overlay design feels right, look at the existing plants and hardscape items on your drawing, and consider where you need to make changes or additions. The next step is to begin selecting plants for each area you've designed.

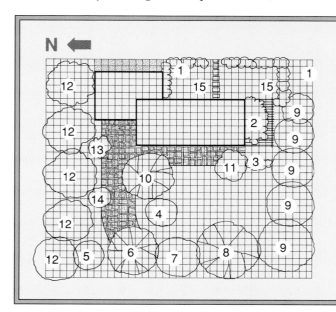

Drawing a Plan

Draw your existing yard on graph paper. Experiment with different arrangements of plants, then create a numbered planting list.

1. *Buxus microphylla* hedge; 2. Wisteria on a pergola; 3. Climbing rose on arch; 4. *Philadephus coronarius*; 5. *Kolkwitzia amabilis* 6. *Kerria japonica*; 7. *Deutzia scabra*; 8. *Buddleia davidii*; 9. *Betula pendula* 'Gracilis'; 10. *Acer palmatum*; 11. *Syringa vulgaris*; 12. *Camellia sasanqua*; 13. *Hydrangea paniculata*; 14. *Hydrangea macrophylla*; 15. Lawn

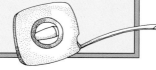

Matching Plants to Sites

Start the plant selection process by thinking about the broad ideas that guided your design. What do you want your design to do, and what types of plants will accomplish your goals? Instead of picking specific plants right away, think first about the type of plant you need—perhaps a fast-growing tree for shade or an evergreen shrub for privacy. From the hundreds of possibilities, keep narrowing down the list until you've picked the best specific plant for each location and function. You'll learn more about picking specific species in "Choosing Your Plants" on page 34; for now, stick to looking for general types of plants with characteristics that appeal to you.

Examine the Possibilities

Growing conditions determine which plants will thrive in your landscape. Wet, poorly drained soil requires different plant choices than dry ground. An exposed area, vulnerable to winter winds, calls for tough plants that can weather the site. Make sure the plants you choose will be at home in the location where you plant them.

A common mistake is to start with a list of specific plants that you absolutely must use. Of course it's nice to include favorites—if they work well in the design and if they're a good choice for the conditions. But if your soil or climate doesn't match their needs, they won't grow well and ultimately will be a disappointment. Fortunately, plants that fit your design and your site will soon become favorites.

Be sure to consider how much space is available before you select plants. Decide how large your plants can grow—in both height and spread—and whether you want a slow grower or one that matures fast. Check the "Plant by Plant Guide," starting on page 78, for the potential mature size of the plants you have in mind. If your selection will outgrow the site, a dwarf cultivar that retains the characteristics that attracted you may be available; ask at your local nursery.

Look for Added Attractions

When you're considering what trees, shrubs, or vines to plant, keep in mind how you're using them in the design and what characteristics would enhance your yard. Be on the lookout for plants that give your landscape a boost in fall and winter. A change in leaf color or some showy fruit adds interest in fall. Evergreen foliage, an unusual branching pattern, or a tree with unusual bark dresses up a barren winter landscape.

Try to include plants with appeal in more than one season. Evergreens—both broad-leaved ones like rhododendrons and needled ones like pines and spruces—add year-round interest. Crab apples provide spring flowers, followed by brightly colored fruit that persists into the fall and winter. Some summer-flowering shrubs, such as crape myrtles (*Lagerstroemia indica*) and oak-leaved hydrangeas (*Hydrangea quercifolia*), also have interesting bark or branch patterns.

Low-maintenance Plants

Although there's no such thing as no-maintenance plants, there's no reason to be a slave to your yard, either. Choose plants that are resistant to pests and diseases, and look for species without the litter problems of large leaves, messy fruit, and lots of dropped twigs. Pick plants that mature at the size you need, so you won't need to keep pruning them back down to size.

Plants native to your area are often among the most low-maintenance choices because they'll generally thrive without any supplemental watering or fertilizing and are often less susceptible to insect and disease problems. Check out local natural areas to see what plants grow well in your area.

Consider a plant's eventual size when siting it. Large plants like forsythia may block paths without regular pruning.

Trees that have attractive bark, like this river birch (*Betula nigra*), can provide year-round interest.

You may choose to highlight the unusual branching structure of a tree you already have.

Using Trees in the Landscape

The biggest investment in your landscape—in both time and money—is the selection, purchase, and planting of trees. Trees dominate the landscape with their size and their effects on the surroundings. A landscape with trees has psychological benefits, too, by making you feel rested and peaceful.

Landscaping with Trees

By horticultural definition, trees are woody plants with one main stem or trunk, although some, such as river birch (*Betula nigra*) and smoke tree (*Cotinus coggygria*), are often grown in multitrunked clumps. Trees generally have a mature height ranging from 15 to 100 feet (4.5 to 30 m) or more. A small tree is defined as one that generally doesn't exceed 25 to 35 feet (7.5 to 10.5 m) in mature height. A medium-sized tree matures at 50 to 65 feet (15 to 19.5 m), and a large tree matures at 75 to 100 feet (22.5 to 30 m) or taller. Growing conditions, climate, competition with grass and other plants, mechanical or animal damage, and pollution can prevent

a tree from reaching its mature height.

These versatile plants frame views, develop patterns for your landscape, and unify your design. To get the most out of the trees you select, consider the following features and what they can add to your design.

Beauty Trees serve as backdrops for other plants or garden features and as focal points, like large, living sculptures. You can use them to screen unwanted views and give you privacy. Your trees establish the walls and ceilings for your outdoor rooms. You can use them to soften the architecture of your house or to call attention to it.

Climate Control By shading your house, trees keep things cool, reducing energy bills. (Don't plant evergreen trees for summer shade, though; they'll block the sun in winter, preventing passive solar heating of your house.) You can use trees as a windbreak, to intercept and buffer prevailing winds. If winter winds are your bane, needle-leaved evergreens are the best choice for a windbreak. If you live near a seacoast, choose salt-tolerant species to soften the sea winds.

Trees come in a wide range of shapes and sizes. Keep these differences in mind when planning your landscape.

either a tree with a columnar shape or a pyramidal needle-leaved evergreen.

Specimen Trees Specimen trees are showy in some way. They may put on an eye-catching display of flowers in spring, like a flowering crab apple, or blaze with autumn color, like the red maple 'October Glory' (*Acer rubrum* 'October Glory'). Or they may have unusually colored leaves, such as purple smoke tree (*Cotinus coggygria* 'Royal Purple'), or bright berries, such as American mountain ash (*Sorbus americana*).

Specimen trees are valuable as focal points in a winter landscape. Fruits that hang on the branches after the leaves drop, such as the fruits of crab apples, are eye-catching. Trees with attractive winter silhouettes, such as flowering dogwoods, also make good specimen trees.

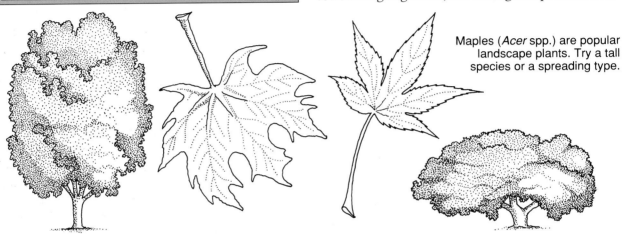

Maples (*Acer* spp.) are popular landscape plants. Try a tall species or a spreading type.

Livability Trees absorb noise and reduce glare, and they purify the air you breathe. Patios or play areas become more usable during hot summers when shaded by trees. Many trees have edible fruits that can feed your family or attract wildlife.

Consider Form and Function

When you select trees for your yard, use your landscape plan to help you decide what shape of tree to select and how each tree will function in the landscape. The arrangement of the branches gives each species of tree a distinctively shaped crown.

Most needle-leaved evergreens, like pines and spruces, tend to have more symmetrical or rigid shapes than deciduous trees, such as oaks or maples. Needle-leaved evergreens often display the familiar conical or pyramidal "Christmas tree" look. Deciduous trees and broad-leaved evergreens can be many shapes, including round, vase-shaped, and columnar.

Trees are often classified according to their intended use—as specimens, shade trees, or street trees. Choose your landscape trees according to their function. For an upright, narrow screen, for example, you might select

Smoke tree (*Cotinus coggygria*) is an attractive specimen plant. Cultivars with purple leaves add extra interest.

Select a specimen tree with multiseasonal interest. A saucer magnolia (*Magnolia* x *soulangiana*) is very showy for a couple of weeks during the spring when in flower, but it fades into the background the rest of the year. A kousa dogwood (*Cornus kousa*), on the other hand, bears showy flowers in spring, raspberry-like red fruits in fall, and attractive peeling bark in winter.

Shade Trees Shade trees may have showy features, but it's their cooling effect that's most important. A tree with a round or vase shape is ideal for use as a shade tree. Decide the location of a new shade tree with care: Make sure the shadow of the tree will shade the area you intend it to.

If you want filtered shade or want to be able to grow grass under your tree, use a tree with small, fine leaves, such as a thornless honey locust (*Gleditsia triacanthos* var. *inermis*), not one with a dense canopy of large, overlapping leaves, such as a Norway maple (*Acer platanoides*).

The prices of trees at your local nursery or garden center won't seem cheap, but think of them as a long-term investment. If you plan for and maintain your trees well, they will repay you by being the longest-lived and often the most maintenance-free plants in your landscape.

Street Trees Street trees are tough species that withstand the difficult growing conditions along the street. They're tolerant of heat and pollution, grow well in poor soils, and can stand drought. Their roots must grow in very limited spaces, and their crowns must fit under overhead utility lines. Street trees have to be neat: Look for trees that don't have messy fruit, falling twigs, or large leaves that can block storm sewers.

In spite of these demands, a number of attractive and adaptable trees are available for roadside planting. Among small trees, consider trident maple (*Acer buergerianum*), thornless cockspur hawthorn (*Crataegus crus-galli* var. *inermis*), or golden-rain tree (*Koelreuteria paniculata*). Suitable medium to large trees include thornless honey locust (*Gleditsia triacanthos* var. *inermis*), Japanese pagoda tree (*Sophora japonica*), and silver linden (*Tilia tomentosa*).

Consider Growth Rates

Trees grow at different rates, ranging from less than 1 foot (30 cm) per year to several feet (about 1 m) per year. Species with a slow-to-medium growth rate, like oaks, generally require less maintenance than fast-growing ones. Fast-growing trees, such as poplars and willows, are often short-lived, surviving only 20 to 30 years, and they also generally have weak wood, which is more susceptible to damage from wind, storms, and pests.

Flowering cherries (*Prunus* spp.) and other spring-blooming trees look great underplanted with colorful bulbs.

Lindens (*Tilia* spp.) can be tough, adaptable street trees. Their yellow fall color is a bonus.

Using Shrubs in the Landscape

Shrubs are hardworking plants in any landscape. They can be used to add a touch of greenery at the foundation of the house, make a thick screen between neighbors, add seasonal color from flowers or fruit, or outline the garden rooms of a landscape design. Even in a well-planted landscape, shrubs sometimes go unnoticed. The glossy, dark green of common boxwood (*Buxus sempervirens*) makes an ideal backdrop for light-colored flowers, but few passersby appreciate the shrub. Instead, their eyes are drawn to the blossoms that the boxwood sets off.

Types of Shrubs

Shrubs are woody plants with multiple stems, ranging from a few inches (centimeters) tall to approximately 15 feet (4.5 m) at maturity. Occasionally an individual shrub is trained to a single tree-like stem, called a standard. And large shrubs are sometimes "limbed up," by removing the lower branches, into small trees.

Like trees, shrubs can be deciduous, evergreen, or semi-evergreen. If all leaves drop each fall, with new leaves each spring through summer, the shrub is deciduous. Deciduous shrubs, including such favorites as roses (*Rosa* spp.) and spireas (*Spiraea* spp.), often have attractive flowers. For heavy flower production, plant them in full sun.

Evergreen shrubs have leaves year-round, though you will notice that each year some of the oldest leaves drop off and are replaced by new leaves. Shrubs with wide, often thick, leaves, such as camellias (*Camellia* spp.) and rhododendrons (*Rhododendron* spp.), are called broad-leaved evergreens. Shrubs with thin, narrow leaves, such as junipers (*Juniperus* spp.) and dwarf mugo pines (*Pinus mugo* var. *mugo*), are classified as needle-leaved evergreens.

A few shrubs are semi-evergreen, holding some of their leaves well into winter. Glossy abelia (*Abelia* x *grandiflora*), for example, is evergreen in the South and semi-evergreen farther north.

Some shrub genera include both deciduous and evergreen species. Hollies (*Ilex* spp.) are a good example. When the deciduous hollies, possum haw (*I. decidua*) and winterberry (*I. verticillata*), drop their leaves in the fall, large clusters of bright red berries are revealed. Their berry display is generally much showier than that of many of the evergreen hollies, such as Chinese holly (*I. cornuta*) and English holly (*I. aquifolium*), whose berries are often hidden by their leaves. Other shrub genera with both deciduous and evergreen species include viburnums (*Viburnum* spp.), rhododendrons and azaleas (*Rhododendron* spp.), and barberries (*Berberis* spp.).

Choosing and Using Shrubs

There are many ways to use shrubs creatively in your landscape. You can use them to define the border of your property, hide an exposed foundation on your house, or block an unwanted view. These useful plants can create privacy, show people where to walk, or just provide an attractive show throughout the year. They also filter noise, break the force of the wind, and provide shade. Of course you can plant a hedge composed of plants from a single species, but one of the most creative

A border of carefully chosen shrubs can provide an attractive, low-maintenance option to flower beds.

Flowering shrubs, like these camellias (*Camellia* spp.), can provide a dramatic show during their bloom season.

and ornamental ways to use shrubs in a landscape is in mixed plantings. Try combining deciduous and evergreen species, interplanting shrubs that bloom at different seasons, or adding flowering shrubs to a perennial border to create year-round interest.

Before making your selections, consider what you want the shrubs for and what season or seasons you need them to work for you. If you need to block the noise of traffic year-round, for example, plant evergreen shrubs, such as yews (*Taxus* spp.), hollies (*Ilex* spp.), or, in warm regions, camellias (*Camellia* spp.). If you need privacy only for summertime barbecues, deciduous shrubs would be a fine choice.

Specimens Shrubs make excellent specimen plants. Use them to call out a special feature in your yard such as the beginning of a path or the end of a border or patio. For specimens, look for shrubs that are attractive for as many months as possible. Many viburnums, for example, have attractive spring flowers, summer fruit, and good fall color.

Backdrops and "Walls" You can use shrubs to mark the garden rooms or the parts of your landscape—to screen a quiet sitting area from an area designed for active play, or to wall utility areas off for trash or storage. You can also use shrubs as a backdrop for plantings of flowers. But if you use shrubs in this manner, look for ones that will complement but not compete with your flowers. Choose green shrubs like boxwoods or junipers, for example, and avoid those with showy blossoms of their own.

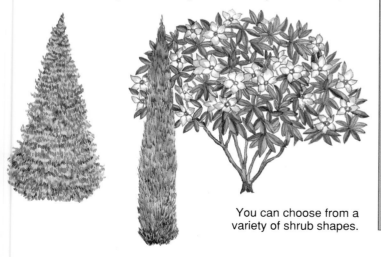

You can choose from a variety of shrub shapes.

Size Up Your Selections

If you want your shrubs to stay short, regular pruning will keep them in bounds. But a better approach is to choose shrubs that mature at the height you need. There are dwarf or miniature cultivars of many popular shrubs, including 'Bronxensis' forsythia, which matures at 2 feet (60 cm) in height. Dwarf cultivars of many trees—especially spruces (*Picea* spp.) and arborvitae (*Thuja* spp.)—are also commonly used as shrubs. Look for plants with names like 'Prostrata', 'Nana', 'Compacta', 'Densa', and 'Pumila', but don't stop there. Be sure to verify mature height before you buy; compact forms of some trees and large shrubs may still be much larger than you want at maturity.

If you like a formal look in your garden, you may choose to include tightly sheared shrubs as accents.

Casual plantings, with a mixture of trees, shrubs, and wildflowers, can produce a charming informal effect.

Screens and Hedges Shrubs are the perfect choice for hedges and screens, to block unattractive views or the sights and sounds of nearby neighbors and traffic. To calculate how many shrubs you need to buy for an effective hedge or screen, determine the mature spread of the species you've selected. Figure on spacing the shrubs closer together than their mature spread so that they'll form an unbroken line. For example, if a particular shrub has a mature spread of 5 feet (1.5 m), plan to space the plants 3 to 4 feet (0.9 to 1.2 m) apart, depending upon how large they are when you buy them and how quickly you want a solid screen or hedge. Divide the total hedge length by the spacing you select to determine the number of shrubs to buy.

Groundcovers Shrubs are an excellent substitute for grass in areas where lawns don't grow well, where mowing is difficult, or where you want less maintenance. Planted in a well-mulched bed, low-growing junipers (*Juniperus horizontalis* and *J. procumbens* 'Nana') or rockspray cotoneaster (*Cotoneaster horizontalis*) will form a low-maintenance cover on a steep hill. Where soil erosion is a problem, use shrubs with creeping underground stolons, such as red-osier dogwood (*Cornus sericea*), or shrubs with arching stems that root when they touch the ground, such as winter jasmine (*Jasminum nudiflorum*).

If you have a sunny yard, consider roses for their beautiful flowers and fragrance.

Seasonal Attractions

In your landscape, shrubs can be utilitarian, but they can also be a focal point. Look for shrubs with multiseasonal interest—especially for use as accents or specimens. Oak-leaved hydrangea (*Hydrangea quercifolia*), for instance, has interesting oak-leaf-shaped leaves that turn purple in fall. Its showy clusters of off-white flowers dry on the plant and persist well into the winter. The peeling bark provides additional winter interest. The fruit on shrubs such as pyracanthas (*Pyracantha* spp.) and viburnums (*Viburnum* spp.) provide food for birds, while the plants serve as protective cover. Fruiting shrubs are also excellent for attracting wildlife.

Some shrubs, like barberries (*Berberis* spp.), offer both flowers and showy fruit for multiseason interest.

A mixture of vines can be quite striking. Shown here is a combination of clematis, grapes, and yellow-leaved hops.

Using Vines in the Landscape

Vines are often used simply for the beautiful flowers and foliage they bring to the garden. But vines have functional uses as well: They are fast-growing and quickly lend an established look to the landscape. They can also soften or hide the harsh architectural lines of buildings, create or define garden spaces, provide privacy, screen unsightly views or noise, cover up ugly masonry, and break up the monotony of long fences and walls.

Types of Vines

While all vines twine or climb, keep in mind that there are three basic types of vines: annuals, herbaceous perennials, and woody perennials. Most vines are fast growers, although some of the woody perennials may take a year or two to get established.

Annual vines, such as common morning glory (*Ipomoea purpurea*), climb a lamppost or trellis in a hurry, making a good show in a single season. You'll need to replant annual vines each year, although some will self-sow. Some vines grown as annuals in the North, including black-eyed Susan vine (*Thunbergia alata*), are perennial in warm climates.

Herbaceous perennial vines, such as crimson starglory (*Mina lobata*), die back to the ground every winter and regrow in spring.

Hardy woody vines include such familiar species as clematis (*Clematis* spp.), honeysuckles (*Lonicera* spp.), and wisteria (*Wisteria* spp.). Most hardy woody vines are deciduous, dropping their leaves each fall but leaving a woody stem from which new leaves, flowers, and fruits grow the following year. Others, including wintercreeper euonymus (*Euonymus fortunei*) and English ivy (*Hedera helix*), are evergreen.

Choosing and Using Vines

You can find a vine for any type of soil—fertile or poor, wet or dry—and any exposure from full sun to deep shade. Just as with trees and shrubs, the best course is to match the plant to your site rather than trying to alter your conditions to suit the plant. Most vines are adaptable plants and accept a wide range of growing conditions. Clematis, for example, need sun for good flower production but do best with cool roots, so plant them in full sun but shade their roots with a groundcover, low-growing perennials, or an organic mulch.

Climbing vines will soften the look of a raw new fence or quickly screen an unsightly view. A hot, sunny porch becomes much more inviting when a trellised vine adds dappled shade. Vines trained on upright supports can fit in spaces too small for most trees and shrubs. They can be used as a vertical accent in flower or herb gardens or to mark the corners of an outdoor living area. Many vines also do well in containers on a deck or patio or in a courtyard garden.

Deciduous vines growing on the south and west sides

Wisterias and clematis are woody deciduous vines. Each year they form new leaves on the old stems.

of your house will shade the walls in summer, reducing your home's energy needs. Where banks are steep or grass is difficult to grow, evergreen vines make excellent groundcovers. Some vines, such as grapes and Chinese gooseberry (*Actinidia chinensis*), provide edible fruit for you or for wildlife.

How Vines Climb

Vines either trail along the ground or climb appropriate supports. If you want your vines to climb, you'll need to know how they do it. Then you can choose an appropriate support for the vine you have in mind. The "Plant by Plant Guide," starting on page 78, will tell you which climbing method each vine uses.

Some vines, such as passionflowers (*Passiflora* spp.) and sweet peas (*Lathyrus* spp.), climb by means of tendrils that grasp any objects they touch. These vines soon blanket a trellis or pergola, with little training from you. Vines that climb with tendrils need supports thin enough for their tendrils to grasp. Some tendrils will coil around supports themselves, while others will loop around supports, then twine around themselves.

Clematis wrap their leaf stems around slender supports. Provide wires or trellises to help plants climb walls.

Other vines, such as wisterias, climb by twining their entire stems around supports. Twining vines need no encouragement to wrap themselves around a pole or porch post. These vines wrap themselves around slender supports, like wires, railings, or other vines, as well as around large objects like columns and tree trunks.

English ivy (*Hedera helix*), wintercreeper euonymus (*Euonymus fortunei*), and climbing hydrangea (*Hydrangea anomala* var. *petiolaris*) use adhesive aerial rootlets along their stems to cling to wood, brick, stone, or other materials. Virginia creeper and Boston ivy (*Parthenocissus quinquefolia* and *P. tricuspidata*) bear tendrils that end in adhesive discs, which attach themselves to surfaces.

Vines use a variety of climbing methods. Boston ivy forms adhesive discs (1), while morning glories produce wrapping tendrils (2). Roses don't actually climb—they must be tied (3). English ivy forms aerial rootlets (4); wisteria has twining stems (5).

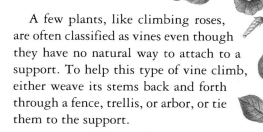

Vine Growers Beware

Fast-growing vines can be a gardener's best friend by quickly providing privacy and screening ugly views. But because of their vigorous nature, some vines can also become a gardener's headache. To avoid common problems such as rampant growth, insufficient support, and structural damage, do some research before you buy, and pick your plants carefully.

Some vines, such as Hall's Japanese honeysuckle (*Lonicera japonica* 'Halliana'), grow very fast, climbing over everything in their path. Unless you are looking for a rampant groundcover for a steep bank, you are better off choosing a less aggressive species, such as scarlet honeysuckle (*Lonicera sempervirens* 'Superba'). If you see a vine spreading out of control, don't hesitate to cut it back severely or remove it.

Other vines, such as wisteria, trumpet creeper (*Campsis radicans*), and bittersweet, can choke or girdle trees, often weakening or killing them. Sometimes the sheer weight of a vine on a tree can topple it. It's best to build a very sturdy support for these heavyweights rather than allowing them to climb your trees.

Vines that climb by holdfasts such as aerial rootlets or clinging discs, including English and Boston ivies and climbing hydrangea, are valuable for cloaking brick or masonry walls. But before you plant, make sure you really want that vine there. Removing the rootlets and discs after tearing down vines can be a frustrating job, requiring a stiff scrub brush and plenty of elbow grease.

Vines with aerial roots and clinging discs may also erode cement between loose bricks. In addition to causing damage from holdfasts, these vines can collect moisture, causing wood beneath them to rot. A safe way to enjoy the look of ivy or other creepers on your house is to train them on a sturdy wood or wire-fencing support, held away from the side of the building to provide air circulation and to prevent the vines from causing damage.

A few plants, like climbing roses, are often classified as vines even though they have no natural way to attach to a support. To help this type of vine climb, either weave its stems back and forth through a fence, trellis, or arbor, or tie them to the support.

Climbing Supports for Vines

If you want your vines to grow upright, begin training them on supports as soon as you plant them. Use a structure big enough to support the mature plant, and put it in place before you plant the vine.

Buy or build freestanding supports that are constructed of sturdy, durable materials. Wood is a traditional and attractive choice for fan-shaped trellises, lattice panels, graceful arbors, or other supports. For longevity and durability, choose cedar or another naturally rot-resistant wood, or keep the support structure painted. Wire fencing framed with two-by-fours is a low-cost option that will give a vine years of sturdy support. Use galvanized or plastic-coated fencing to prevent rust. Copper or aluminum wire and tubing can also be fashioned into rustproof supports.

Training Vines

Use string to guide young vines to the structure you want them to climb. Fasten one end of the string to the support and tie the other end around a rock or a stick. Place the rock at the base of the plant, or poke the stick into the ground nearby, making sure to avoid the vine's rootball. Use string or soft fabric strips to tie vines to their supports until they begin to twine or cling.

Wisteria can quickly outgrow its supports. Make sure the structure is strong enough to hold the mature plant.

CHOOSING YOUR PLANTS

Now that you have identified the types of plants you need and want in your landscape, and the ones that will grow well there, it's time to get specific. This chapter will help you narrow down your choices of plants and will also provide guidelines for selecting and buying specific plants. Use the "Plant by Plant Guide," starting on page 78, to help you select the trees, shrubs, and vines that best meet your needs—practically and aesthetically.

There are also other places you can look for ideas and suggestions. If you haven't already done so, drive around your neighborhood and look at which plants are growing successfully and under what conditions. Ask at your local garden center for advice and recommendations, too. Be sure to focus on plants that are pest- and disease-resistant. Your county extension agent is another good resource for helping you select plants that will thrive. The Cooperative Extension Service is usually aware of which species are trouble-free in your area, and which may be plagued by pests or diseases. In some regions, for example, insect problems have decimated the hemlock (*Tsuga* spp.) population, while in other areas, a hemlock is still a good choice.

This is one of the most enjoyable parts of the landscaping process, a time when that design you sketched on paper starts coming to life. Take your time with the selection process. Cross out and make new choices until you're satisfied with your list. Choose the best plant for each site, and make sure your selections complement each other as well.

If your design calls for a planting of shrubs and small trees to screen your backyard, try to think about what your selections will look like next to one another and how interesting and attractive they will be from week to week and month to month. For example, look for plants that will provide several seasons of interest. You may want to mix evergreens and deciduous trees and shrubs, and include plants with ornamental berries, bark, or foliage. If you have room for several spring-flowering shrubs, try to find ones that bloom early, midseason, and late, so you'll have color for many weeks. And don't forget summer-blooming shrubs like hydrangeas (*Hydrangea* spp.) or winter-blooming witch hazels (*Hamamelis* spp.). You can even plan to allow vines like clematis or climbing roses to grow up through shrubs and small trees for an added show.

When you are satisfied with your list and plan, make a note of the number of each plant you need. You can always change your mind later, but having a specific list is a good idea when you begin to shop for specimens.

Opposite: As you choose your plants, start by considering their growing requirements, such as temperature, soil, and moisture needs. Once you know that the plants are adapted to your site, you can consider factors like color. The white blooms of 'Miss Bateman' clematis (*Clematis* 'Miss Bateman') add a cool touch to the summer garden.

Selecting and Buying Plants

When you start to shop for trees, shrubs, and vines, look for the best plants you can find. They are a long-term investment, and it's well worth the effort to find good-quality plants. Look for healthy, vigorous plants, with leaves of proper size and color (unless plants are dormant). Buds should be plump and firm, and the bark on the stems should be undamaged.

Inspect all plants for signs of insects and diseases; if the leaves are spotted or chewed, or if the stems have indentions or cankers, don't buy them. Be sure the plant is labeled with species and cultivar names. Be careful when buying from discount, grocery, and hardware stores. The plants may be in bad condition because they often receive minimal care. In addition, selection is generally limited.

Bareroot, Balled-and-burlapped, or Container-grown?

Trees, shrubs, and vines are produced and harvested in several ways. You'll find bareroot, balled-and-burlapped, container-ized, and container-grown stock to choose from. Each method has advantages and disadvantages. The planting techniques you use will depend on the way the plants were grown and sold (see "Planting Techniques" on page 4). Whatever type you buy, keep plants protected from wind and sun when you transport them home.

Bareroot plants usually cost less than other types of nursery stock, and they adapt quickly to your soil. Buy and plant bareroot stock in fall or early spring.

Buying Bareroot Stock   Bareroot plants are just that—they're dug from the field and sold with bare roots. Bareroot plants are less expensive than other nursery stock; they may cost half as much as the same plant grown in a container. Bareroot plants offer another advantage: After planting, the roots will easily adjust to your garden's soil, whereas the roots of container-grown plants have to make the transition from the nursery soil to yours.

Most deciduous trees, shrubs, and vines can be successfully grown from bareroot stock. Don't buy large trees or any evergreens bareroot; their roots can dry out easily, causing damage that's hard to overcome. Buy and plant bareroot stock when it is dormant, from late fall to early spring. If you can't plant immediately, temporarily "heel in" your plants by laying them along a

Larger trees and shrubs are often sold balled-and-burlapped. Look for firm, moist root balls.

shallow trench in a shady, protected area and covering their roots with soil.

Buying Balled-and-burlapped Stock   Balled-and-burlapped (B&B) stock is dug from the field with a ball of soil around the roots. B&B plants are often the most expensive, and the soil ball makes them heavier to handle. Be sure the root ball is large enough to support and anchor your plant. Properly handled root balls should be well wrapped, firm, and moist. Avoid lifting B&B plants by the trunk, and handle them carefully or the root ball might break apart and damage the roots.

Since B&B stock comes with soil, plants have to make the transition from the nursery soil to yours. The difference in soil type can cause uneven water distribution, either soaking the root ball or leaving it drier than the surrounding soil.

Buying Containerized Stock   Not to be confused with container-grown plants, containerized or processed-balled plants are initially dug bare-root. Their roots are then packed or potted in organic matter or potting medium, not

Check the roots of container-grown stock by inverting the plant and slipping off the pot.

field soil. As with bareroot stock, most of the roots are left behind in the field. When you buy, check inside the packing or slip the pot off and look for new roots. If all you find are a few large, cut roots but no fine, small roots, don't buy the plant. The nursery didn't hold it long enough for new roots to grow, and the plant will be slow to establish.

Buying Container-grown Stock   Unlike containerized plants, container-grown plants are grown from the start in a container. Since you get 100 percent of the root system, transplant shock is minimal. You can set container-grown stock aside until you're ready to plant (keeping it watered) without fear of damaging it.

When you shop for a container-grown plant, gently slip it out of the container to inspect the root ball. Well-cared-for plants have many roots showing on the outside of the ball. The roots should be white or light tan in color; brown or black roots are probably diseased or rotting from overwatering. If the potting medium is very dry, roots may be damaged or dead from underwatering. If the roots have begun to circle

Root balls should have many light-colored roots; avoid those with circling roots.

around inside the pot, look for another specimen. Circling roots will continue to circle in their planting hole. They won't anchor into the soil adequately and eventually may strangle the plant.

Where to Buy

Shopping for trees, shrubs, and vines at local garden centers or nurseries allows you to inspect the plants before you buy. And if you're in the market for large plants, those outlets are probably the best bet. But local retailers may not have a wide selection of plants. Specialty mail-order nurseries are good places to find unusual species or the newest cultivars of plants. If you buy by mail, be sure to find out what size and type of plants you'll be receiving.

Wherever you shop, ask about a warranty before you buy. Find out under what conditions a return is accepted, for how long a period after the sale, and whether the refund will be in cash or trade. Some nurseries offer guarantees only on plants they install themselves, especially when it comes to larger trees.

Container-grown plants should have healthy top growth that is in proportion to the container. You can plant them anytime during the growing season.

Nurseries sell a wide variety of shrubs and trees in containers. Shop early for the best selection and quality.

Species Charts

Choosing your trees, shrubs, and vines can be one of the most enjoyable steps to creating a beautiful landscape, but it can also be one of the most challenging. With so many plants to pick from, how do you decide which ones will meet your needs?

Start by making a wish list. Here you'll write down all the plants you've ever wanted to have—those that you've read about in books or magazines or that you've seen and admired in catalogs or neighbors' gardens. As you create your list, don't forget to look at your landscape plan and think of plants that will fulfill your needs. If you want a formal trimmed hedge, for example, look for plants that can tolerate severe pruning. Or if you're planning a foundation planting, consider a combination of naturally slow-growing plants to reduce pruning chores. Take notes as you come up with possibilities. Record each plant's name (both common and botanical), the growing conditions it prefers, and the seasons it is attractive in the garden.

The next step is to narrow down your list. Start by eliminating any plants that won't tolerate the conditions your garden has to offer. Then match the remaining plants on your wish list to specific places and uses in your landscape. Consider factors such as size, season of interest, and flower and foliage color. When you are done, you'll have a list of plants that will thrive and look wonderful in your landscape for years to come.

Below you'll find lists of plants for special purposes, such as foundation plantings and hedges, or with special features, like multiseason interest or fast growth. Use these lists to get ideas for plants that would be suitable for your landscape. To learn more about specific plants, look them up in the "Plant by Plant Guide," starting on page 78.

Plants for Flowering Hedges

A flowering hedge can provide seasonal or year-round interest. Flowering shrubs generally look best when you let them grow in their natural arching or spreading forms, without extensive pruning. Besides shaping plants into awkward cubes and globes, heavy pruning can remove flower buds, reducing or eliminating the blooms.

If you think you'd enjoy the informal look of a flowering hedge, peruse the list of suggested plants given below. The botanical name of each is followed by the common name, description, and hardiness zone.

Abelia x *grandiflora* (glossy abelia): Semi-evergreen. Lightly fragrant pale pink flowers in spring and summer. 4 to 6 feet (1.2 to 1.8 m) tall. Zones 6–10.

Chaenomeles speciosa (flowering quince): Deciduous. Single or double red, pink, or white flowers in spring; yellow fruit ripen in fall. 4 to 10 feet (1.2 to 3 m) tall. Zones 4–8.

Deutzia spp. (deutzias): Deciduous. White flowers in summer. 2 to 10 feet (0.6 to 3 m) tall. Zones 4–9. (Height and hardiness vary among species.)

Forsythia spp. (forsythias): Deciduous. Yellow flowers in early spring. 6 to 8 feet (1.8 to 2.4 m) tall. Zones 4–9.

Hibiscus syriacus (rose-of-Sharon): Deciduous. White, pink, red, or violet flowers in summer. 8 to 15 feet (2.4 to 4.5 m) tall. Zones 5–9.

Hydrangea paniculata var. *grandiflora* (peegee hydrangea): Deciduous. Large clusters of creamy white flowers in late summer. 4 to 10 feet (1.2 to 3 m) tall. Zones 4–8.

Philadelphus coronarius (sweet mock orange): Deciduous. Fragrant white flowers in late spring. 6 to 8 feet (1.8 to 2.4 m) tall. Zones 4–9.

Potentilla fruticosa (shrubby cinquefoil): Deciduous. Lemon yellow flowers in late spring and again in summer to fall. 2 to 4 feet (0.6 to 1.2 m) tall. Zones 2–8.

Prunus laurocerasus (cherry-laurel): Evergreen. Fragrant white flowers in spring. 10 to 15 feet (3 to 4.5 m) tall. Zones 6–9.

Rosa spp. (roses): Deciduous. Shrub, grandiflora, and floribunda roses come in a range of colors. Height and hardiness vary among species.

Spiraea spp. (spireas): Deciduous. White flowers in spring. 3 to 6 feet (0.9 to 1.8 m) tall. Zones 4–9. (Height and hardiness vary among species.)

Syringa spp. (lilacs): Deciduous. Fragrant white, pink, or purplish flowers in spring. 5 to 20 feet (1.5 to 6 m) tall. Zones 3–7. (Height and hardiness vary among species.)

Viburnum spp. (viburnums): Deciduous or evergreen. White flowers in spring or summer. 5 to 12 feet (1.5 to 3.6 m) tall. Zones 3–8. (Height and hardiness vary among species.)

Foundation Plantings

If you've incorporated a traditional foundation planting into your landscape plan, take some time to choose the plants carefully. To minimize pruning and to produce a natural-looking planting, look for low-growing and dwarf species and cultivars. Choose a combination of foliage and flowering plants for year-round interest. Listed below are some suggested plants. These shrubs usually stay below 5 feet (1.5 m) with minimal trimming so they won't grow up to block your windows. The plants are listed by botanical name, followed by the common name, description, and hardiness zones.

Berberis thunbergii (Japanese barberry): Deciduous. Egg-shaped green leaves turn reddish in fall. Zones 4–10.

Buxus sempervirens 'Suffruticosa' (edging boxwood): Evergreen. Dark green foliage may bronze in winter. Zones 6–10.

Cotoneaster horizontalis (rockspray cotoneaster): Deciduous or semi-evergreen. Tiny pink flowers in spring, followed by bright red berries in fall. Zones 4–9.

Daphne spp. (daphnes): Evergreen or semi-evergreen. Clusters of pale pink, purple, or white flowers in spring. Zones 4–9.

Deutzia gracilis (slender deutzia): Deciduous. White flowers in late spring. Zones 4–9.

Fothergilla gardenii (fothergilla): Deciduous. Clusters of fragrant white bottlebrush-like flowers in spring. Zones 5–9.

Ilex crenata 'Compacta' (dwarf Japanese holly): Evergreen. Small glossy green leaves. Zones 5–8.

Itea virginica (Virginia sweetspire): Deciduous. Long, densely packed clusters of small white flowers in early summer. Zones 5–9.

Juniperus horizontalis (creeping juniper): Evergreen. Needle-like green, blue-green, or gray-green foliage. Zones 3–8. (Hardiness varies among species.)

Kerria japonica (Japanese kerria): Deciduous. Bright yellow flowers in spring; green stems all winter. Zones 4–8.

Leucothoe fontanesiana (drooping leucothoe): Evergreen. Clusters of fragrant white flowers in spring. Zones 4–9.

Mahonia spp. (mahonias): Evergreen. Spiky clusters of drooping yellow flowers in spring. Zones 6–9. (Hardiness varies among species.)

Myrica pensylvanica (northern bayberry): Deciduous or semi-evergreen. Fragrant dark green leaves and small, waxy gray fruit. Zones 2–7.

Pinus mugo var. *mugo* (dwarf mugo pine): Evergreen. Medium to dark green needle-like leaves. Zone 2–7.

Potentilla fruticosa (shrubby cinquefoil): Deciduous. Yellow flowers in summer. Zones 2–8.

Rhododendron 'P. J. M.' ('P. J. M.' hybrid rhododendron): Evergreen. Lavender-pink flowers in spring; dark green leaves turn purplish in fall. Zones 5–8.

Trees and Shrubs for Windbreaks

Plants can be a great alternative to a solid fence for dividing a property or blocking an unpleasant view. The plants listed below tolerate close planting—they form an effective barrier or screen. The botanical name is followed by the common name, foliage description, and hardiness zones.

Juniperus virginiana (eastern red cedar): Evergreen. Medium to dark green foliage. 40 to 80 feet (12 to 24 m) tall. Zones 3–7.

Picea abies (Norway spruce): Evergreen. Bright green foliage when young; darker green when older. 70 to 100 feet (21 to 30 m) tall. Zones 2–7.

Pinus spp. (pines): Evergreen. Medium to dark green or bluish green foliage. 30 to 100 feet (9 to 30 m) tall. Zones 3–8. (Height and hardiness vary among species.)

Populus spp. (poplars): Deciduous. Dark green leaves with white or bright green undersides. 40 to 90 feet (12 to 27 m) tall. Zones 2–8.

Tsuga spp. (hemlocks): Evergreen. Fine-textured with dark green foliage. 80 to 100 feet (24 to 30 m) tall. Zones 4–7. (Height and hardiness vary among species.)

Plants with Multiseason Interest

When you only have room for a few trees and shrubs, you need to choose plants that will provide the greatest effect for the space they take up. Listed below are some deciduous trees and shrubs that can provide attractive features in more than one season. The plants are listed by botanical name, followed by the common name, special features, and hardiness zones.

Abelia x *grandiflora* (glossy abelia): Lightly fragrant pale pink flowers in spring through summer; glossy green leaves turn reddish in fall. Zones 6–10.

Acer spp. (maples): Many species have outstanding red to yellow fall color; some have striped bark. Zones 3–9. (Hardiness varies among species.)

Amelanchier spp. (serviceberries): White flowers in spring; red to black berries in summer; yellow to red fall color. Zones 3–8.

Berberis spp. (barberries): Small yellow flowers in spring; red to black berries in late summer into winter; red or purple fall color. Zones 4–10. (Hardiness varies among species.)

Betula spp. (birches): Many species have bright yellow fall color and peeling bark. Zones 3–8. (Hardiness varies among species.)

Callicarpa spp. (beautyberries): Pinkish purple flowers in late summer; bright purple berries in fall and winter. Zones 5–9.

Chionanthus virginicus (white fringe tree): White flowers in early summer; females produce blue berries in summer; yellow fall color. Zones 5–8.

Cladrastis lutea (American yellowwood): Fragrant white flowers in late spring; yellow fall color; smooth gray to tan bark. Zones 3–8.

Cornus florida (flowering dogwood): White flowers in spring; red berries in late summer to fall; reddish fall color. Zones 4–9.

Cornus kousa (kousa dogwood): White flowers in late spring; red fruit in late summer; red fall color; peeling bark. Zones 5–9.

Cornus mas (cornelian cherry): Yellow flowers in early spring; red berries in late summer; peeling bark. Zones 4–8.

Cotinus coggygria (smoke tree): Airy masses of pinkish flowers in summer; yellow, orange, or reddish purple fall color. Zones 5–8.

Eucalyptus spp. (eucalyptus): Yellow, red, or white flowers in summer to fall; aromatic bluish leaves; peeling bark. Zones 9–10.

Fagus spp. (beeches): Smooth gray bark. Dark green leaves turn coppery in fall. Zones 4–8.

Fothergilla spp. (fothergillas): White flowers in spring; bright yellow to orange-red fall color. Zones 5–9.

Hamamelis spp. (witch hazels): Yellow, orange, or reddish flowers in fall or early spring; yellow to orange fall color. Zones 5–9.

Hydrangea quercifolia (oak-leaved hydrangea): White flowers in summer; burgundy red fall color. Zones 5–8.

Itea virginica (sweetspire): White flowers in late spring to early summer; bright red to purplish fall color. Zones 5–9.

Lagerstroemia indica (crape myrtle): White, pink, red, or purplish flowers in summer; peeling bark. Zones 7–10.

Liquidambar styraciflua (sweet gum): Lobed leaves turn red in fall; deeply ridged bark. Zones 3–8.

Magnolia stellata (star magnolia): White flowers in spring; red seeds in summer. Zones 5–9.

Malus spp. (crab apples): White or pink flowers in spring; red or yellow fruit in summer. Zones 4–8.

Oxydendrum arboreum (sourwood): White flowers in summer; bright red fall color. Zones 5–9.

Parrotia persica (Persian parrotia): Yellow, orange, and scarlet fall color; gray-and-white mottled bark. Zones 5–10.

Prunus serrulata (Japanese flowering cherry): Small white flowers in spring; yellow fall color; peeling reddish brown bark. Zones 5–8.

Pyracantha spp. (firethorns): White flowers in late spring to summer; red fruit in fall. Zones 6–9.

Rosa rugosa (rugosa rose): Fragrant white, pink, or red flowers in summer; orange-red fruit in late summer. Zones 3–10.

Stewartia spp. (stewartias): White flowers in summer to fall; yellow, red, or purplish fall color; showy peeling bark. Zones 5–9. (Hardiness varies among species.)

Viburnum spp. (viburnums): White flowers in spring or summer; red or blue berries; red to purple fall color. Zones 3–9. (Hardiness varies among species.)

Fast-growing Vines

Don't overlook the value of vines and climbing plants in your outdoor living spaces. These versatile plants can help you to solve various problems in your yard. They can merge the boundaries between different areas or to soften the harsh edges of new walls and fences. Use vines and climbers on an arbor as a decorative entrance or on a trellis or pergola to provide shade.

Listed below are some particularly fast-growing vines and climbers that can cover a space quickly. The botanical name is followed by the common name, description, and hardiness zones.

Actinidia spp. (kiwis): Deciduous. Woody-stemmed vining climbers need a strong support. Female plants produce edible fruit. Zones 4–10. (Hardiness varies among species.)

Ampelopsis brevipedunculata (porcelain ampelopsis): Deciduous. Variable dark green leaves; bright blue berries. Climbs by tendrils. Zones 4–9.

Aristolochia durior (Dutchman's-pipe): Deciduous. Twining vine with dark green heart-shaped leaves and pouched flowers in summer. Zones 4–8.

Clematis maximowicziana (sweet autumn clematis): Deciduous. Twining woody vine with fragrant white blooms in late summer into fall. Zones 5–9.

Humulus lupulus (hops): Deciduous. Twining vine with lobed green leaves. Zones 3–8.

Ipomoea spp. (morning glories): Annual. Twining vine with trumpet-shaped blue, white, or pink flowers from summer into fall.

Mina lobata (crimson starglory): Annual in most climates. Twining vine with lobed leaves and showy clusters of red buds and orange-and-yellow flowers.

Passiflora spp. (passionflowers): Dramatic purple, pink, or white flowers from summer to fall. Climbs by tendrils. Zones 7–10. (Hardiness varies among species.)

Thunbergia alata (black-eyed Susan vine): Annual. Twining vine with heart-shaped leaves and orange-yellow flowers in summer.

Shrubs and Trees for Sheared Hedges

If you're willing to invest the maintenance time, a closely trimmed hedge can add a dramatic touch to the landscape. A formal hedge is a perfect way to enclose a garden, providing wind protection and serving as a background for colorful flowers. Listed below are several plants that can stand the severe pruning needed to produce dense hedges. The botanical name is followed by the common name, description, and hardiness zones.

Berberis thunbergii (Japanese barberry): Deciduous. Thorny stems make an impenetrable hedge. Red berries in winter. Zones 4–10.

Buxus sempervirens (common boxwood): Evergreen. Dark green foliage may bronze in winter. Zones 6–10.

Carpinus betulus (European hornbeam): Deciduous. Dark green leaves that are usually pest-free. Good as tall hedges. Zones 5–9.

Chamaecyparis lawsoniana (lawson cypress): Evergreen. Flat scale-like leaves in a variety of colors (depending on the cultivar).

Fagus sylvatica (European beech): Deciduous. Green leaves turn golden-brown in fall. Good as tall hedges. Zones 4–8.

Ilex crenata (Japanese holly): Evergreen. Shiny dark green leaves. Very adaptable. Zones 5–8.

Ligustrum spp. (privets): Deciduous. Glossy dark green leaves. Needs frequent trimming. Zones 4–9. (Hardiness varies among species.)

Photinia spp. (photinias): Evergreen. Reddish new leaves turn dark green when mature. Zones 6–9. (Hardiness varies among species.)

Pyracantha coccinea (scarlet firethorn): Evergreen or semi-evergreen. Dark green leaves, spiny stems, and persistent red fruit. Zones 6–9.

Taxus spp. (yews): Evergreen. Dark green foliage. Seeds and leaves are poisonous. Zones 4–8. (Hardiness varies among species.)

Thuja spp. (arborvitae): Evergreen. Flat scale-like leaves; color varies with cultivar. Zones 2–9. (Hardiness varies among species.)

Tsuga canadensis (Canada hemlock): Evergreen. Fine-textured dark green foliage. Zones 4–7.

PLANTING YOUR LANDSCAPE

Proper planting is a critical step if your trees, shrubs, and vines are going to flourish in your landscape. Your new plants won't grow well if you handle them improperly or if you prepare a poor planting site. You have put time into carefully planning your landscape and matching individual plants to each site. Now take the time to do a good job of planting.

In this chapter, you will find instructions on how to prepare a proper planting site and how to deal with problem sites, as well as how to properly handle different types of nursery stock—bareroot, balled-and-burlapped (B&B), containerized, and container-grown plants. You'll also find guidelines on whether you should amend the soil when you plant, how and when to stake, and how to care for your plants after they're in the ground so they'll get off to a vigorous start.

Keep in mind that good care at planting time begins at the nursery. Once you've purchased your plants, be sure to protect them from wind and sun when you transport them home. Wind will desiccate the needles or leaves of plants in short order and can also tear the foliage. Hot sun can easily scorch foliage and twigs of plants. When you load your plants in the car, be sure to protect twigs and stems that might rub against windows or doors or be otherwise damaged. Wrapping tree trunks with a cushioning layer of burlap or other soft fabric will help prevent such injuries.

If you can't plant your new trees, shrubs, and vines immediately, find a shady, sheltered location in which to store them. Keep plants in containers and B&B stock moist. Heel-in bareroot plants in a shallow trench, laying them against the wall of the trench and covering their roots with soil until you can plant them properly.

The care you take at planting time affects the ultimate health of your trees, shrubs, and vines more than any other care you will ever give them. Preparing the planting area and eliminating soil compaction at planting time is essential to the long-term growth of your plants. Proper site preparation encourages plants to develop a healthy, vigorous root system and to extend their roots quickly into the surrounding soil. This is especially important with field-dug specimens like B&B stock. Since these plants have lost a large portion of their active root systems, it's important that they replace lost roots as quickly as possible. The amount of time, energy, and money you spend preparing a proper planting area will be well worth it in the long run. That's because healthy plants will require less maintenance than stressed ones.

Before you turn over a shovelful of soil, it's a good idea to position your new trees, shrubs, and vines in their designated places according to your landscape plan. No matter how good a plan looks on paper, it always looks different in the real world. Move your new plants around until you're happy with how they look, and then start digging.

Opposite: It's smart to group plants with similar needs together in the landscape. These azaleas (*Rhododendron* spp.), for example, are all thriving in the well-drained, acid soil of this raised bed.

Preparing the Planting Site

Most trees, shrubs, and vines are planted one by one in individual holes. But before you plant, you should think about creating planting areas, not just digging holes. You'll want to prepare a large enough growing area so the roots of your new plants can spread easily for at least a few years, until they get well established. In this section, you'll learn how to create the best possible conditions for the roots of your new plants.

Soil Improvement

Average garden soil is fine for most trees, shrubs, and vines—especially if you've picked ones that are well adapted to the site. But if you have less-than-ideal soil, suspect a nutrient deficiency, or are gardening in an area where topsoil has been removed, a soil-improvement program may be in order.

A soil test can tell you the relative amounts of the major nutrients in your soil: phosphorus (P) and potassium (K). Soil tests can also provide details on the amounts of minor nutrients in your soil and the percentage of organic matter.

If you know where you will be planting several months in advance, there are a few ways to improve the soil in the planting area before you plant. Grow a cover crop such as ryegrass, alfalfa, or beans in that location. About 3 weeks before you're ready to plant, dig or till your cover crop into the soil as a green manure. You can also add compost, well-rotted manure, or an organic nitrogen fertilizer such as bloodmeal or fish meal to increase fertility. Mix these materials into your soil to a depth of 6 to 12 inches (15 to 30 cm).

If you are preparing a large planting area, mix in a generous helping of compost to improve the soil.

Roses thrive in deep, humus-rich, well-drained soil. Add any needed amendments, like bonemeal, before planting.

Planting Hole Preparation

Dig the planting hole before you remove your stock from its container or wrapping to prevent the roots from drying out. Make the hole as wide and as deep as necessary to accommodate the roots of the plant without crowding. Angle the sides of the hole to about 45 to 60 degrees so it's wider at the top. Most tree, shrub, and vine roots grow out rather than down, and the hole's wide top encourages them to reach into the surrounding soil.

Dig your planting hole no deeper than the depth of the root ball—or slightly shallower in heavy soils. Measure the plant and the hole with a yardstick to avoid strain—on you and the plant—from constantly lifting it in and out of the hole to check depth.

If your soil is clayey, the walls of the planting hole may get slick or glazed as you dig. To prevent a barrier from forming that roots won't be able to penetrate, roughen the sides of the hole by scratching with a hoe or a claw-type hand tool.

The last step is to loosen the soil around the hole, so the roots of your new plant will be encouraged to spread out from the planting area. To do this, fluff up the soil 2 to 5 feet (0.6 to 1.5 m) out from the hole with a spading fork or rotary tiller. You can also dig a layer of compost into the soil in this area to add organic matter.

Soil Amendment Guidelines

Traditional advice recommends filling a planting hole with an improved, nutrient-rich soil. But current research shows this is not a good idea. Here's why: New plants must develop a strong root system as soon as possible for both nourishment and structural support.

Check Your pH

Soil pH, the relative measure of how acid or alkaline your soil is, can affect nutrient availability for plants in your yard. Soil pH is measured on a scale from 1.0 (strongly acid) to 14.0 (strongly alkaline). Most trees, shrubs, and vines are not particularly demanding about the pH of the soil, provided the soil isn't extremely acid or alkaline. Most garden plants thrive within a range of 6.0 to 7.0, from slightly acid to neutral. Nutrients tend to be most accessible to plant roots at this pH range.

If you suspect your soil is extremely acid or alkaline, it's wise to get your soil tested. If the test results confirm your suspicions, choose plants that are naturally adapted to that condition. Gardeners with acid soils, for example, will do well with rhododendrons, azaleas, mountain laurels, and blueberries. Gardeners with alkaline soils will do best with locally native trees and shrubs or those adapted to dry-land conditions. Alkaline-tolerant plants include black locust (*Robinia pseudoacacia*), honey locust (*Gleditsia triacanthos*), and sycamores (*Platanus* spp.); ask neighbors or local botanic gardens for more suggestions.

You can make small changes to your soil's pH by incorporating compost or soil amendments such as powdered sulfur to lower pH or ground limestone to raise it. A soil test report will include recommendations on the types and quantities of amendments to use. But, again, the best solution is to select plants that do well in your natural conditions.

A highly amended soil in the planting hole gives the roots no reason to seek nutrients in the surrounding soil. Because the roots stay in the hole instead of spreading out into the surrounding soil, the first strong wind or driving rain can dislodge the plant. In addition, the plants are less drought-tolerant because their roots have a small volume of soil from which to absorb water.

If the soil on your site is similar to the soil in the root ball, there's no need to amend the soil in the planting hole. But if the soil in the root ball is significantly different from your local soil, your tree may grow better if you amend the soil before planting. For example, if you planted a balled-and-burlapped (B&B) tree that was grown in sandy loam in a landscape where the soil is a heavy clay and didn't amend the soil, you would probably find that water pooled up in the hole. Since most nurseries are growing trees in sandy or loamy soil, but lots of gardeners have clayey soils, this is a common problem. The best approach is to evaluate your specific conditions—comparing your soil to the soil the plant is growing in—and decide what to do on a case-by-case basis.

Preparing a Planting Bed

One good way to create a site for planting shrubs and small trees as screens or hedges is to prepare the soil in an entire bed. In this case, you can improve the soil just as you would for a vegetable garden or flower bed, working it to remove clods and lumps and adding compost or other organic matter for better soil structure and fertility. This is also an ideal way to plant shrubs and vines in a mixed border with perennials.

The first step when preparing to plant a bed is to

For easier planting and maintenance, group plants into larger beds rather than dig separate holes.

As you dig a planting hole, use a measuring stick to compare the depth of the hole with the depth of the root ball.

Dealing with Problem Soils

Planting naturally well-adapted species is the best way to handle problem soils, particularly those with slow drainage. Building raised beds and filling them with improved soil is an option for shallow-rooted vines and even some small shrubs. But the roots of trees and many shrubs and vines will soon outgrow the beds. If your soil is extremely sandy or clayey, save your raised beds for flowers and vegetables, and choose species of trees, shrubs, and vines that are compatible with your soil conditions.

remove the grass growing in that area. You'll want to clear a big enough area so the roots of the new plants won't have to compete with the grass for water and nutrients for the first few years. A good rule of thumb is that the grass should be no closer than the drip line (the farthest lateral reach of the branches).

Now you're ready to loosen the soil. Before you start, squeeze a handful to check moisture. The soil should be lightly moist, holding its shape loosely. If the soil forms a wet, sticky ball, it's too wet to work. Digging or working in wet soil can ruin soil structure, causing large clumps to form that will dry rock-hard and leave few pore spaces for air and water. At the other extreme, avoid working extremely dry soil. If your handful of soil crumbles to dust, wait for a rain

shower or wet the soil a day or so before you dig to prevent the topsoil from blowing away.

Dig your soil by hand, using a garden fork or a shovel, or cultivate the bed with a rotary tiller. Loosen the soil to a depth of 8 to 12 inches (20 to 30 cm), breaking up large clods. Remove any rocks or debris, such as buried building material, that turn up. Spread 1 or 2 inches (2.5 to 5 cm) of finished compost over the bed and work it in to a depth of 4 to 6 inches (10 to 15 cm).

Preparing the area in fall for spring planting, or spring for fall planting, is the ideal situation. This gives the soil time to settle back to its normal level before planting. If you're not that organized, try to wait at least a few weeks before planting. If you must plant right away, set plants slightly higher to allow for soil settling.

To look their best, azaleas need humus-rich soil and good drainage. If you want to grow azaleas and don't already have a well-drained site in your garden, build a large raised bed for them instead.

Planting Techniques

You can plant anytime the ground isn't frozen. Plant bareroot stock when it's dormant, from late fall to as early in spring as possible. Balled-and-burlapped (B&B) stock does best when planted in the cooler months of spring or fall. You can plant container-grown stock anytime during the growing season, but if you plant during summer, be sure to pay extra attention to watering. Below you'll find some hints on preparing different types of trees, shrubs, and vines for planting.

Bareroot Plants Before you plant, soak the roots of bareroot trees, shrubs, or vines in water overnight and plant the stock the next day. Don't soak the roots too long or they will begin to decay.

Container-grown and Containerized Plants Remove your new plants from their containers and any labels, tags, or wires. Add durable, weatherproof labels near each plant for identification purposes or mark the botanical and cultivar names on your landscape plan.

Inspect the roots of your plants and prune any that are broken, soft and mushy, or diseased, cutting back to healthy tissue. If the roots are snarled and matted when you remove the pot, comb them out with your fingers and clip off any that appear to be permanently kinked.

Balled-and-burlapped Plants Remove any rope, twine, or nails from B&B stock. If your B&B stock is wrapped in synthetic material, wait until the plant is in the hole, then snip the wrapping into pieces, removing as much of it as you can. If the root ball begins to shatter, cut slits in the remaining material and leave it in place. Natural burlap can be left on, as it will rot away after planting. If your plant came in a wire basket, remove any loop handles and the first few wires at the top.

How to Plant

Keep a firm, level area of soil in the bottom of the hole on which to set the plant, and dig a few inches deeper around it so that extra water can drain away from the roots easily. Now set the plant into the hole. (If you're planting bareroot stock, build a cone of soil in the hole to support the roots. Firm the soil well and settle the plant on top of the cone, spreading the roots over it.) Stand back and make sure the plant is straight.

Now start refilling, or backfilling, with the soil you removed when you dug the hole. Backfill half the hole, then water the soil to remove large air pockets. Once the water drains away, finish backfilling and water again. With the leftover soil, build a well around the planting hole to trap and hold water over the plant's roots.

Planting a Tree or Shrub

Small container-grown trees and shrubs are easy to buy and plant. Fall and spring are ideal planting times, but container-grown stock will adapt to a new home almost any time the ground isn't frozen. If you plant during hot weather, remember to keep the soil evenly moist to promote root growth and avoid heat stress.

1. Dig a hole large enough to hold the root ball with space around it.

2. Remove the plant from the pot. Prune away broken or circling roots.

3. Place the plant in the hole, making sure that it is straight.

4. Backfill half the hole, then water the soil.

5. Finish backfilling and water again. Build a well around the edge.

Aftercare

Prune the top of your newly planted tree, shrub, or vine only to correct problems. Remove branches that are crossing, rubbing, broken, narrow-angled, or diseased. If you want a single-trunked tree, prune away any multiple main stems. Apply a 2- to 3-inch (5 to 7.5 cm) deep layer of mulch over the entire planting area, keeping it a few inches away from the stem to prevent rodent damage and to allow air circulation. Water regularly for the next year or two, keeping the root ball and surrounding soil moist but not wet, as your plant gets established. See "Care and Maintenance," starting on page 51, for more details on pruning, mulching, and other maintenance techniques.

Staking

Staking holds trees and shrubs in place while their roots grow out from the root ball into the surrounding soil. Trees taller than 8 feet (2.4 m) or top-heavy trees with a large crown or top in relation to the size of the root ball benefit from the support of stakes to prevent them from falling over. Trees with straight, strong trunks that are less than 8 feet (2.4 m) tall and have small crowns usually need no staking unless they are planted in a windy location. Unstaked trees, or those staked with some slack, develop thicker, stronger trunks faster than staked trees.

If staking is necessary, use one or two stakes for small trees, two or three for large trees. Select stakes that are tall and strong enough to support your trees. Locate the first stake facing the prevailing wind. If more than one stake is used, space the stakes equally around the trees.

Drive the stakes several inches into firm soil on the

Avoid ties like this that don't allow slack between the tree and stake. Movement encourages strong wood to develop.

outside of the root ball before you finish backfilling the planting hole. Attach the stakes to your trees with materials that won't cut, rub, or damage the trees' bark. Plastic bands, nylon webbing, and strips of man-made fabric are good choices. Also provide some sort of spacer between the tender bark and the stake. Allow a few inches of slack when you attach these materials so that your trees can move slightly in the wind. This movement promotes the development of strong wood, so the tree will be able to support itself when you remove the stakes.

Unstake your trees one year after planting. By that time, a healthy tree will be well anchored into the ground with its own roots.

Planting a Bareroot Plant with Support

Tall or top-heavy trees often benefit from staking for the first year after planting. It's best to add the stake at planting time so you can insert it into the soil without damaging any roots. By the following year, the new roots will have anchored the plant into the soil.

1. Dig a hole large enough to hold the roots without bending them.

2. Drive the stake into the soil, avoiding any roots; backfill.

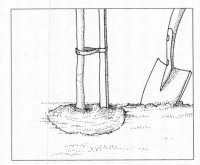

3. Attach the trunk to the stake with a loose tie.

Tree Wraps

To prevent damage from gnawing rodents, such as mice or rabbits, you can install a loose-fitting plastic or wire guard around the trunks of your new trees and shrubs. Apply the guard to a height of about 18 inches (45 cm), which is out of range for most hungry rodents. If your area gets deep snow, wrap the trunk to a higher level. Guards are commercially available, or you can wrap a piece of fine-gauge wire mesh loosely around the trunk. Be sure the guard is loose enough to allow plenty of air movement and room for growth. Avoid paper wraps, which hold in moisture and keep bark soft; they provide ideal conditions for wood-boring insects to tunnel into young trees.

Tree wraps can protect tender young bark from sunscald, chewing animals, and lawn mower nicks.

A loose-fitting wire guard is a great way to protect young trees from damage caused by rabbits and woodchucks.

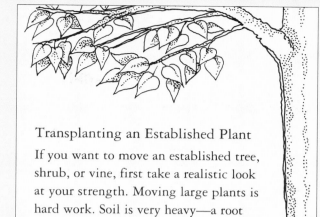

Transplanting an Established Plant

If you want to move an established tree, shrub, or vine, first take a realistic look at your strength. Moving large plants is hard work. Soil is very heavy—a root ball for a tree with a 2-inch (5 cm) trunk can easily weigh a few hundred pounds. If it's too big a job for you, a nursery owner or arborist can give you an estimate on moving it professionally.

To transplant an established tree, shrub, or vine, root-prune in advance. Six months to a year before transplanting, outline a root ball around your plant with a sharp shovel. Allow 1 foot (30 cm) for each inch (2.5 cm) of stem diameter. For example, mark off a 4-foot (1.2 m) diameter root ball for a tree with a 4-inch (10 cm) trunk. Dig a narrow trench, 8 to 12 inches (20 to 30 cm) deep, around the outline. Fill the trench with sphagnum moss so that any roots that regrow will lift out easily.

When you're ready to transplant, dig a root ball, beginning just outside your trench so you take all the new roots. Dig deep enough to lift beneath most of the roots. Tip the ball and slide a piece of burlap or other sturdy material under the ball. Work it around the ball and secure it with rope or nails. Call in strong-shouldered helpers to lift the plant out of its hole and move it to its new location. Plant as you would a B&B specimen. Give the plant some extra care for the first few years—regular watering and lots of organic mulch—to help it settle into its new surroundings. Large or top-heavy plants may also benefit from staking the first year.

CARE AND MAINTENANCE

Maintaining your landscape doesn't have to be an exhaustive or expensive undertaking. Preventing problems before they get started is a simple but important part of the plan—and one that depends on you. Be alert to signs of stress that might be a result of pests or diseases. Perform any maintenance as soon as you see that it's needed and you will keep your labor and expense to a minimum.

Whenever possible, try to carry out your landscape maintenance on a preventive basis. Not only is it less work that way, but you can also perform routine tasks when you have time rather than on an emergency basis when your plants are in dire need of attention. As you think about the maintenance activities you need to perform each year, jot notes on your calendar to remind yourself when the best time is to accomplish them. For example, plan on replenishing mulch before the dry season approaches to conserve soil moisture. Or note when Japanese beetles normally appear so you can start your control program before they get out of hand.

Here is a list of activities you'll need to consider as you draw up a maintenance plan for your property. You'll find more information on each of these topics in the pages that follow.

Composting Making and using compost is at the heart of any successful organic garden. Compost makes a great soil amendment and fertilizer, and it's also an ideal way to recycle yard wastes and kitchen scraps.

Mulching A thick layer of organic mulch around trees, shrubs, and vines cuts down on all other maintenance chores. Mulch is a laborsaving way to control weeds, and it also helps retain moisture and improve your soil, encouraging healthy root growth.

Watering New trees, shrubs, and vines require regular watering, from the hose or the skies, for at least 1 full year after planting. When rainfall is inadequate during the growing season, you will need to provide supplemental irrigation until plants become established.

Feeding Most trees, shrubs, and vines don't need much in the way of supplemental fertilizers. In fact, a layer of compost applied over the soil to the drip line will offer all the added nutrition most plants need. If your soil is low in nutrients, plants may grow slowly, have few flowers, or have leaves that are small and pale. In this case, you may need to apply fertilizers.

Controlling Weeds Weeds are an eyesore and compete with your plants for nutrients. In addition, they can harbor pests and diseases. Use mulch as the basis of your weed-control program and whenever possible, pull weeds while they're young.

Controlling Pests and Diseases Keeping a watchful eye for insects, diseases, or pesky animals doesn't take much time, but it goes a long way toward protecting your landscape investment. When problems arise, you can take care of them with safe organic methods.

Pruning Careful plant selection will free you from pruning foundation shrubs that grow up over your windows or trees that are too tall for utility wires. But don't throw away your pruning shears—you'll still need them for correcting structural problems and training young plants into well-shaped trees and shrubs.

Opposite: If you perform small maintenance tasks regularly, they won't become overwhelming. This wisteria (*Wisteria* spp.), for instance, needs to be pruned back severely after flowering to control its rampant growth.

Making and Using Compost

Compost is the best thing you can do for your garden. No matter what kind of soil you have, compost will improve it. Compost loosens compacted clay and helps sandy soils retain moisture. It also stimulates the activities of the living soil community by giving microorganisms plenty of organic matter for raw material and by increasing the supply of air and water. It buffers the pH level of soil, moderating conditions that are highly acid or alkaline. Depending on what you put in the mix, most compost is a well-balanced source of the nutrients plants need for good growth.

Materials for Composting

Composting is a great way to reduce the amount of household and garden wastes you haul to the curb. Through the alchemy of a simple compost pile, you can turn kitchen scraps, garden trimmings, and other organic matter into rich, dark, crumbly compost.

Keep a bucket with a lid in your kitchen and make it a habit to toss peelings and other organic waste in the bucket instead of in the trash. Avoid meat scraps and grease, however; they decompose slowly and attract animals. Also avoid tossing seed-bearing weeds, diseased plants, or any weeds that regenerate from pieces of root on your compost pile—the pile may not heat up enough to kill them. And don't compost manure from humans, dogs, and

Keep your composting area close to the garden so you can easily dump in trimmings or haul out finished compost.

cats—this material can carry disease organisms.

If you plan to build a hot compost pile, you'll need a mix of materials that are high in carbon and materials that are high in nitrogen. High-nitrogen materials, such as grass clippings, vegetable scraps, young weeds, and fresh manure, tend to be green, moist, and often sloppy. High-carbon materials, like dead leaves, sawdust, newspaper, and straw, are brown or yellow, bulky, and dry.

You'll soon gain a feel for whether your materials are high in nitrogen or high in carbon by the way they look, smell, and feel. Mixing them together isn't an exact science; it's a matter of experience and observation. A pile made of only grass clippings and kitchen scraps will soon begin to smell bad; since there's not enough carbon, the excess nitrogen escapes into the air in the form of strong-smelling ammonia. A large pile of dry leaves—very high in carbon but low in nitrogen—will eventually decompose, but it may take years.

It's easy to remedy a pile with too much nitrogen by

Build a handy homemade bin out of posts and wire fencing.

A simple wire-fencing cylinder is fine for smaller bins.

Concrete blocks make a convenient, easy-to-build container.

You can make compost from two basic ingredients almost all gardens have—fallen leaves and grass clippings.

mixing in a wheelbarrowful of high-carbon materials. Similarly, a pile that is decomposing slowly because of too much carbon can be reactivated by adding a few forkfuls of high-nitrogen material.

Composting Systems

Your composting system can be as simple as an open pile tucked in an out-of-the-way corner. An open pile 3 feet (1 m) wide by 3 feet (1 m) deep by 3 feet (1 m) high will produce fine compost. However, many gardeners prefer to use bins. Bins protect the pile from the weather and scavenging animals and help to conserve heat during composting.

The container you use is unimportant, as long as the volume of the pile is at least 3 cubic yards (3 cubic meters). You can use a circle of wire fencing or construct bins from wooden pallets, concrete blocks, snow fence, or any other materials you have. Wire or plastic bins are also available ready-made, as are barrel or drum composters.

Hot Composting

A hot compost pile—built all at once with a balanced mixture of high-carbon and high-nitrogen materials—can reach temperatures between 113° and 158°F (45° and 70°C). It decomposes quickly, producing finished compost in only a few weeks. Aeration is the key to maintaining this temperature range, at which decomposing organisms proliferate and work best. Frequent turning with a garden fork is the best way to mix air into the pile.

Building the Pile Air and water are critical to a successful hot compost pile. Start with a well-drained spot for your pile. Build a 3- to 4-inch (7.5 to 10 cm) base of coarse materials, such as brush, wood chips, or chopped dry cornstalks, to allow air to penetrate the pile from below. A wooden pallet also makes a suitable base.

Your compost pile should be a mix of both high-carbon and high-nitrogen materials. Use as many different types of organic matter as possible to produce compost with a wide variety of nutrients. Add a thin layer of soil, old compost, or a commercial compost starter every 6 to 8 inches (15 to 20 cm) to introduce the microorganisms needed for decomposition.

The more finely cut or chopped the organic material you start with, the faster it decomposes. Run your lawn mower over large leaves to cut them smaller, and

For a more formal look, trim block bins with wooden edges and fronts.

When the original ingredients are unrecognizable, the compost is done.

tear newspapers into strips to keep them from settling into a dense mat. Woody branches from trees and shrubs decompose slowly unless you run them through a chipper first.

As you build, water the pile periodically with a garden hose. A good compost pile should feel like a moist sponge. Make a small depression on the top of the pile to catch rain, and sprinkle your pile to keep it moist. If your pile gets too wet and smells like ammonia, add some high-carbon materials and turn the pile to help dry it out.

A properly built compost pile will begin to heat within a few days. If your pile doesn't feel hot, water it thoroughly or add a high-nitrogen material like grass clippings. Remember to turn your pile every few days to speed up decomposition.

Cold Composting

If you're not in a hurry for compost, if your back isn't up to turning the pile every few days, or if you just want a less-demanding system, try cold composting. A cold compost pile—one left to decompose naturally without frequent turning—will produce compost just as well as a hot pile, but at a much slower rate. Just pile up your organic materials as they become available and wait a year or so until they have broken down. Finished compost smells earthy and is dark and crumbly like good topsoil. If any large pieces of twigs or other materials remain, screen them out and return them to your pile for further composting.

Compost Tea

Brewing up a batch of compost tea is easy, and your plants will thank you for it! To make a large amount, put a shovelful of finished compost in a burlap sack and tie the sack closed. Hang the bag in a barrel or a large bucket of water for up to a week. (For a smaller batch, put a handful or two of compost in a square of cheesecloth and let it soak in a watering can—ready for application.) Remove the bag and dilute the remaining liquid to a weak-tea color. You can add the soaked compost to the garden or simply return it to the compost pile. Apply the nutrient-rich solution with a watering can to seedlings, young plants, and newly planted stock. Or strain it well and mist it onto the foliage—it will provide some nutrients directly to the leaves and can help prevent some fungal diseases, too.

Using Compost

Compost is so versatile that you'll soon find you never have enough to go around. Use your finished compost as an all-purpose fertilizer and soil conditioner. Incorporate it into new planting beds to improve soil structure and moisture retention, as well as a balanced supply of plant nutrients. Apply a layer of it beneath another organic mulch for a fertility boost.

Add a layer of compost under the mulch around trees, shrubs, and vines, or poke holes into the soil around the drip line of trees and fill them with compost as a fertilizer. Scatter screened compost on the lawn beneath trees, shrubs, and vines to feed far-reaching roots. Wherever you need additional nutrients or a soil improver, make compost your first choice.

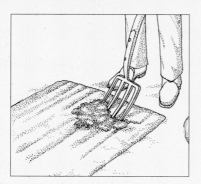

Dig or till in generous amounts of compost when you are preparing new planting areas.

Apply a layer of compost around the base of plants before adding a more permanent mulch.

Scatter finished compost along beds of young plants to get them off to a good start.

A thick layer of loose organic mulch will help keep the soil cool and moist—ideal conditions for new plantings.

Selecting and Using Mulch

Mulch is the number-one time-saver in your home landscape. Mulch saves on weeding chores because it discourages weeds and makes sprouting weeds easy to pull. By keeping grass and weeds away from your plants, you also prevent weeds from competing for water and nutrients.

Mulch also creates a good soil environment for plant roots. It helps hold water in the soil, making plants less prone to drought stress. Mulch also moderates soil temperatures, keeping soil warmer or cooler depending on the type of mulch you select. As organic mulches—such as wood chips and shredded leaves—break down, they add nutrients and organic matter to your soil.

Mulch also helps reduce soil erosion, and it keeps soil from splashing up on your house or plants when rain falls. Finally, a wide ring of mulch around trees, shrubs, or vines is good protection against accidental nicks and bangs from string trimmers and lawn mowers, which can cause trunk wounds.

Selecting a Mulch

There are two general types of mulch—organic and inorganic. Both help control weeds and hold moisture in soil, but organic mulches also add all-important organic matter to soil. Inorganic mulches don't improve soil, but they last longer than organic types.

Organic Mulches Shredded leaves, grass clippings, and bark chips are all examples of organic mulches. In addition to keeping soil cool and moist, organic mulches help improve soil structure by encouraging the activity of earthworms and other soil organisms. They also add nutrients and organic matter to soil as they decompose. Good organic mulches for use around trees, shrubs, and vines are wood and bark chips, shredded bark, pine needles, and chopped leaves. Hay, straw, and grass clippings are also good mulches, and you can top them with a layer of wood chips or shredded bark to improve their appearance.

The larger the particle size, the more slowly the mulch will decompose and need to be replenished. Grass clippings decompose quickly and need frequent renewal, while large bark chips will last several seasons. Flat, leathery tree leaves such as oak and sycamore will last a long time but can mat and shed water: Chop these leaves in a chipper or with your lawn mower before using them as mulch.

Some organic materials are unsuitable for use as

Grass clippings also make a great mulch. Apply them in thin layers so they don't mat down.

Straw is not the most attractive mulch. You may want to top it with a layer of another material, like wood chips.

mulch because they are too attractive to weeds. Compost, aged manure, or other finely shredded organic materials act like potting soil to weed seeds. In a frequently tended vegetable or flower garden, these mulches are fine. But select a less-hospitable mulch for your low-maintenance permanent plantings, or use these mulches as a base and top them with wood chips.

You can collect materials like leaves and pine needles for mulches. Wood chips and bark are widely available in bags at garden or home centers. Composted yard waste and wood chips are sometimes available for little or no cost from municipal composting facilities or tree-care companies.

Inorganic Mulches Inorganic mulches include stones, marble chips, and lava rock, as well as black plastic and various landscape fabrics. Inorganic mulches don't decompose, so they won't need renewing like organic mulches. But they also don't improve soil as organic mulches do.

Since you won't be disturbing stone or gravel mulches with fresh applications, weeds can become a problem. You will have to hand pull weeds that sprout in these materials. These mulches are often used in combination with a weed barrier such as landscape fabric to greatly reduce the chance of weed problems.

Dark-colored inorganic mulches heat soil, sometimes too much. A plant that prefers cool roots (such as clematis) or one that is growing in full sun may suffer stress from the heat retained by the dark stones. Light-colored inorganic mulches, such as marble or quartz chips, reflect sunlight and heat, which can cause leaf damage.

Whan applying mulch, keep it a few inches away from the stems, to avoid rot and pest damage.

Applying Mulch

Before laying down any mulch, get rid of all existing weeds by pulling, digging, or smothering them. Then spread a layer of mulch that is thick enough to discourage new weeds from sprouting. If your mulch has large particles, such as large wood or bark chips, use a 3- to 5-inch (7.5 to 12.5 cm) thick layer. Mulches with smaller-sized particles, such as grass clippings or shredded bark, allow less space for sprouting weeds, so you can apply them in a thinner layer of 2 to 3 inches (5 to 7.5 cm). Cover the soil with a uniformly thick layer, but taper the depth of the layer near the trunks or stems of

Fallen leaves make an attractive, natural-looking mulch. They break down quickly, so replace them often.

Clematis thrive when their roots are cool and moist. Provide the conditions they need with a thick organic mulch.

Chopped leaves are a gardener's gold mine. Use them as a beautiful, nutrient-rich mulch for all kinds of plants.

Shredded bark and wood chips are popular mulches. They provide a pleasing neutral background to show off plants.

plants. Never pile mulch against your plants' trunks or stems. Mulch can hold excessive moisture around them and also reduce the amount of oxygen that reaches the crowns of the plants. To prevent this problem and to keep rodents from nesting nearby and feeding on the bark, leave about 6 to 12 inches (15 to 30 cm) between the mulch and tree and shrub trunks, and 4 to 6 inches (10 to 15 cm) between mulch and vines.

How frequently you need to renew the mulches depends on which kind you use. Long-lasting materials like wood chips may need refreshing only every 2 to 3 years. Finer materials, like compost or grass clippings, should be renewed once or twice a year. Top these materials with coarse mulches to help them last longer.

Weed Barriers

Several materials, including black plastic and landscape fabrics, are sold for use as weed barriers. These materials are designed to be used under inorganic mulches to provide better weed control. (If you use a thick layer of organic mulch and renew it as needed, weed barriers are generally unnecessary.)

Black plastic is fine for a vegetable garden, but it's not good to use around permanent plantings like trees, shrubs, and vines. Water can't pass through it, and it also prevents oxygen from reaching plant roots.

Landscape fabrics, which are spunbonded or woven geotextiles, have pores through which water and gases can pass. They're relatively expensive but control weeds for several years because they don't readily decompose unless left uncovered. Landscape fabrics sound like the perfect solution to weeds, but new research indicates that surface roots of plants grow into the fabric. These roots are more susceptible to drought than those in the soil. In addition, weeds that grow in the mulch covering the fabric may root into the fabric. When you pull out the weeds, you'll rip the fabric, leaving a space for more weeds to sprout up.

Using the News

If your mulch supply is limited and your weeds are rampant, newspaper makes an excellent weed barrier. Lay it down in sections, several pages thick, and cover it with organic mulch to smother weeds. The organic mulch keeps the newspaper from blowing away and also covers the unattractive paper. The newspaper will gradually decompose over the next year or two, adding organic matter to the soil.

A spring topdressing of compost or well-rotted manure will give plants the nutrients they need for good growth.

Fertilizing

Unlike smaller garden plants like vegetables and annuals, well-chosen, established trees, shrubs, and vines generally do just fine in searching out their own nutrients. There will be times, however, when you want to give your plants a boost. The first few years after planting is an important time, since the young root system may not yet be able to reach all the necessary nutrients. Plants that are near paving or in pots, where the soil is limited, often need supplemental feeding. If growth seems slow or stunted—look for short stems, small or distorted leaves, and few flowers or fruits—you may need to supply additional nutrients.

Types of Fertilizers

When you fertilize, you can supply nutrients in either a dry or a liquid form or a combination of the two.

Dry Fertilizers These materials are applied to the soil around your plant and release their nutrients into the soil gradually. You can buy commercially prepared, balanced organic fertilizers, which usually come in a granulated form. Compost is an excellent all-around fertilizer. It supplies small amounts of the macro-nutrients nitrogen (N), phosphorus (P), and potassium (K), as well as important trace nutrients and organic matter.

Liquid Fertilizers Liquid fertilizers are generally applied directly to the plants, so they can absorb the nutrients through their leaves. You can apply a single dose as a quick but temporary fix for nutrient deficiencies or make regular applications 2 to 4 weeks apart for a general nutrient boost.

Applying Fertilizers

How you physically apply the nutrients depends on the type of fertilizer you choose. Broadcasting, drill-hole application, irrigation, and foliar feeding are all fairly easy methods.

Broadcasting Broadcasting involves spreading the fertilizer material evenly onto the soil over the roots. Before you apply fertilizer, pull back the layer of mulch around your plants; then scatter the material over the soil and replace the mulch.

Drill-hole Application If the soil around your plants is compacted or clayey, broadcasting may not be effective in getting the nutrients where they're needed. In this situation, use an auger or steel pipe to punch holes into the ground around and a few feet out from the

Applying Fertilizer

Whichever fertilizing method you use, make sure you always follow the application rates given on the package. Adding too much fertilizer can actually harm your plants.

You can punch holes in the soil and fill them with dry fertilizer.

Sprinkling dry fertilizer around the base of the plant is also effective.

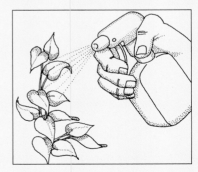

Liquid fertilizers are easy to mist right onto plant leaves.

drip line. Make the holes 4 to 6 inches (10 to 15 cm) deep and fill them with fertilizer or compost. The holes help break up the compaction, get needed oxygen to the roots, and place the fertilizer directly into the root zone.

Irrigation If you have a drip or soaker-hose irrigation system, you can use it to apply liquid fertilizer. Be sure to use a product such as kelp that dissolves thoroughly to avoid clogging your emitters or pipes.

Foliar Feeding You can apply liquid fertilizers with a hand-held sprayer or mister or with a knapsack sprayer. Set the nozzle to release the finest spray possible. A surfactant such as ¼ teaspoon of mild soap per gallon (3.8 l) of spray will improve coverage, preventing the spray from beading up on the leaves. Spray in early morning or late afternoon to avoid leaf burn. Be sure to follow the instructions and suggested application rates on the labels of commercial foliar sprays.

Fertilizing Guidelines

Roots absorb nutrients from the soil when it is adequately moist and when its temperature is between 40° and 80°F (4° and 27°C). In temperate regions, apply fertilizers in spring or in mid- to late fall. In warmer areas where plants grow year-round, apply fertilizers when plants are most actively growing.

Established Plants Once trees, shrubs, and vines are established, your fertilizing chores will be minimal. Regular applications of organic mulch are all that most

of these plants need. If you have extra compost on hand, you can apply an even layer of it underneath the mulch.

New Plants Apply an even layer of compost around the base of a new plant in a circle extending 2 to 3 feet (60 to 90 cm) past the drip line. Then cover the compost with a 2- to 3-inch (5 to 7.5 cm) deep layer of mulch. Keep both the compost and the mulch a few inches away from the stem to prevent rodent damage and to allow air circulation.

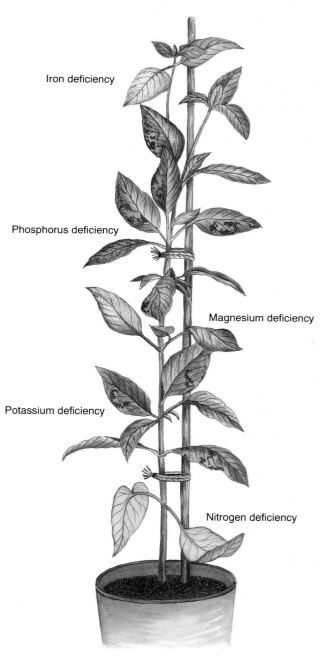

Iron deficiency

Phosphorus deficiency

Magnesium deficiency

Potassium deficiency

Nitrogen deficiency

Thankfully, plants rarely show all of these nutrient deficiencies at once. If one of your plants shows any of these symptoms, try seaweed spray for a quick fix. Then amend the soil with compost for a long-term solution.

Watering

Water stress, a result of both too little or too much water, is one of the major causes of poor plant growth or even death. Selecting trees, shrubs, and vines that are adapted to your site and climate is the best thing you can do to avoid problems with water stress—and to reduce watering chores. A deep layer of mulch will also help reduce water-stress problems because it helps soil retain water and controls competition from grass and weeds.

Newly planted trees, shrubs, and vines will need special watering attention for at least the first full year of growth after planting—or better yet, 2 years. After that—provided you've selected plants adapted to your site, prepared the planting area properly, and kept the plants well mulched—their roots should be far-reaching enough to collect adequate moisture during times of drought.

Even if you live where 40 inches (1 m) of rain or other precipitation falls per year, you may still need to water new plantings. Most trees, shrubs, and vines should receive 1 to 1½ inches (25 to 37 mm) of water per week during the growing season. A rain gauge, available for a few dollars at hardware stores or garden centers, will give you an exact measure of your rainfall. Or check the weekly totals reported in your local newspaper.

Test for moisture by digging a small hole and looking at the soil.

If less than 1 inch (25 mm) of rain falls in a week, test the soil for moisture before watering. Pull aside the mulch and wiggle your finger into the soil in the root area to see how wet it is, or remove a slice of soil with a hand trowel so you can judge deep moisture. If only the top 1 inch (25 mm) is dry, you don't need to water. If your soil is dry several inches down, start watering. Don't wait for signs of plant stress—wilting, leaf drop, and bud drop—before you water. Once a plant is suffering visibly, it will take longer to recover.

Water Wisely

The key to wise watering is to water slowly and deeply. Watering slowly ensures that all the water soaks into the soil—you don't want any water to run off or cause soil erosion. Deep watering encourages deep rooting, which makes plants more drought-tolerant. Whenever you water, wet the soil to a depth of at least 6 inches (15 cm) or more, a process that usually takes several hours. Water early or late in the day when temperatures and winds are generally lower, decreasing evaporation.

If your soil has a crust that reduces water penetration, cultivate shallowly with a trowel or hand fork. Then apply a layer of organic mulch around your plants to conserve soil moisture and to prevent future crusting.

Watering Methods

The best way to irrigate new trees, shrubs, and vines, without wasting water, is by using soaker hoses. That's because they deliver water directly to the root zone of a plant, where it seeps slowly into the soil.

Soaker hoses are perforated along their length or are simply designed to leak all over (in which case they're often called leaky pipe). Since they release water at ground level, very little is lost to runoff or evaporation. Look for a flexible hose that can be coiled around trees, shrubs, and vines, and install it beneath your mulch.

Avoid using overhead sprinklers. They often put water where you don't need it, and most of it evaporates before it reaches the soil. Hand-watering is an option for small, newly planted stock, but avoid it for established plants. Sprinkling just the surface encourages shallow rooting, making plants more drought-prone. But if you dump on enough water to wet the soil deeply, you may also end up washing soil away from the roots.

Choose the watering equipment that fits your needs and budget.

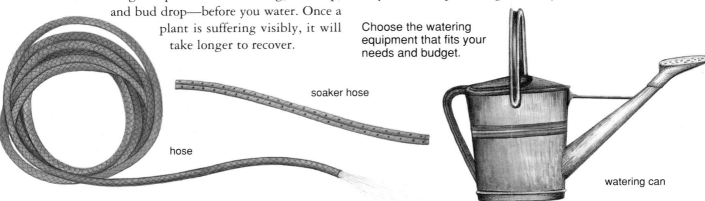

hose

soaker hose

watering can

Controlling Weeds

Identifying and controlling weeds is a critical part of landscape maintenance. Weeds detract from the appearance of your yard, making it look neglected and untidy. They also compete with your trees, shrubs, and vines for space, light, water, and soil nutrients. Many weeds develop extensive root systems very quickly that will interfere with the growth of newly planted trees, shrubs, and vines. Climbing weeds may overgrow or twine around and strangle your desired plants.

Besides directly competing with or harming your plants, weeds can also serve as alternate hosts or habitats for insects and diseases that bother your trees, shrubs, and vines. Problems may first develop on the weeds, then move to your landscape plants.

The Ways of Weeds

Understanding the growth habits of weeds is the key to choosing the right control measure.

Annuals   Weeds that grow in one year, like ragweed and lamb's-quarters, are annuals. If they sprout in the spring, flower in the summer, and set seed in the fall (like pigweed and crabgrass), they're summer annuals. If they sprout in the fall, flower in the winter, and set seed in the spring (like chickweed and henbit), they're winter annuals. Summer annuals are usually the bigger problem of the two because they're competing with your trees, shrubs, and vines during their time of active growth. Winter annuals grow at a less-competitive time and are killed off by summer heat.

Since annual weeds can produce thousands of seeds

Bindweed is a real garden menace. The roots of this perennial spread quickly; remove them all when weeding.

per plant, the trick to controlling them is to remove the plants before they go to seed. Scrape them out of the soil with a hoe or hand weeder or, if the soil is moist or loose, carefully pull them out roots and all.

Biennials and Perennials   Biennial weeds like Queen Anne's lace and mullein and perennial weeds like dock and dandelion have persistent roots. Even if you cut or pull off the tops, they grow back. Many perennial weeds spread not only by seed but also by creeping roots or stems; thistles, bindweed, and ground ivy are good examples.

The secret to controlling biennials and perennials is removing the roots. A dandelion fork (also known as an asparagus knife) is handy for prying taproot weeds like Queen Anne's lace out of the soil. A hand or spading fork is useful for digging up the root systems of spreading weeds. Remove all the root pieces you can find from the soil; any pieces that you leave can quickly sprout into new plants.

Preventing Weed Problems

Preventing weeds from getting started is the best way to keep your weeding chores to a minimum. When you remove the turf as you prepare a planting hole, shake out the soil and add the grass or weeds to your compost pile. If you just work them into the planting area, there's a good chance they will sprout up again.

Prepare the soil for planting; then wait a week and use a hoe to slice off any weeds that have grown. If your planting site is plagued by perennial weeds that spread by creeping roots, such as quack grass, carefully and thoroughly weed out the roots by hand before planting.

A deep layer of mulch around trees, shrubs, and vines is the best weed-control method for established plants.

Dandelions may be unsightly in the lawn, but they're easy to remove. Use a fork to pry out the plant, root and all.

Wood-boring beetles produce larvae that mine into bark, causing limbs to die or break. Prune affected branches.

Preventing Pest and Disease Problems

Here's where all that planning you did to choose well-suited, naturally resistant plants pays off. Plants that are situated in the right site and growing well are less susceptible to attack than weakened plants that are stressed by poor growing conditions. Healthy plants shrug off diseases and pests more easily than sickly plants, for which such problems can be the final blow.

The organic approach to pests and diseases emphasizes prevention. Selecting species and cultivars that are naturally resistant to diseases and pests will make your life easier. Good housekeeping in the garden is another part of the program: Weeds and plant debris can harbor pests and diseases, so keep your garden clean.

If problems do get out of hand, then it's time to choose a control measure. Organic pest management (OPM) is a pest-control concept that combines cultural, biological, and physical controls. In OPM, organically acceptable chemical controls, including botanicals such as pyrethrins and rotenone, are considered only after all other approaches have failed.

Planning for Action

Start your pest-control program with a plant-and-pest list. First, list all the species of trees, shrubs, and vines in your landscape. If you don't know what some of them

are, take a sample to your local garden center or nursery for help in identification. Then research the problems you might expect to have with each plant. Your local Cooperative Extension Service agent is a good place to start. She or he is usually well aware of any diseases or pests that are a problem in your area. Garden center personnel are also a good source of advice on which pests and diseases to watch for.

List the problems each plant in your landscape might have, along with a brief description of symptoms. Note the general time of year when the problems usually occur. Keep in mind that weather variations, such as a late-spring or summer drought, affect the rate of growth of your trees, shrubs, and vines. This in turn affects the occurrence of pest problems.

Organic-gardening books are an excellent resource for identifying pests and diseases and for determining methods of control. Local nursery owners and your county Extension agent may also be able to suggest appropriate measures. (Many Extension agents and

Trap gypsy moth caterpillars in tree bands or spray with BT.

At night, shake black vine weevils off plants onto a cloth; then destroy.

Carefully scrape off scale insects or spray with horticultural oil.

You'll often find aphids clustered on buds and shoot tips. Prune off infested parts or spray with soap.

nurseries routinely recommend synthetic chemicals, so be sure to ask for advice on organic methods of control.)

Using Your Eyes

For most gardeners, walking through their garden is a regular and enjoyable habit. Incorporate your garden strolls into your pest-control program by using this time to scout for garden pests.

Walk through your landscape at least once each week looking closely for any sign or symptom of a problem. Some symptoms are obvious—deformed leaves, discolored or wilted foliage, buds that blacken or fail to open, or webbing. Look for the not so obvious, too; pests are adept at hiding from view. Turn leaves over and look at their undersides, stand back from your trees and look at the top of their canopies, and examine flower and leaf buds closely.

If you see abnormal growth but can't identify the pest or disease problem yourself, get a positive identification before selecting control measures. Keep in mind that far

more landscape plant problems are caused by physiological factors such as drought, compacted soil, chemicals, equipment damage, or lightning than by insects, fungi, bacteria, and other pathogens.

A small number of insects or a few leaf spots may not warrant any control measure. Keep in mind that your plants are home to a host of insects all the time. If you're new to organic gardening, you may find it unusual not to reach for the chemical artillery at the first sign of pests or diseases, especially if you have invested a considerable amount of money in the plant. But give natural biological controls a chance to work before you step in. Often beneficial insects will prey on the undesirables, keeping a natural balance. If you detect an infestation of aphids, for example, hold off for a few days and see if green lacewings or other aphid-eating beneficials are drawn to the feast.

If the symptom spreads or the number of insects increases, take control measures before the infestation or disease is severe. One skeletonized leaf on your grapevine may be the work of a single feeding caterpillar and nothing to worry about, but it could also be a forewarning of a Japanese beetle invasion. Keep an eye on any plant that shows symptoms. Pest and disease problems are easier to control when they first develop.

Cultural Controls

If pests or diseases seem serious, turn to cultural controls first. Take a careful look at your plant and see if it has been stressed by a lack of water or nutrients. Thrips, for example, are attracted to wilted plants. A good soaking in the root zone or a foliar spray of nutrients is an immediate first step you can take.

Too much water or fertilizer can cause just as many problems as a deficiency. Waterlogged soil is a breeding ground for soilborne diseases. Overfertilized trees, shrubs, and vines produce soft, lush growth that is very attractive to pests with sucking mouthparts, such as aphids.

Japanese beetles feed on many plants, skeletonizing leaves. Handpick pests.

Prune out or scrape off and destroy the webs of tent caterpillars.

Tiny spider mites cause yellowed leaves. Spray with water or soap.

Overcrowded plants are also more prone to insect infestations and diseases. They're often weak and spindly, and the lack of air movement is an invitation to disease. Pull out weeds that crowd plants and restrict free air flow, and transplant specimens that were planted too close together. Mulch can also be useful in pest prevention. Mulch helps to control disease by preventing soil-borne pathogens from splashing onto leaves and stems. Beneficial insects live in mulch, providing a ready army to feed on pests. Mulching also helps keep the soil moist, moderating drought that can stress plants.

Try a baking soda spray (1 teaspoon baking soda in 1 quart [1 l] water) to stop the spread of powdery mildew.

Physical Controls

Physical controls—trapping or otherwise removing the problem from the plant—are an immediate and effective way of dealing with many pests and with some diseases. For example, a blast of water from a garden hose washes away soft-bodied aphids.

Pruning is another way to get rid of pests in a hurry, as long as the symptoms are limited to a few leaves, shoots, or branch tips. As soon as you see signs of poor health, snip off the leaf or stem. Don't add diseased foliage and plants to your compost pile; it may not heat up enough to kill pathogens. Bury or burn infected plant material or put it in a closed paper bag for disposal with the household trash.

Handpicking and insect traps keep pests at a manageable level. If Japanese beetles are defoliating your roses, tap them into a bucket of soapy water. Tree bands fashioned from cloth trap crawling pests. Tie a 15-inch (37.5 cm) wide strip of burlap to the trunk with a string around the middle, then pull the top section down over the lower half to trap caterpillars and other crawlers.

Check daily and destroy your catch. A physical barrier of copper sheet metal deters creeping pests like slugs and snails. Fasten a strip of copper around the trunks of trees, shrubs, or vines.

Biological Controls

Biological control of pests and diseases depends on naturally occurring beneficial insects and animals as well as microbial insecticides like *Bacillus thuringiensis* (BT) and other measures introduced by the gardener. A landscape that is well balanced naturally includes a large force of beneficial lacewings, ladybugs, ground beetles, tachinid flies, and others. Beneficial insects such as ladybugs and praying mantids are also sold commercially.

BT and other microbial insecticides control pests by making them sick and die. Use these measures sparingly because they can harm beneficial or desirable insects as well as pests. BT, for example, will kill the larvae of many beautiful butterflies and moths as well

Prevent rust on apples and crabapples by planting resistant cultivars.

Pick off rose leaves affected with black spot; try a baking soda spray.

If you find leaf galls on azaleas, pick off and destroy affected leaves.

When you spot a pest problem, look for beneficial insects nearby. Ladybugs often feed on aphids.

as pest caterpillars. Except for unusually severe infestations—such as invasions of gypsy moths—your trees, shrubs, and vines can shrug off insect pests quite well without microbial insecticides.

Birds do their part in controlling pests, too. Even the maligned starling is a superb pest controller—a large part of this stocky bird's diet consists of Japanese beetle grubs. Add a bird feeder and nesting boxes to attract feathered helpers to your yard.

Organically Acceptable Chemical Controls

Consider organic pesticides and fungicides, such as insecticidal soap sprays or bordeaux mixture, as a last resort. Even though they don't persist in the environment as long as some synthetic pesticides do, they also have drawbacks. Like synthetic controls, organic pesticides kill insects nonselectively, annihilating beneficials as well as pests. And like synthetic chemicals, organically acceptable chemicals can be extremely toxic to you as well as to pests. Wear protective clothing, including

Animals and People are Pests, Too

As more land is swallowed up for buildings, the habitat for wildlife continues to diminish. Rabbits and deer that move into suburbia can become serious pests. A strong, secure fence is the best line of defense. Ask your neighbors and your local Cooperative Extension Service or wildlife conservancy which trees, shrubs, and vines are unpalatable to the deer in your neighborhood. A trunk wrapping of wire mesh will protect your trees, shrubs, and vines from rodents that gnaw or strip bark.

People can also be pests as far as plants are concerned. When you run into the trunk of your tree with a lawn mower, you open up a wound to insect and disease attack. When you nail things onto trees or wrap wire around them or carelessly pull on branches or strip off bark, you're causing damage. Use care as you work and play around your landscape to avoid harming your plants.

gloves and a face mask, when applying them.

You can make an all-purpose garden insecticide with 1 to 3 tablespoons of liquid dish soap (not detergent) per gallon (3.8 l) of water. Use this mixture as a spray for aphids, whiteflies, and other pests. Commercial insecticidal soaps are also effective. Pyrethrins, rotenone, and sabadilla dust are other weapons in the organic gardener's last-resort arsenal of insecticides. Copper sulfate and other copper mixtures, sulfur, and antitranspirants can be used to prevent or control the spread of fungal diseases. Consult organic-gardening reference books, local nursery staff, or other organic gardeners for specific control suggestions.

Praying mantids will catch and eat both pest and beneficial insects.

Lacewings and their larvae eat many kinds of pests, including aphids.

Burlap tree bands are an easy way to trap many kinds of caterpillars.

A Pruning Primer

Pruning your plants at the right time, with the right tools, and for the right reasons is a vital part of keeping your landscape looking good. Proper pruning can promote healthy growth on ailing plants, improve the form of poorly shaped ones, show off the natural beauty of good-looking plants, and encourage the production of more or better fruits or flowers. By taking the time to learn the proper techniques, you'll be amply rewarded with a healthy, attractive landscape.

Why Should You Prune?

There are many reasons you may want or need to prune. Judicious pruning at planting time defines the shape of your new trees, shrubs, and vines. As your new plants grow, they will occasionally need pruning to correct structural problems that develop, such as branches that rub or grow at tight angles, or to remove vertical water sprouts and suckers.

Maintenance pruning is also necessary to remove damage caused by weather, animals, people, or insects and diseases. You may need to direct growth, especially of fast-growing vines, or control the height or spread of your plants. Some vines, especially vigorous growers like trumpet creeper (*Campsis radicans*) and wisteria (*Wisteria* spp.), need heavy pruning to keep them a manageable size and to increase the number of flowers.

When to Prune

Timing is critical to successful pruning. Adapt your pruning schedule depending on what you want to accomplish. Here are the benefits and drawbacks to

Pruning forsythia while it's blooming gives you a good view of the plant's form. Enjoy the cut branches indoors.

pruning in each season:

- Spring pruning stimulates a flush of vigorous growth. It's a good time for heavy pruning because plants will recover fast.
- Summer pruning is a good time for tidying up, but avoid heavy pruning, which can stress plants in hot weather.
- Fall is a good time to make thinning cuts, removing branches back to a main stem. Don't prune back branch tips in fall because the tender new growth that results can be easily damaged by freezes.
- In winter, dormant plants are easy to prune since the lack of leaves makes it easy to see the plant's structure.

There are times when you need to ignore the season and pick up the pruners, however. If damage from storms, equipment, or disease occurs, you should prune

Pruning Pointers for Trees and Shrubs

Prune spring-flowering trees and shrubs, such as deutzias (*Deutzia* spp.), forsythias (*Forsythia* spp.), and spireas (*Spiraea* spp.), after they finish blooming. If you wait too long, it will be too late for the plant to produce flower buds for next year. If you prune spring bloomers in fall or winter, you'll remove the flower buds; in spring, you'll see leafy new growth but few flowers.

Summer-flowering shrubs and trees, including old-fashioned weigela (*Weigela florida*), hydrangea (*Hydrangea* spp.), and butterfly bush (*Buddleia davidii*), should be pruned soon after bloom or in late winter. These plants form buds on the current year's growth.

Prune other types of deciduous shrubs and trees any time of year, except for those species that bleed too much sap if pruned in the spring. Wait until summer to prune beeches, birches, elms, and maples.

Winter is a good time to prune evergreen trees, shrubs, and vines. Plus, you can use the trimmings for Christmas greenery!

Hedge clippers are handy for shearing back heaths and heathers after flowering.

immediately, removing all damaged wood. For more tips on when to prune particular kinds of plants, see "Pruning Pointers for Trees and Shrubs" on page 66 and "Pruning Vines" on page 69.

Pruning Tools

The pruning tools you'll need depend on what you will be trimming. Hedge clippers are the traditional choice for formal hedges. Pruning shears are best for stems and twigs. As the diameter of the branches increases, switch

Flowering shrubs, like this weigela, are often most attractive when allowed to grow in a natural arching form.

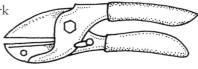

to loppers, which work well on branches that are finger-sized or larger. When loppers aren't large enough, use a pruning saw.

Pruners and loppers are available in two types. Bypass pruners cut with a scissor action; anvil pruners cut with a sharp blade that closes against a metal plate. Lopping shears have long handles to give you leverage and a longer reach. Test pruning tools before buying them to make sure the grip is comfortable and the mechanism is easy to work.

Pruning Techniques

Start any pruning job by removing dead wood. Dead wood is easy to spot during the growing season because it bears no leaves. It snaps easily, revealing no green under the bark.

After removing the dead wood, prune your trees and shrubs to improve their structure, making them more attractive and stronger. Remove any branches that are badly crossed or rubbing, leaving the best of the pair. Thin out or head back misplaced branches that crowd walkways or other plants.

Pruning Cuts Pruning basically comes down to two types of cuts: thinning and heading. A thinning cut removes branches where they join the stem. Be sure to cut just outside the branch collar—the raised or otherwise distinct area at the branch base. Cuts that are flush to the stem, removing the collar area, don't heal (close) well. Use thinning cuts to open the interior of a shrub or tree or to remove misplaced branches.

Heading cuts stimulate regrowth. Save them until the end of the pruning job. A nonselective heading cut slices off branch tips in midstem, bringing on a thick flush of uniform growth. Selective heading snips off the tip of a branch back to a bud or side branch. Cut slightly above a bud pointed in the direction in which you want new stems to grow. In general, prune above buds that face outward, not inward.

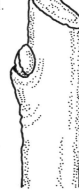

Make a sloping heading cut slightly above a bud (left). Don't cut too close (middle) or leave a stub (right).

Pruning a Large Limb

1. Start with a cut from underneath the branch, out from the trunk.

2. Make another cut a few inches in from the first; saw off the branch.

3. Finish by sawing off the stub just outside the branch collar.

Pruning Large Limbs To prune a large limb, first cut halfway through the branch from underneath, about 1 foot (30 cm) out from the trunk. Move your saw a few inches in toward the trunk from the first cut and saw down from the top until the branch drops. Finish the cut by sawing just outside the branch collar. If the crotch (the angle between the branch and the trunk) is too tight for easy maneuvering, saw from the bottom up. Pruning cuts, even on large branches, need no paint or other wound dressings applied. They will heal fastest on their own.

Renewal Pruning If your plants grow too large or if they contain many old or dead stems, drastic measures are often effective. Many vigorous vines, including autumn clematis (*Clematis maximowicziana*) and perennial sweet pea (*Lathyrus latifolius*), can be pruned to within a few inches of the ground in late winter if they have grown much too large. In spring, the vines will regrow at a manageable size.

Multistemmed deciduous shrubs, such as forsythia (*Forsythia* x *intermedia*) and lilacs (*Syringa* spp.), which have grown old and woody with limited bloom, can also be given this drastic treatment to stimulate new growth. However, it will take several years after this treatment for the shrub to recover completely and flower again. A less-stressful renewal method for reclaiming overgrown deciduous flowering shrubs is to prune one-third of the plant each year over a period of 3 years. Selectively cut a few of the old stems to the ground each year until you finally have an entirely new plant.

Topping Topping is a favorite technique of utility crews and, sometimes, of desperate homeowners: Large trees that interfere with wires or grow too tall

Sharp pruning shears are also handy for removing spent blooms. Deadheading often encourages more flowers.

Large shrubs like lilacs can be "limbed up" (by removing the lower branches) to look like small trees.

Prune wisteria back severely just after flowering to control rampant growth and promote future bloom.

for their site are simply sliced off across the top. Large branches are sawed off in midlimb instead of being pruned at main stems.

Topping disfigures and weakens trees, stimulating undesirable water sprouts that actually accelerate the rate of top regrowth. The slow-to-heal wounds of topping are open invitations to insects and diseases, and limbs that die from these causes will soon fall in a storm, creating a danger to people and property. If your trees are so badly out of place that you would consider topping, remove them entirely and plant a better-suited species.

Pruning Hedges How you prune your hedges depends on the effect you're looking for. If you want a natural-looking screen, a bit of selective pruning is all

your hedge really needs. Prune flowering shrubs after they bloom. To keep the hedge vigorous, cut two or three of the oldest stems down to the ground each year.

Many gardeners appreciate the formal look of neatly trimmed hedges. But before you decide to go this route, consider whether you'll be eager to do the frequent pruning that is necessary to maintain them. After planting, the new shoots of broad-leaved plants should be trimmed back by one-third or more each year until the plants reach the desired size. After that, shear often during the growing season to keep the hedge neat.

Needle-leaved evergreens, such as yews (*Taxus* spp.), require a different technique. Allow the plants to grow untrimmed until they reach the desired height. Then shear the tips back no more than once a year. Don't cut into the bare wood; it won't resprout.

Pruning Vines Most vines require little special care other than pruning to train them, limit their growth, or encourage flower or fruit production. Prune away dead wood at any time during the year. To control growth or to shape a vine grown for foliage, such as Virginia creeper (*Parthenocissus quinquefolia*) or Boston ivy (*P. tricuspidata*), prune in late winter or early spring. Cut back flowering vines shortly after bloom. Trim spring-blooming vines, such as wisteria and Carolina jasmine (*Gelsemium sempervirens*), by early summer—before the next year's flower buds develop. Summer bloomers, such as honeysuckles and climbing hydrangeas, produce flowers on new stems that grow during the spring. Prune summer-blooming vines from late fall until late winter.

Rounded hedges have a slightly more casual look; tightly trimmed hedges provide a very formal effect.

Summer-blooming honeysuckles flower on wood produced in the spring. Prune these vines in late fall or winter.

PROPAGATING TREES, SHRUBS, AND VINES

Propagating your own trees, shrubs, and vines takes a little longer to fill the landscape than buying nursery stock, but the savings are considerable. A single forsythia (*Forsythia* x *intermedia*), for example, can easily father a whole hedge and the only cost to you is that of the original plant.

There are other good reasons to grow your own: You may want to start your own bush from your grandmother's favorite rose, or you may admire an uncommon apple cultivar that grows in a friend's backyard. A handful of pinecones collected on a family trip to the mountains might yield seeds for a souvenir tree at home. Home-propagated plants, especially those with a sentimental history, make great gifts, too. But most important, starting your own plants is satisfying and fun.

Propagating plants is easier than you think. In this chapter, you'll learn all the techniques you'll need to grow a garden full of trees, shrubs, and vines. Many of the techniques are simple enough that even a first-timer can succeed. Some methods require no special equipment; others, only a few inexpensive tools or supplies.

There are two basic types of propagation: asexual, or vegetative, and sexual. The method you choose depends on the species of plant you want to propagate, how patient you are (some seed-grown trees can take years to reach 12 inches [30 cm] tall), and whether it's important that the resulting offspring are an exact duplicate of the parent plant.

Vegetative propagation uses a piece of stem, leaf, bud, or root—one of the plant's vegetative parts—to produce a new plant. Division, cuttings, layering, and grafting are all asexual, or vegetative, methods.

A big advantage of the vegetative method is that you'll get larger plants faster than if you start from seed. Another plus is that the offspring will be exact replications of the original plants. Young shrubs started from clippings of a hybrid azalea, for example, will have the same flower shape and color as their parent.

Sexual propagation uses the reproductive parts of a plant—its seeds, with or without the protective fruit—to produce new plants. If you use seeds, you may get plants very much like your original or, due to genetic variability, you may get plants that are very different in size, shape, flower, or leaf color from the parent plant. Bald cypress trees (*Taxodium distichum*) grown from seed, for example, will be nearly identical to the tree that supplied the seed. Colorado spruce (*Picea pungens*) seedlings, on the other hand, will vary from the parent; their needles will have a range of colors from greenish blue to gray. To maintain the exact needle color, the spruce must be vegetatively propagated.

As any gardener who's planted an acorn knows, it is gratifying to grow a tree from a single seed. But trees, shrubs, and vines grown from seed may take years longer to reach a good size than the same plants started by vegetative propagation. Some trees, shrubs, and vines are easy to grow from seed, while others have seeds that are difficult for a home gardener to germinate. A few trees, shrubs, and vines don't produce any seeds, so you must propagate them vegetatively.

Each species of tree, shrub, or vine can generally be propagated in more than one way. Consult the "Plant by Plant Guide," starting on page 78, for the best way to propagate your trees, shrubs, and vines.

Opposite: Many plants can be propagated by more than one method. To reproduce rugosa rose (*Rosa rugosa*), you can take stem cuttings in summer or remove the seeds from the fleshy red "hips" and sow outdoors in fall.

Layering

Layering is the simplest method of propagation—Mother Nature does the work for you. Some plants with long vines or sweeping stems, such as forsythia (*Forsythia* x *intermedia*) and winter jasmine (*Jasminum nudiflorum*), layer naturally with no tinkering from the gardener. Their stems bend over, touch the ground, and root. Other plants, such as red-twig dogwood (*Cornus sericea*), form horizontal stems called stolons that root along their length, spreading the clump of plants. You can cut these rooted sections from the parent and transplant them as new plants. A little help from you will induce many other plants to root.

Simple Layering

Simple layering is just what its name promises—simple. You can use this technique anytime during the growing season, although roots form fastest in spring.

Start by selecting a young, flexible, vigorous branch, about as thick as a pencil, to layer. A branch of the previous season's growth works best. Measure back about 12 inches (30 cm) from the branch tip, bend the shoot down, and mark the spot where that point on the stem touches the ground. Release the shoot and dig a small hole, 3 to 5 inches (7.5 to 12.5 cm) deep at the marked point. Work a few handfuls of finished compost into the loosened soil.

Strip the leaves and any side shoots from the section of branch to be buried. With a sharp knife, make a short, shallow notch or slit on the underside of the branch, about 10 inches (25 cm) from the tip and just above a node (the swollen area on the stem where a leaf emerges). Insert a toothpick to keep the cut open. Then bend the stem into the hole and anchor it with a hairpin or bent wire, letting the branch tip stick up from the hole. Fill the hole with the enriched soil mixture and water well.

Roots may form in as little as a few weeks for vigorous vines, or as long as 2 years for some rhododendrons. Gently uncover the stem to check for visible roots. If you see none, cover it back up and check in another month or two. If you see roots, unpin the anchor and give the stem a tug to make sure it is well rooted. Sever the rooted stem from the parent plant but leave it in place until the following spring. Then transplant it.

Step-by-step Layering

Layering is a slow but reliable method for propagating many kinds of trees, shrubs, and vines.

1. Select a young, flexible, healthy branch about as thick as a pencil.

2. Cut off any leaves and side shoots from the section to be buried.

3. Make a slit on the underside, and insert a toothpick to keep it open.

4. Bend the stem into the hole and anchor it with bent wire.

5. Fill the hole with the enriched soil mixture and water thoroughly.

6. After a couple of months, cut off and transplant the new plant.

Taking Cuttings

Plants have an amazing capacity for regenerating themselves from small pieces of tissue. You can use this potential to create many new plants from stem sections, also known as cuttings. Depending on the species you're propagating and the time of year, your cuttings may be from softwood, semihardwood, or hardwood stems.

Getting Started

A sharp knife, a plastic bag, clean pots, and a well-drained soilless growing medium are all you need. Be sure your knife (or pruning shears) is sharp; a dull blade will crush plant tissue and invite disease. Scrub your pots—clay and plastic are both suitable—and rinse with a solution of 1 part bleach to 9 parts water.

Use a lightweight, moisture-retentive propagation medium, free of insects, diseases, and weed seeds. Garden soil is not a good choice. Use a 50-50 mix of peat moss and perlite, peat and vermiculite, or peat and sand.

Softwood Cuttings

Take softwood cuttings from the succulent new growth that occurs in the spring. Softwood stems snap easily when bent. Some plants have spurts of new growth later in the year that can also be used for softwood cuttings. Many species of shrubs and vines, and some trees, root well from softwood cuttings, including crab apples (*Malus*

Crabapples usually root easily from softwood cuttings. Take cuttings from stem tips in late spring.

spp.) and crape myrtle (*Lagerstroemia indica*).

Take softwood cuttings from April to June, when stems are soft and new leaves are fully open. Have ready a container of moist propagation medium. Snip 3- to 6-inch (7.5 to 15 cm) cuttings, including the branch tip, on a cool overcast morning, cutting just below a node (the swollen area on the stem where a leaf emerges). Remove leaves from the bottom half of the stem with pruning shears. Carefully insert the cutting into the medium to about one-third of its length and tamp it into place. When the tray or pot is full, gently water the cuttings to settle the medium, then enclose the container in plastic or in a cold frame.

Roots will usually form in 2 to 5 weeks. If the cuttings resist when you gently tug on them, they have rooted. Harden off rooted cuttings, gradually increasing the light intensity and decreasing the humidity to adjust them to normal growing conditions. Transplant the cuttings to a nursery bed or to individual containers.

Semihardwood Cuttings

Once the flush of spring growth is over, stem wood becomes firmer and leaves become fully expanded or mature. Pieces taken from this maturing wood are called semihardwood cuttings. Use semihardwood cuttings to propagate broad-leaved evergreens, such as hollies (*Ilex* spp.) and rhododendrons

Move rooted cuttings to individual pots or plant them in a nursery bed until they're big enough for the garden.

Snip off the bottom of your cutting to just below a node. Remove the lower leaves.

Encourage rooting on rhododendrons and hollies by wounding the base of the cutting with a sharp knife.

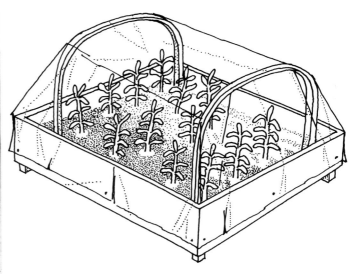

Make a minigreenhouse by covering a tray with clear plastic. Wire supports keep the plastic off the cuttings.

(*Rhododendron* spp.), or deciduous shrubs that don't root very well from softwood cuttings, such as winged euonymus (*Euonymus alata*).

Take 3- to 6-inch (7.5 to 15 cm) cuttings of semihardwood in late summer and remove the leaves from the bottom half. Cut the foliage of broad-leaved evergreens in half to save space and to reduce water loss. Some cuttings, like hollies and

rhododendrons, benefit from having a small sliver of bark sliced off the side of the base. This wounding encourages new roots to form.

Insert the cuttings into a tray or pot of moist propagation medium, spacing them far enough apart so the leaves don't touch. Keep the air around the cuttings moist by misting them frequently, or enclose the whole container in clear plastic. (Use bent wire hangers to keep the plastic from resting on the cuttings and encouraging rot.) Set the cuttings where they will get bright light but no direct sun. Semihardwood cuttings usually root in 1 to 3 months. Transplant rooted cuttings into individual pots or a nursery bed.

Semihardwood Cuttings

Semihardwood cuttings are a good way to propagate broad-leaved evergreen trees and shrubs, like hollies, rhododendrons, and camellias. Take cuttings from partially hardened wood in late summer. Keep the finished cuttings in a humid environment to promote rooting.

1. Take cuttings from healthy, vigorous growth and remove the leaves from the bottom half.

2. Cut large leaves in half to reduce evaporation and to save space in the container.

3. Insert cuttings halfway into moist potting mix and place them in a shady position.

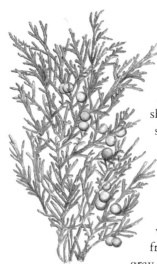

Hardwood Cuttings

Take hardwood cuttings from mature wood in mid- to late fall or in winter. Deciduous shade trees and needled evergreen shrubs, such as arborvitae (*Thuja* spp.), junipers (*Juniperus* spp.), and yews (*Taxus* spp.), can be propagated successfully from hardwood cuttings.

Look for mature, 1-year-old wood with bark that has turned from green to (usually) brown or gray. For deciduous plants, take stem pieces 4 to 8 inches (10 to 20 cm) long starting a few inches below the terminal bud. Make a straight cut at the top of each piece just above a node or bud and a sloping cut at the base just below a node or bud. To propagate evergreens, take 4- to 6-inch (10 to 15 cm) tip cuttings and clip off the bottom leaves.

Take simple cuttings from stem ends. Some plants root better with older wood at the base.

Stick the cuttings right-side up (with the straight-cut end up) in your propagation medium. The top bud should be about 1 inch (2.5 cm) above the soil surface. Set the pots

Big-leaved hydrangea (*Hydrangea macrophylla*) will root from softwood, semihardwood, or hardwood cuttings.

outdoors or in a cold frame. Keep the propagation medium evenly moist, but don't worry about misting the cuttings or enclosing them in plastic; since they're not actively growing, the cuttings won't lose much water. After the ground freezes, cover your cuttings with a 6- to 8-inch (15 to 20 cm) deep layer of loose mulch, like straw. Remove the mulch in spring.

Hardwood cuttings often take several months to root. Tug gently on them to check for roots the summer or fall after planting. Transplant rooted cuttings to individual pots or to a nursery bed for a few years. When the rooted cuttings have reached the size you need, move them to their final place in the garden.

Arborvitae (*Thuja* spp.) will root from cuttings taken anytime from late summer through early winter.

Creating the Right Environment

It is vital to prevent most cuttings from drying out while roots develop. If you have just a few cuttings, you can enclose them, pot and all, in a plastic bag; for large numbers, a cold frame may be more practical. Set your pots in a bright place out of direct sunlight, or cover your cold frame with wooden lattice to shield the cuttings from the full brunt of the sun.

Starting from Seed

If you have space for a nursery bed and don't mind waiting a few years for trees to reach transplanting size, you can have fun by propagating trees, shrubs, and vines from seed. Be aware, though, that some tree seeds are frustratingly slow to germinate, and remember that many of your seedlings won't look exactly like the parent tree, shrub, or vine from which you harvested the seed. That's the bad news. The good news is that seedling variations sometimes yield interesting new plant forms. Growing woody plants from seed can be a most satisfying process.

Planting Seeds

Many gardeners designate a corner of the garden for a seedbed, where the slow-germinating and slow-growing seeds of trees, shrubs, and vines can be left undisturbed. You can also plant these seeds in a cold frame or in pots. Many woody plants develop deep roots fast and resent transplanting, so use at least a 1-gallon (3.8 l) pot.

Fill your cold frame or pots with a planting medium that retains moisture but doesn't stay soggy. Fine soil mixed with compost, peat moss, and vermiculite makes a good seed-starting mixture. You may prefer to use a sterile mix to fill containers in order to reduce weeding. Premoisten the seedbed or growing medium before sowing.

Plant ripe tree and shrub seeds in outdoor seedbeds, cold frames, or pots in fall or early spring. Be sure to pretreat as necessary before planting. Sow your seeds in the moist medium, covering them to a depth of once or twice their diameter. You don't need to cover fine seed at all; press it into the soil lightly. Make sure you keep the seedbed moist. Seedlings of woody plants

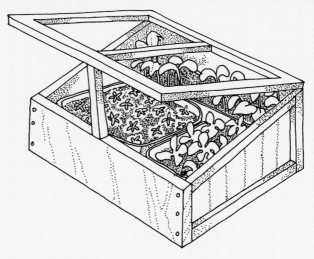

If you set seedlings in a cold frame, make sure you open the top on sunny days—the heat can build up quickly!

grow slowly. Keep them well watered, and give them a dose or two of diluted compost tea for a nutrient boost.

When the seedlings are large enough to handle, pot them up individually or transplant them to a nursery bed, where they can grow on for a few years. Move your new plants into the landscape when they are the desired size. Use a spade to lift the young plants with some surrounding soil, making sure you dig deeply to avoid damaging the roots. Carry the plant on the spade to the prepared planting hole. With proper care, your new plants should settle in quickly and provide years of pleasure.

Use a shovel or trowel to lift small plants, so you'll keep some soil around the roots.

For More Information

Propagating from seeds you collect in your own landscape or from those you pick up elsewhere is certainly worth a try. Because trees, shrubs, and vines vary so greatly in their requirements, it's best to check a propagation reference like *Foolproof Planting* (by Anne Moyer Halpin and the Editors of Rodale Press) as to time of seed maturation and when to collect ripe seeds. This reference can also tell you if the seeds you've collected require any special treatments, such as cleaning, nicking, or chilling, prior to germination. Your local Cooperative Extension Service may have information, too.

Grafting

Grafting is the process of uniting two related plants using the root system of one to nourish the top of the other. An alternative to propagating by layering, cuttings, or seed, grafting produces large plants quickly because the roots are already well established. The technique is used to propagate species and cultivars of flowering cherries (*Prunus* spp.) and pears (*Pyrus* spp.), dwarf conifers, and Japanese maples (*Acer palmatum*) that won't come true from seed and don't root easily from cuttings or layering.

Getting Started

The key to grafting is to match the cambium layers—the actively growing green tissue under the bark—of the rooted plant (called the rootstock) and the new top (called the scion). Once these two cambium layers unite, the graft grows as one plant.

Choosing a Rootstock Grafting joins two or more pieces of different plants together to form a new plant. Compatibility between rootstock and scion is a must. Select closely related plants of the same genus or cultivars within the same species or, sometimes, species within the same family. You can grow your own rootstocks from seeds or cuttings or graft onto a mature tree.

The multiflora rose (*Rosa multiflora*), for example, is a hardy, pest-resistant species that is grown easily from seed. Because of its vigor, it makes a good rootstock for a hybrid tea or an heirloom rose.

Tools and Supplies For most home gardeners, a very sharp knife, a pair of pruners that makes clean cuts, and materials to tie and seal off the graft are all that's needed. Tying and wrapping materials hold the rootstock and scion together and keep the cambium layers from drying out. Wide rubber bands or waxed string are good for tying. Sealing materials, such as grafting wax or rubber tape, are widely available at garden centers, or you can improvise with plastic tape or petroleum jelly.

Grafting Techniques

Learning to make successful grafts requires practice. Several grafting techniques are available for you to try, including whip-and-tongue, side veneer and cleft grafts, and T and chip buds. Consult a propagation reference and choose the best method depending on the amount of scion wood you have, the size of the rootstock, the time of year, and the effect you want to obtain. Grafting is usually done from late winter to early spring depending on the method used. Most grafts, properly done, will unite within 1 to 2 months.

Whip-and-tongue Grafting

With some practice, you'll be able to graft a wide variety of trees, shrubs, and vines successfully.

1. Make a long sloping cut at the top of the rootstock.

2. Make a shallow cut down through the middle of the rootstock stem.

3. Prepare the scion with a matching sloping cut at the base.

4. Cut shallowly into the middle of the scion's base.

5. Slip the stock and scion together so the "tongues" interlock.

6. Wrap the graft with tape to provide support and hold in moisture.

PLANT BY PLANT GUIDE

The "Plant by Plant Guide" is arranged in an easy-to-use, quick-reference format. This handy alphabetical listing contains all you need to know to successfully plant and maintain a wide variety of trees, shrubs, and vines. (See "How to Use This Book" on page 10 for further details on how to use this guide.)

The guide is divided into three sections—trees, shrubs, and vines. Within each section, the trees, shrubs, and vines are listed alphabetically by botanical name with their common names displayed prominently. Each entry is illustrated with a full-color photograph to make identification easy.

The entries include information on the ideal growing conditions for each plant. You need to refer to the USDA Plant Hardiness Zone map on page 154 to find out which zone you live in. It's important to choose trees, shrubs, and vines that grow well in your area. There is also information on the best possible site for your trees, shrubs, or vines—whether they need sun or shade and the type of soil they prefer.

For each tree, shrub, and vine you'll find details on flower color, flowering time, and height and spread—essential information to make garden planning easier. You'll also learn about the cultivation requirements, including when you should prune and transplant.

Each entry gives details on how and when to propagate your plants. Seed-sowing times are given, and other propagation methods like cutting, layering, and grafting are also covered.

In addition, the entries tell you how to deal with pests and diseases using organic methods. Being able to identify common problems will help prevent pests and diseases from becoming a big problem.

"Landscape Use" will help you with your garden planning. This is where you'll find details on how to use your trees, shrubs, or vines in your overall garden design. Some trees, shrubs, or vines look best as specimen plants, while others are more suited to hedges, woodland plantings, or tree and shrub borders.

To get the most out of this guide, you should refer to it regularly. Trees, shrubs, and vines are important elements in landscape design, and because they live for such a long time, you should give careful thought to where they are placed and make sure you give them the correct growing conditions. This guide will enable you to have confidence in your planting and know that the trees, shrubs, and vines you have planted will still look good in the garden for years to come.

Opposite: For bright color, you can't beat the berries of firethorns (*Pyracantha* spp.). These and other fruiting shrubs, like chokeberries (*Aronia* spp.) and hollies (*Ilex* spp.), add splashes of color to winter landscapes.

Abies homolepis   Pinaceae

NIKKO FIR

Like all firs, Nikko fir is a coniferous evergreen tree that grows best in cool, moist climates. It has a columnar habit and glossy needle-like leaves held in whorls on the branches.

FLOWER COLOR AND SEASON: Insignificant green or yellowish flowers in spring; followed by upright tannish cones in summer to winter.

HEIGHT AND SPREAD: To 100 feet (30 m) tall and 30 feet (9 m) wide.

BEST CLIMATE AND SITE: Zones 4–7. Deep, moist, well-drained soil. Full sun to light shade.

CULTIVATION: Best transplanted in spring or winter, balled-and-burlapped. Pruning not necessary.

PROPAGATION: Sow seed in fall. Take cuttings in winter. Graft in late winter and early spring.

PEST AND DISEASE PREVENTION: Heat- and water-stressed plants are more attractive to pests and susceptible to diseases. Mulch regularly with organic matter to keep soil moist. Avoid planting in hot, dry areas.

COMMON PROBLEMS: Intolerant of city pollution.

LANDSCAPE USE: Specimen tree; screens.

OTHER SPECIES:

A. concolor, white or Colorado fir, has curving, claw-shaped needles that are gray-green or blue-gray. It grows to 100 feet (30 m) tall and 40 feet (12 m) wide. 'Conica' is a dwarf pyramidal form. 'Violacea' has blue leaves. 'Wattezii' has golden yellow leaves when young.

MAPLE

A. saccharum, *sugar maple, is a handsome shade tree for a large yard. Prized in the landscape for its outstanding fall color, it is also the chief source of maple syrup and sugar.*

FLOWER COLOR AND SEASON: *A. griseum:* yellow-green flowers; *A. palmatum:* purple flowers; *A. platanoides:* yellow flowers; *A. rubrum:* red flowers; *A. saccharum:* greenish yellow flowers. All bloom in early spring.

HEIGHT AND SPREAD: *A. griseum:* to 12 feet (3.6 m) tall and 15 feet (4.5 m) wide; *A. palmatum:* to 15 feet (4.5 m) tall and slightly wider; *A. platanoides:* to 90 feet (27 m) tall and 60 feet (18 m) wide; *A. rubrum:* to 100 feet (30 m) tall and nearly as wide; *A. saccharum:* to 100 feet (30 m) tall and 70 feet (21 m) wide.

BEST CLIMATE AND SITE: *A. griseum:* Zones 5–8; *A. palmatum:* Zones 5–9; *A. platanoides, A. rubrum,* and *A. saccharum:* Zones 3–7. Adaptable to a variety of soil conditions. *A. rubrum* tolerates poor drainage. Partial shade for *A. palmatum;* other species prefer full sun.

CULTIVATION: Transplant bareroot, container-grown or balled-and-burlapped plants in spring. Prune in winter only to shape the young tree initially.

PROPAGATION: Sow seed in fall or spring. Take cuttings in late spring or winter. Graft in late winter or early spring.

PEST AND DISEASE PREVENTION: Avoid damaging the bark with gardening tools such as lawn mowers. Wounds are entry points for pests and diseases.

Japanese maples, such as A. palmatum *'Atropurpureum', are ideal for small gardens. Their colorful leaves and graceful branching habit provide year-round interest.*

COMMON PROBLEMS: Many maple species have shallow, spreading roots that make growing other plants under them difficult.

LANDSCAPE USE: Specimen plant; shade trees. *A. platanoides* and *A. rubrum:* street trees.

SPECIES:

A. griseum, paperbark maple, has compound leaves and grows to wide-spreading rounded form. Its cinnamon brown bark peels in long strips, providing year-round color interest.

A. palmatum, Japanese maple, is a small rounded tree with picturesque branching. Its leaves may be lobed or very finely dissected and vary in color with the cultivar. 'Senkaki' (coral-bark maple) has coral red young stems.

A. platanoides, Norway maple, is a large round-headed tree with large, five-lobed leaves that turn bright yellow in fall. 'Crimson King' has red leaves throughout the growing season.

A. rubrum, red maple, is native to eastern and central North America. It is a large, broadly columnar tree. Its leaves are three- to five-lobed and turn brilliant scarlet in fall.

A. saccharum, sugar maple, is native to eastern North America. Its habit is oval or rounded; its leaves are three- to five-lobed and turn yellow, orange, and scarlet in fall.

Aesculus x *carnea*   Hippocastanaceae

RED HORSE CHESTNUT

Red horse chestnut is a deciduous tree that grows to a rounded form. It bears dark green compound leaves and showy clusters of red flowers in late spring.

FLOWER COLOR AND SEASON: Deep red flowers in upright clusters in late spring; followed by slightly spiny fruit.

HEIGHT AND SPREAD: To 40 feet (12 m) tall and as wide.

BEST CLIMATE AND SITE: Zones 3–8. Tolerant of a variety of soil conditions. Full sun.

CULTIVATION: Transplant balled-and-burlapped plants in fall or spring. Keep well watered until established. Pruning not necessary.

PROPAGATION: Sow seed in spring. Take cuttings in winter.

PEST AND DISEASE PREVENTION: Clean up leaves to remove overwintering sites for disease spores. Irrigate in very dry seasons to avoid leaf browning.

COMMON PROBLEMS: Spiny fruit can be a problem when it falls to the ground. Brown scorched leaves are the result of lack of water, excessive heat, or fungal infection.

LANDSCAPE USE: Specimen tree; street trees; shade trees.

OTHER SPECIES:

   A. hippocastanum, common horse chestnut, is a large round-headed tree. The upright pyramidal clusters of white late spring flowers are followed by spiny fruit. Plants can grow up to 80 feet (24 m) tall and nearly as wide.

Albizia julibrissin   Leguminosae

MIMOSA

Native to the Near East, mimosa is a deciduous tree with doubly compound leaves that give it a ferny, almost tropical effect. The fluffy pink flowers are borne in midsummer.

FLOWER COLOR AND SEASON: Pink flowers with numerous prominent stamens borne in dense, terminal culsters in midsummer.

HEIGHT AND SPREAD: To 40 feet (12 m) tall and as wide.

BEST CLIMATE AND SITE: Zones 7–10. Best in poor, dry soil; widely tolerant of different pH conditions. Thrives planted near a warm wall. Full sun.

CULTIVATION: Plant in winter or spring. Withstands dry conditions but benefits from extra watering for the first year or two. Pruning is not necessary except for shaping the tree.

PROPAGATION: Sow scarified seed in spring. (Scarify seed by shaking in a jar lined with sandpaper to break the hard seed coat.) Take cuttings in winter.

PEST AND DISEASE PREVENTION: In warm climates plants are subject to mimosa wilt, a soil fungus. Choose resistant cultivars and avoid wet, poorly drained soil.

COMMON PROBLEMS: Webworms bind leaves together with webs and skeletonize foliage. Remove and destroy any webs that are noticeable.

LANDSCAPE USE: Specimen tree; shade trees for small gardens.

OTHER COMMON NAMES: Silk tree.

CULTIVARS: 'Charlotte' and 'Tryon' are wilt-resistant. 'Ernest Wilson' is hardier than the species.

Amelanchier laevis   Rosaceae

ALLEGHENY SERVICEBERRY

Allegheny serviceberry is a multistemmed deciduous tree with white spring flowers and black berries. The leaves are reddish in spring, green in summer, and red-orange in fall.

FLOWER COLOR AND SEASON: White five-petaled flowers in spring; followed by edible blue berries.

HEIGHT AND SPREAD: To 40 feet (12 m) tall and as wide.

BEST CLIMATE AND SITE: Zones 3–7. Moist, acid soil.

CULTIVATION: Plant in winter or early spring. Pruning is seldom necessary except to shape the tree when it is young. This may be carried out after flowering. Mulch while young to keep the soil evenly moist.

PROPAGATION: Sow seed in fall.

PEST AND DISEASE PREVENTION: Avoid overfeeding, which can produce succulent growth prone to pests and diseases.

COMMON PROBLEMS: Intolerant of dry, alkaline soils.

LANDSCAPE USE: Specimen tree; shade trees.

OTHER SPECIES:

A. arborea, downy serviceberry, is a large shrub or small tree growing to 20 feet (6 m) tall, with white spring flowers, purple-black berries, and red or orange fall color. Zones 3–8.

A. x *grandiflora*, apple serviceberry, is a hybrid of *A. laevis* and *A. arborea*. It grows to 25 feet (7.5 m) tall and has clusters of larger white flowers from pink-tinged buds. Zones 4–8.

Betula papyrifera   Betulaceae

CANOE BIRCH

Native to northeastern North America, canoe birch is a tall deciduous tree that grows best in cool climates. Its mature trunks and branches are white with distinct black markings.

FLOWER COLOR AND SEASON: Tannish green flowers in catkins in early to midspring.

HEIGHT AND SPREAD: To 60 feet (18 m) tall and 30 feet (9 m) wide.

BEST CLIMATE AND SITE: Zones 2–6. Moist, well-drained, deep soil. Full sun to partial shade.

CULTIVATION: Plant in spring. Prune only in late summer or fall, as pruning at other times can cause excessive "bleeding." Pruning is only necessary initially to shape the tree.

PROPAGATION: Sow seed in fall. Graft in late winter and early spring.

PEST AND DISEASE PREVENTION: Drought stress can weaken trees, making them more susceptible to pests and diseases. Plant in evenly moist soil and water during extended drought periods.

COMMON PROBLEMS: Can be short-lived, especially in hot, dry areas.

LANDSCAPE USE: Specimen tree; group plantings.

OTHER SPECIES:

B. nigra, river birch, is a pyramidal tree with reddish brown exfoliating bark. It is tolerant of swampy conditions. Zones 4–8.

B. pendula, European white birch, has pendulous branch tips and silvery white bark marked with black. It is particularly prone to birch borers, which weaken and kill trees. Zones 2–6.

Carpinus betulus   Betulaceae

EUROPEAN HORNBEAM

European hornbeam is a slow-growing deciduous tree with an upright oval form and serrated green leaves. This easy-care tree tolerates heavy pruning and is often used for hedges.

FLOWER COLOR AND SEASON: Yellowish green flowers in catkins in early to midspring.

HEIGHT AND SPREAD: To 60 feet (18 m) tall and 30 feet (9 m) wide.

BEST CLIMATE AND SITE: Zones 5–9. Moist, well-drained soil. Full sun to partial shade.

CULTIVATION: Plant in spring. Prune in winter for hedges.

PROPAGATION: Sow seed in fall. Graft in late winter or early spring.

PEST AND DISEASE PREVENTION: May be subject to scale infestation. Prune and destroy affected parts. Plants in fertile soil with adequate moisture tolerate attacks better than plants that are water-stressed, nutrient-deficient, and overcrowded.

COMMON PROBLEMS: Difficult to transplant; plant young container-grown plants.

LANDSCAPE USE: Specimen tree; group plantings; hedges.

OTHER SPECIES:

C. caroliniana, American hornbeam, is a small bushy tree that provides excellent red fall foliage. 'Pyramidalis' grows to a pyramidal shape. Zones 2–7.

C. japonica, Japanese hornbeam, is a small pyramidal tree with wide-spreading branches and furrowed bark; its leaves turn red in fall. Zones 5–8.

Cedrus deodara   Pinaceae

DEODAR CEDAR

Deodar cedar is a graceful coniferous evergreen tree of pyramidal habit with pendulous branches. Its needle-like leaves vary in color from green to silvery blue.

FLOWER COLOR AND SEASON: Inconspicuous, upright yellowish tan flowers in fall; followed by purplish cones.

HEIGHT AND SPREAD: To 100 feet (30 m) tall and 65 feet (19.5 m) wide.

BEST CLIMATE AND SITE: Zones 7–9. Moisture-retentive, humus-rich, well-drained soil. Full sun.

CULTIVATION: Transplant container-grown or balled-and-burlapped plants in spring. Stake *C.deodara* in the first year or so until it develops a strong leading shoot. Occasionally a competing leader must be pruned away. Thereafter no pruning is necessary.

PROPAGATION: Sow seed in spring. Take cuttings in fall. Graft in spring.

PEST AND DISEASE PREVENTION: Avoid overfeeding, which promotes succulent growth attractive to aphids. Cedars grow best and suffer less problems when grown in deep rich soil in a moist climate.

COMMON PROBLEMS: Foliage may be damaged by strong winds.

LANDSCAPE USE: Specimen tree.

OTHER SPECIES:

C. atlantica, atlas cedar, is an evergreen tree with long curving needles. It is pyramidal when young and later flat-topped with horizontal branching. 'Glauca' has silvery blue-gray leaves. 'Pendula' has pendulous branches. Zones 6–9.

| *Cercidiphyllum japonicum* | Cercidiphyllaceae | *Cercis canadensis* | Leguminosae |

KATSURA TREE

Katsura tree is a deciduous tree from China and Japan. Its leaves are heart-shaped and mostly opposite; they turn yellow, orange, or red in fall and become sweetly fragrant.

FLOWER COLOR AND SEASON: Small reddish flowers without petals in mid- to late spring.

HEIGHT AND SPREAD: To 60 feet (18 m) tall and 3–50 feet (0.9–15 m) wide.

BEST CLIMATE AND SITE: Zones 4–8. Very moist, well-drained soil. Full sun to light shade.

CULTIVATION: Transplant container-grown or balled-and-burlapped plants in early spring. Prune only to shape when young.

PROPAGATION: Sow fresh seed as soon as available. Take cuttings in winter.

PEST AND DISEASE PREVENTION: Water during prolonged periods of drought to maintain vigor. Healthy plants are less susceptible to pests and diseases.

COMMON PROBLEMS: Usually trouble-free.

LANDSCAPE USE: Specimen tree; street trees; screens. If it grows to a single trunk, the form is markedly columnar; if multiple trunks form, the result is a wide-spreading tree.

EASTERN REDBUD

Eastern redbud is a flat-topped, broadly spreading deciduous tree native to eastern North America. It produces masses of pink flowers in spring; the foliage may turn yellow in fall.

FLOWER COLOR AND SEASON: Pink flowers in mid- to late spring before leaves appear. Blooms are produced profusely at the joints of old wood (even along the trunk).

HEIGHT AND SPREAD: To 30 feet (9 m) tall and 20 feet (6 m) wide.

BEST CLIMATE AND SITE: Zones 4–9. Tolerant of a variety of soil conditions. Full sun to light shade.

CULTIVATION: Difficult to transplant; best moved in winter when young.

PROPAGATION: Sow seed immediately upon ripening in late summer or fall.

PEST AND DISEASE PREVENTION: Keep vigorous by regular watering and feeding. Healthy plants are less susceptible to pests and diseases.

COMMON PROBLEMS: Sometimes subject to canker and verticillium wilt.

LANDSCAPE USE: Excellent small specimen tree; use alone or in combination with *Cornus florida* as shade tree.

OTHER SPECIES:

C. siliquastrum, Judas tree, is very similar but is native to the eastern Mediterranean and Asia Minor. It produces purplish rose flowers and yellow fall foliage. Zones 6–9.

Chamaecyparis obtusa   Cupressaceae

HINOKI FALSE CYPRESS

Hinoki false cypress is a slow-growing coniferous evergreen tree with flat sprays of waxy, dark green scale-like foliage. It grows in a broadly pyramidal form.

FLOWER COLOR AND SEASON: Inconspicuous flowers in spring; followed by brown cones in fall.

HEIGHT AND SPREAD: To 100 feet (30 m) tall and 40 feet (12 m) wide.

BEST CLIMATE AND SITE: Zones 5–8. Deep, loamy, moisture-retentive soil. Full sun.

CULTIVATION: Transplant container-grown or balled-and-burlapped plants in spring. Prune plants to shape in spring.

PROPAGATION: Take cuttings in fall.

PEST AND DISEASE PREVENTION: Avoid damaging plant with lawn mowers or sharp gardening tools; these wounds are common entry points for pests and diseases.

COMMON PROBLEMS: Plants may be subject to a fungal disease that attacks roots. Dig out and destroy diseased plants. Plant in moist but well-drained soil to help prevent injury.

LANDSCAPE USE: Specimen tree; background trees.

OTHER SPECIES:

C. lawsoniana, Lawson false cypress, is a slender to broadly pyramidal tree with horizontal branches. The scale-like leaves differ widely in color. 'Allumii' is a conical spreading form with blue foliage. 'Aurea' has golden yellow leaves.

CULTIVARS: 'Aurea' has yellow young shoots. 'Nana Gracilis' has dark foliage and a compact habit.

Chionanthus virginicus   Oleaceae

WHITE FRINGE TREE

White fringe tree is a deciduous small tree or large shrub with medium green leaves that turn yellow in fall. The loose clusters of white flowers bloom from late spring into summer.

FLOWER COLOR AND SEASON: Slightly fragrant white flowers borne in loose clusters from late spring to early summer; followed by blue grape-like fruit on female plants.

HEIGHT AND SPREAD: To 30 feet (9 m) tall and as wide.

BEST CLIMATE AND SITE: Zones 5–8. Humus-rich, moisture-retentive, well-drained soil. Full sun.

CULTIVATION: Transplant balled-and-burlapped or container-grown plants in spring. Prune after flowering only if shaping is required.

PROPAGATION: Sow seed in fall; may take 2 years to germinate. Take semihardwood cuttings in late summer.

PEST AND DISEASE PREVENTION: No serious pests or diseases.

COMMON PROBLEMS: Slow-growing.

LANDSCAPE USE: Specimen tree or shrub.

OTHER SPECIES:

C. retusus, Chinese fringe tree, is native to China, Korea, and Japan. It has smaller leaves and grows to 8 feet (5.4 m) tall with a rounded bushy form.

Cladrastis lutea   Leguminosae

AMERICAN YELLOWWOOD

Native to the southeastern United States, American yellow-wood is a deciduous tree growing to a wide-spreading rounded form. The bark is pale gray and glossy; the leaves are compound.

FLOWER COLOR AND SEASON: Bell-shaped slightly fragrant white flowers, marked with yellow, borne in 1-foot (30 cm) long terminal clusters from late spring to early summer; flowers attractive to bees.

HEIGHT AND SPREAD: To 40 feet (12 m) tall and slightly wider.

BEST CLIMATE AND SITE: Zones 3–8. Tolerates a wide range of soil conditions but needs good drainage. Full sun to light shade.

CULTIVATION: Transplant young balled-and-burlapped or container-grown plants in fall or spring. No pruning necessary unless shaping is desired.

PROPAGATION: Sow seed in fall. Take root cuttings in winter.

PEST AND DISEASE PREVENTION: No serious pests or diseases.

COMMON PROBLEMS: Bleeds profusely if pruned in winter or spring. Prune only in late summer or fall.

LANDSCAPE USE: Specimen tree; woodland plantings.

CULTIVARS: 'Rosea' has light pink flowers.

Cornus spp.   Cornaceae

DOGWOOD

Cornus florida, *flowering dogwood, is often considered to be the finest native North American flowering tree. It produces showy white blooms in spring and red berries in fall.*

FLOWER COLOR AND SEASON: *C. alternifolia:* small white or yellow flowers in flat clusters in late winter to early spring; followed by black fruit. *C. florida:* inconspicuous yellow flowers with four broad, rounded white bracts in mid- to late spring; followed by clustered brilliant red fruit in fall. *C. kousa:* similar flowers to *C. florida* from late spring to early summer, but bracts are pointed at the tips; followed by red strawberry-like fruit. *C. mas:* profuse yellow flowers from late winter to early spring; followed by edible red fruit.

HEIGHT AND SPREAD: *C. alternifolia:* to 20 feet (6 m) tall and 12 feet (3.6 m) wide; *C. florida:* to 40 feet (12 m) tall and as wide; *C. kousa:* to 20 feet (6 m) tall and almost as wide; *C. mas:* to 40 feet (12 m) tall and as wide.

BEST CLIMATE AND SITE: *C. alternifolia:* Zones 3–7; *C. florida:* Zones 4–9; *C. kousa:* Zones 5–9; *C. mas:* Zones 4–8. Moisture-retentive, humus-rich, well-drained soil; keep well watered during periods of drought. Full sun to partial shade.

CULTIVATION: Young plants transplant best during early spring. Prune trees only if necessary to shape.

PROPAGATION: Remove seed from its fleshy covering and sow in fall. Take cuttings in late spring. Graft in late winter and early spring.

PEST AND DISEASE PREVENTION: Stressed plants are

DOGWOOD—CONTINUED

C. kousa var. chinensis *has larger flower bracts than the species. Its flattened branches are covered with masses of flowers in late spring to early summer.*

more prone to problems. Plant in evenly moist soil, water during extended droughts, and avoid damaging the plant with sharp gardening tools like lawn mowers, which cause wounds that are entry points for pests and diseases.

COMMON PROBLEMS: Anthracnose has become a severe problem for *C. florida* in parts of North America. Using *C. kousa* or hybrids between *C. florida* and *C. kousa* that are resistant or immune to the disease may be a necessary alternative.

LANDSCAPE USE: Excellent specimen or lawn tree, used singly or in groups.

SPECIES:

C. alternifolia, pagoda dogwood, is native to eastern North America. It is a flat-topped deciduous shrub with horizontal branches and is one of the few dogwoods with alternate leaves.

C. florida, flowering dogwood, is a flat-topped, horizontally branching deciduous tree with leaves that turn brilliant scarlet in fall. *C. florida* var. *rubra* has pink bracts. 'Cherokee Chief' has red bracts. 'White Cloud' is unusually free-flowering.

C. kousa, kousa dogwood, is native to China, Korea, and Japan. It is a deciduous shrub or tree. *C. kousa* var. *chinensis* 'Milky Way' is very free-flowering.

C. mas, cornelian cherry, is an early-blooming, spreading deciduous tree or shrub native to Europe.

SMOKE TREE

Smoke tree is a rounded bushy deciduous tree or shrub with glossy green or purplish leaves that turn yellow or red in fall. Showy plumes appear in summer.

FLOWER COLOR AND SEASON: Large, feathery pink, purple, or gray plumes that look like puffs of smoke (hence the common name) from midsummer to fall.

HEIGHT AND SPREAD: To 12 feet (3.6 m) tall and slightly wider.

BEST CLIMATE AND SITE: Zones 5–9. Moist, well-drained soil. Full sun.

CULTIVATION: Plant in spring. Water frequently until plants are established. Do not overfeed, as excessive nutrients produce vegetative growth at the expense of flowers.

PROPAGATION: Sow seed in fall. Take cuttings in summer.

PEST AND DISEASE PREVENTION: Few serious pests or diseases.

COMMON PROBLEMS: Heavy pruning tends to force undesirable long, thin shoots. A light trim after flowering will produce more compact growth.

LANDSCAPE USE: Shrub borders.

CULTIVARS: 'Flame' has brilliant orange-red fall foliage. 'Royal Purple' has dark purple leaves.

OTHER SPECIES:

C. obovatus, American smoke tree, is a small tree with reddish purple young shoots and summer flowers. It grows to 30 feet (9 m) tall.

Eucalyptus globulus   Myrtaceae

BLUE GUM

The young leaves of evergreen blue gum are oval and silvery blue; they mature to glossy green with a long, narrow shape. The trunk is bluish white with bark that peels off in strips.

FLOWER COLOR AND SEASON: White flowers from winter to spring.

HEIGHT AND SPREAD: To 150 feet (45 m) tall and 40 feet (12 m) wide.

BEST CLIMATE AND SITE: Zones 9–10. Adapts to a wide range of soil conditions. Full sun. Tolerates drought.

CULTIVATION: Transplant smallest possible trees in winter or spring. Pruning is not necessary.

PROPAGATION: Sow seed in spring.

PEST AND DISEASE PREVENTION: No serious pests or diseases.

COMMON PROBLEMS: Can be injured by strong, cold winds.

LANDSCAPE USE: Specimen tree; shade trees; windbreaks.

OTHER COMMON NAMES: Eucalyptus, ironbark.

OTHER SPECIES:

E. ficifolia, red-flowering gum, has coarse, red-tinged broadly lance-shaped leaves and grows quickly to 40 feet (12 m) tall with a dense rounded form. Its pink or red flowers bloom in summer.

E. leucoxylon, white ironbark, has pendulous branches, grayish narrow leaves, and flaking gray bark. It bears white, pink, or red flowers from winter to spring and grows to 50 feet (15 m) tall.

Fagus sylvatica   Fagaceae

EUROPEAN BEECH

European beech is a magnificent long-lived deciduous tree with smooth gray bark. It varies considerably in growth habit and in the form and color of its large leaves.

FLOWER COLOR AND SEASON: Inconspicuous greenish flowers in midspring; followed by small triangular nuts.

HEIGHT AND SPREAD: To 100 feet (30 m) tall and spread varying with cultivar.

BEST CLIMATE AND SITE: Zones 4–8. Deep, loamy, moist, humus-rich, well-drained soil.

CULTIVATION: Transplant balled-and-burlapped plants in spring. Prune in summer only when young enough to establish a straight, upright trunk.

PROPAGATION: Graft in late winter and early spring. Sow seed in fall.

PEST AND DISEASE PREVENTION: Avoid overfeeding, which results in succulent growth that is attractive to aphids. Protect the shallow roots from compaction and other forms of disturbance.

COMMON PROBLEMS: Intolerant of poor drainage. The shallow roots and dense shade make it difficult to grow other plants under these trees.

LANDSCAPE USE: Specimen tree; shade trees; hedges.

CULTIVARS: 'Laciniata' has ferny and deeply incised leaves. 'Pendula' has a weeping habit.

OTHER SPECIES:

F. grandifolia, American beech, has light gray bark and larger leaves that turn yellow-bronze in fall. It tends to sucker from the roots. Zones 3–8.

Fraxinus ornus   Oleaceae

FLOWERING ASH

Flowering ash is a deciduous tree with attractive compound leaves. Its fragrant white spring flowers are much more conspicuous than those of other ash species.

FLOWER COLOR AND SEASON: White flowers in early to late spring.

HEIGHT AND SPREAD: To 60 feet (18 m) tall and nearly as wide.

BEST CLIMATE AND SITE: Zones 6–7. Deep, loamy, humus-rich, moisture-retentive, well-drained soil. Tolerates lime.

CULTIVATION: Plant in spring or fall. Prune in fall if necessary. Mulch with organic matter to keep soil evenly moist.

PROPAGATION: Graft in spring. Sow seed in fall.

PEST AND DISEASE PREVENTION: Adequate moisture, especially during summer, will help keep plants healthy.

COMMON PROBLEMS: Scales may attack, sucking sap and weakening the tree. Avoid overfeeding, which produces succulent growth attractive to pests.

LANDSCAPE USE: Specimen tree; shade trees; woodland plantings.

OTHER SPECIES:

F. americana, white ash, is a fast-growing tree with furrowed gray bark, growing in a rather upright form to 120 feet (36 m). Zones 4–9.

F. excelsior, European ash, is a large tree of oval form, growing to 120 feet (36 m) tall. It has glossy dark green leaves and deeply incised bark. Zones 5–8.

Ginkgo biloba   Ginkgoaceae

GINKGO

Native to China, ginko is a pyramidal deciduous tree with fan-shaped leaves that turn bright yellow in fall. Male and female flowers are borne on separate plants.

FLOWER COLOR AND SEASON: Inconspicuous greenish flowers in early spring; followed by small, orangish evil-smelling seeds.

HEIGHT AND SPREAD: To 80 feet (24 m) tall and 40 feet (12 m) wide.

BEST CLIMATE AND SITE: Zones 4–8. Deep, moist, humus-rich, well-drained soil. Full sun.

CULTIVATION: Plant in fall or early spring. Prune in spring if necessary.

PROPAGATION: Take cuttings of male trees in summer. Sow seed in fall (although you cannot determine a tree's sex from seed, and female trees are undesirable in the landscape).

PEST AND DISEASE PREVENTION: Virtually no pests or diseases. Mulch with organic matter to keep soil evenly moist especially while the plant is young.

COMMON PROBLEMS: Fruit of female trees is malodorous; plant males only.

LANDSCAPE USE: Specimen tree; street trees.

OTHER COMMON NAMES: Maidenhair tree.

CULTIVARS: 'Autumn Gold' is a male with good spreading habit and bright golden fall color. 'Fastigiata' is a tree of columnar habit. 'Laciniata' has deeply incised leaves. 'Pendula' has weak-growing pendulous branches.

| *Gleditsia triacanthos* | Leguminosae | *Halesia carolina* | Styracaceae |

HONEY LOCUST

CAROLINA SILVERBELL

Honey locust is a deciduous tree with compound leaves and trunks and branches armed with sharp thorns. 'Sunburst' is a thornless cultivar with golden yellow young leaves.

Native to the southeastern United States, Carolina silverbell is a deciduous tree or shrub with elliptical leaves. The delicate bell-shaped white flowers bloom in spring.

FLOWER COLOR AND SEASON: Greenish flowers borne in clusters in late spring. The female flowers are followed by long scimitar-shaped brown pods.

HEIGHT AND SPREAD: To 100 feet (30 m) tall and 60 feet (18 m) wide.

BEST CLIMATE AND SITE: Zones 4–8. Moist, loamy, well-drained soil. Full sun.

CULTIVATION: Plant in winter or spring. Prune in fall if necessary.

PROPAGATION: Graft in late winter or spring. Sow seed in spring.

PEST AND DISEASE PREVENTION: Honey locusts are prone to many pests and diseases. Healthy plants are more resistant to pest invasion. Mulch to keep the soil evenly moist. Look for resistant cultivars.

COMMON PROBLEMS: The thick, sharp thorns can be hazardous; choose a thornless cultivar. Self-sown seedlings can be a nuisance; plant male cultivars.

LANDSCAPE USE: Specimen tree; shade trees.

CULTIVARS: 'Moraine' is a thornless male cultivar that is somewhat resistant to webworm.

FLOWER COLOR AND SEASON: Bell-shaped white flowers in clusters of three to five from mid- to late spring.

HEIGHT AND SPREAD: To 30 feet (9m) tall and as wide.

BEST CLIMATE AND SITE: Zones 5–8. Moisture-retentive, humus-rich, well-drained soil. Full sun to light shade; shelter from strong winds.

CULTIVATION: Transplant balled-and-burlapped or container-grown plants in spring. Rarely needs pruning.

PROPAGATION: Sow seed in fall; may take 2 years to germinate.

PEST AND DISEASE PREVENTION: No serious pests or diseases. Keep soil moist with organic mulch.

COMMON PROBLEMS: Loses leaves very early.

LANDSCAPE USE: Specimen tree, most effective against an evergreen background; woodland plantings.

OTHER COMMON NAMES: Snowdrop tree.

CULTIVARS: 'Rosea' has light pink flowers.

BLACK WALNUT

Native to the eastern and central United States, black walnut is a deciduous tree with a wide-spreading head. The bark is dark brown and deeply furrowed; the leaves are compound.

FLOWER COLOR AND SEASON: Inconspicuous yellow-green catkins from late spring to early summer; followed by nuts enclosed in green husks.

HEIGHT AND SPREAD: To 100 feet (30 m) tall and 75 feet (22.5 m) wide

BEST CLIMATE AND SITE: Zones 4–8. Widely tolerant of varying soil conditions. Full sun.

CULTIVATION: Transplant small plants in early spring. Trees bleed badly when large branches are cut, so thin out only small branches when crowded. Prune in fall.

PROPAGATION: Sow seed in fall.

PEST AND DISEASE PREVENTION: Clean up fallen leaves to reduce overwintering sites for disease spores.

COMMON PROBLEMS: Roots give off a substance toxic to many other plants.

LANDSCAPE USE: Specimen tree; shade trees for large gardens.

CULTIVARS: 'Laciniata' has deeply incised foliage.

GOLDEN-RAIN TREE

Golden-rain tree is a deciduous tree with compound leaves that turn bright yellow in fall. Its showy yellow summer flowers come at a time when few other trees are blooming.

FLOWER COLOR AND SEASON: Rich yellow flowers borne in dense, terminal racemes in midsummer; followed by bladder-like greenish pods.

HEIGHT AND SPREAD: To 50 feet (15 m) tall and 40 feet (12 m) wide.

BEST CLIMATE AND SITE: Zones 5–9. Adapts to a variety of soil conditions; tolerant of heat, drought, and air pollution. Full sun.

CULTIVATION: Transplant container-grown or balled-and-burlapped plants in fall and spring. No pruning is necessary unless you want to shape the tree; then prune in winter.

PROPAGATION: Sow seed in fall. Take root cuttings in winter.

PEST AND DISEASE PREVENTION: No serious pests or diseases.

COMMON PROBLEMS: Will flower poorly, or not at all, in shade.

LANDSCAPE USE: Good specimen tree for midsummer color.

CULTIVARS: 'Apiculata' has finely divided leaves. 'Fastigiata' has a narrow columnar habit. 'September' is late-blooming with exceptionally large flower clusters.

OTHER SPECIES:
K. bipinnata is a similar but later-blooming species. Zones 8–10.

Laburnum x *watereri*   Leguminosae

GOLDEN-CHAIN TREE

*Golden-chain tree is a deciduous tree with trifoliate leaves.
L. x* watereri *'Vossi', a cultivar of this hybrid, has a denser
habit and exceptionally long flower clusters.*

FLOWER COLOR AND SEASON: Golden yellow flow-
    ers borne in long, pendulous clusters in late
    spring; followed by 2–3-inch (5– 7.5 cm) pods.

HEIGHT AND SPREAD: To 30 feet (9 m) tall and
    18 feet (5.4 m) wide.

BEST CLIMATE AND SITE: Zones 5–9. Virtually any
    well-drained soil. Full sun.

CULTIVATION: Transplant container-grown or balled-
    and-burlapped plants in spring. Prune after flow-
    ering only as necessary to remove unwanted or
    crowded shoots.

PROPAGATION: Sow seed in fall. Graft in spring.

PEST AND DISEASE PREVENTION: No serious pests or
    diseases.

COMMON PROBLEMS: Tend to be short-lived. Re-
    move whatever seedpods you can to counteract
    this. Seeds are poisonous when ingested

LANDSCAPE USE: Particularly effective grouped against
    a background of evergreens; shrub borders.

OTHER SPECIES:
    L. anagyroides is a wide-spreading tree with branches
    close to the ground. It grows to 20 feet (6 m) tall.
    'Aureum' has golden yellow leaves. 'Involutum'
    has curled leaves. 'Pendulum' is a form with weep-
    ing branchlets. 'Quercifolium' has lobed leaves.

Larix decidua   Pinaceae

EUROPEAN LARCH

*European larch is a deciduous conifer with scaly bark and
light green needle-like leaves that turn yellow in fall. This
tree has a pyramidal habit with drooping branchlets.*

FLOWER COLOR AND SEASON: Insignificant yellow
    male and reddish female flowers in spring; fol-
    lowed by upright brownish cones.

HEIGHT AND SPREAD: To 100 feet (30 m) tall and
    40 feet (12 m) wide.

BEST CLIMATE AND SITE: Zones 2–6; Tolerant of a
    variety of soil, but prefers cool, moist conditions.
    Full sun to light shade.

CULTIVATION: Transplant in late fall or winter. Prune
    in winter to shape if necessary.

PROPAGATION: Sow seed in fall. Graft in early spring.

PEST AND DISEASE PREVENTION: Mulch with or-
    ganic matter to keep the soil moist. Strong, healthy
    trees are less prone to pest and disease problems.

COMMON PROBLEMS: Intolerant of dry, alkaline soils
    and air pollution.

LANDSCAPE USE: Screens; background plantings.

CULTIVARS: 'Fastigiata' is an upright columnar form.
    'Pendula' is an attractive weeping form.

OTHER SPECIES:
    L. laricina, tamarack, has reddish scaly bark, very
    small cones, and bright yellow fall color. It grows
    to 60 feet (18 m) tall. Zones 1–4.

Liquidambar styraciflua　　　Hamamelidaceae

SWEET GUM

Native to the eastern United States, sweet gum is a deciduous tree growing to pyramidal form. It has star-shaped leaves that turn shades of purple, crimson, and orange in fall.

FLOWER COLOR AND SEASON: Insignificant yellow-green flowers in downy spikes in late spring; followed by ball-shaped fruit.

HEIGHT AND SPREAD: To 100 feet (30 m) tall and 50 feet (15 m) wide.

BEST CLIMATE AND SITE: Zones 3–8. Moist well-drained soil. Full sun to light shade.

CULTIVATION: Transplant balled-and-burlapped or container-grown plants in spring. Prune in early winter only if necessary to shape young trees or to remove dead wood.

PROPAGATION: Sow seed in fall. Take cuttings from semihardwood in summer.

PEST AND DISEASE PREVENTION: No serious pests or diseases.

COMMON PROBLEMS: Difficult to transplant and slow to become established. The persistent spiny fruit can be a nuisance.

LANDSCAPE USE: Specimen tree; woodland plantings.

CULTIVARS: 'Pendula' has pendulous branches. 'Variegata' has leaves marked with yellow.

Liriodendron tulipifera　　　Magnoliaceae

TULIP TREE

Tulip tree is a stately deciduous tree with lobed leaves that turn golden yellow in fall. The yellowish flowers are borne high up in the crown, so they're often hard to see.

FLOWER COLOR AND SEASON: Yellow tulip-shaped flowers from late spring to early summer.

HEIGHT AND SPREAD: To 100 feet (30 m) tall and 60 feet (18 m) wide.

BEST CLIMATE AND SITE: Zones 4–8. Deep, moist, humus-rich, well-drained soil.

CULTIVATION: Transplant balled-and-burlapped plants in spring. Prune in early winter only to shape if necessary.

PROPAGATION: Sow seed in fall. Graft in early spring. Take cuttings in summer.

PEST AND DISEASE PREVENTION: Avoid damaging the trunk with sharp gardening tools, such as the lawn mower; these wounds are common entry points for pests and diseases.

COMMON PROBLEMS: Somewhat weak-wooded; too large for most small properties.

LANDSCAPE USE: Specimen tree for a large property.

CULTIVARS: 'Arnold' has a dense columnar habit. 'Aureo-marginatum' has leaves margined with yellow. 'Compactum' is a dwarf form.

Magnolia spp. Magnoliaceae

MAGNOLIA

Magnolias are deciduous or evergreen trees and shrubs with simple leaves. M. stellata, *star magnolia, is a bushy shrub or small tree with starry white spring flowers.*

M. x soulangiana, *saucer magnolia, is a spreading tree with smooth gray bark. The dark green leaves emerge after the spring display of white or rosy purple flowers.*

FLOWER COLOR AND SEASON: *M. grandiflora:* fragrant, waxy, creamy white flowers from late spring to midsummer; followed by red strawberry-like fruit. *M. kobus:* white six-petaled flowers in midspring; followed by pink fruit. *M. x soulangiana:* saucer-shaped white or rosy purple flowers in early spring; followed by greenish fruit. *M. stellata:* white flowers with strap-shaped petals in early spring; followed by pink fruit. *M. virginiana:* fragrant creamy white flowers from late spring to early fall; followed by red conical fruit.

HEIGHT AND SPREAD: *M. grandiflora:* to 90 feet (27 m) tall and 55 feet (16.5 m) wide; *M. kobus:* to 25 feet (7.5 m) tall and nearly as wide; *M. x soulangiana:* to 20 feet (6 m) tall and slightly wider; *M. stellata:* to 15 feet (4.5 m) tall and nearly as wide; *M. virginiana:* to 60 feet (18 m) tall and 30 feet (9 m) wide.

BEST CLIMATE AND SITE: *M. grandiflora:* Zones 7–10; *M. kobus:* Zones 4–8; *M. x soulangiana:* Zones 5–9; *M. stellata:* Zones 5–9; *M. virginiana:* Zones 5–9. Moist, humus-rich, well-drained soil. Partial shade.

CULTIVATION: Transplant balled-and-burlapped or container-grown plants in spring. Prune after flowering only if necessary to shape the tree.

PROPAGATION: Layer in spring. Remove seed from its covering and sow in fall. Take cuttings in mid- to late summer. Graft in winter.

PEST AND DISEASE PREVENTION: If scales attack, causing yellow leaves, prune out badly infested growth and spray the remaining stems with horticultural oil.

COMMON PROBLEMS: Early-blooming plants may have flowers spoiled by late frosts.

LANDSCAPE USE: Specimen tree.

SPECIES:

M. grandiflora, southern magnolia, is native to the southern United States. It is a pyramidal evergreen tree with oval 10-inch (25 cm) long leaves that are glossy dark green above, downy below. 'Goliath' has extra-large flowers.

M. kobus is a deciduous tree native to Japan, pyramidal at first and maturing to rounded form.

M. x soulangiana, saucer magnolia, is a deciduous tree that often grows in a multistemmed form. *M. stellata,* star magnolia, is a much-branched deciduous shrub or small tree with a rounded, compact habit. 'Lennei' has deep magenta flowers. 'Verbanica' is a late bloomer with flowers that are white on the inside and pink on the outside.

M. virginiana, sweet bay, is a shrub or small tree. It is evergreen in the warmer portions of its range, deciduous in the colder ones.

Malus floribunda   Rosaceae

CRAB APPLE

Japanese flowering crab apple is a round-headed deciduous tree. It is prized for its profuse display of pink spring flowers, followed by showy yellow-red fruit in fall.

FLOWER COLOR AND SEASON: Deep pink flowers in spring; followed by red or yellow fruit.

HEIGHT AND SPREAD: To 20 feet (6 m) tall and slightly wider.

BEST CLIMATE AND SITE: Zones 4–8. Deep, humus-rich, moist, slightly alkaline soil. Full sun.

CULTIVATION: Plant in early spring. Prune soon after flowering.

PROPAGATION: Graft in spring. Take softwood cuttings in late spring.

PEST AND DISEASE PREVENTION: Avoid overfeeding, which results in succulent growth attractive to aphids and other insects. To reduce possibility of rust, keep at least 500 feet (150 m) from eastern red cedar (*Juniperus virginiana*). Prune to keep the center of the plant open to light and air to reduce disease problems. Choose disease-resistant cultivars.

COMMON PROBLEMS: Many cultivars bloom heavily only in alternate years.

LANDSCAPE USE: Specimen tree; shade trees for small gardens.

OTHER SPECIES:
> *M. baccata,* Siberian crab apple, is a tall spreading tree with white flowers. Zones 2–7.
> *M. coronaria,* wild sweet crab apple, has an open habit and fragrant white flowers. Zones 4–8.

Metasequoia glyptostroboides   Taxodiaceae

DAWN REDWOOD

Dawn redwood is a coniferous deciduous tree with opposite, soft, green needle-like leaves that turn coppery brown in fall. It has an upright pyramidal form and grows rapidly.

FLOWER COLOR AND SEASON: Inconspicuous yellow male and greenish female flowers in spring; followed by a rounded green cone that ripens to brown.

HEIGHT AND SPREAD: To 100 feet (30 m) tall and 25 feet (7.5 m) wide.

BEST CLIMATE AND SITE: Zones 5–10. Deep, moist, well-drained soil; dry or alkaline soil results in slower growth. Full sun and sheltered position.

CULTIVATION: Transplant balled-and-burlapped or container-grown plants in spring. No pruning is necessary.

PROPAGATION: Sow seed in fall or early spring. Take cuttings in late summer.

PEST AND DISEASE PREVENTION: No serious pests or diseases.

COMMON PROBLEMS: Can be injured by early fall frosts. To avoid this, plant on a slope.

LANDSCAPE USE: Because of its size, it is best for large properties. Most effective when planted in groups.

OTHER COMMON NAMES: Water fir.

CULTIVARS: 'National' is a narrow pyramidal form.

| *Nyssa sylvatica* | Nyssaceae | *Ostrya virginiana* | Betulaceae |

BLACK TUPELO

AMERICAN HOP HORNBEAM

Black tupelo is a deciduous tree of pyramidal form. The branches are somewhat pendulous; the leaves are leathery and glossy dark green, turning brilliant orange or scarlet in fall.

American hop hornbeam is a slow-growing deciduous tree with alternate simple leaves and graceful horizontal or drooping branches. It ultimately forms a round-headed tree.

FLOWER COLOR AND SEASON: Greenish white flowers in late spring; followed in midsummer by small blue fruits on the female trees.

HEIGHT AND SPREAD: To 90 feet (27 m) tall and 45 feet (13.5 m) wide.

BEST CLIMATE AND SITE: Zones 4–8. Moist, humus-rich, well-drained soil. Full sun.

CULTIVATION: Transplant small balled-and-burlapped or container-grown plants in early spring.

PROPAGATION: Sow seed when ripe in fall.

PEST AND DISEASE PREVENTION: Few serious pests or diseases. Mulch with organic matter to keep soil moist and to provide a home for beneficial insects.

COMMON PROBLEMS: Intolerant of alkaline soil.

LANDSCAPE USE: Specimen tree; woodland plantings; chiefly valued for its fall color.

OTHER COMMON NAMES: Black gum, pepperidge.

FLOWER COLOR AND SEASON: Inconspicuous greenish catkins in early spring.

HEIGHT AND SPREAD: To 40 feet (12 m) tall and 30 feet (9 m) wide.

BEST CLIMATE AND SITE: Zones 4–9. Tolerant of a variety of well-drained soil. Full sun to partial shade.

CULTIVATION: Transplant balled-and-burlapped or container-grown plants in spring.

PROPAGATION: Sow seed when ripe in fall.

PEST AND DISEASE PREVENTION: No serious pests or diseases.

COMMON PROBLEMS: Difficult to transplant and slow to establish.

LANDSCAPE USE: Specimen or street tree; chiefly valued where other trees will not grow.

OTHER COMMON NAMES: Ironwood.

Oxydendrum arboreum   Ericaceae

SOURWOOD

Native to the eastern United States, sourwood is a slow-growing deciduous tree or shrub with oval leaves that turn vivid scarlet in fall. The tree usually grows in pyramidal form.

FLOWER COLOR AND SEASON: White flowers borne in pendulous clusters in midsummer.

HEIGHT AND SPREAD: To 50 feet (15 m) tall and 20 feet (6 m) wide.

BEST CLIMATE AND SITE: Zones 5–9. Moist, well-drained, humus-rich, acid soil. Full sun.

CULTIVATION: Transplant small balled-and-burlapped or container-grown plants in late winter or early spring. Plant in permanent position as established plants are difficult to move. Rarely needs pruning.

PROPAGATION: Sow seed indoors in spring. Take cuttings in midsummer. Cuttings should be 2–3 inches (5–7.5 cm) long and made of short sideshoots with a thin heel of old wood. Bottom heat promotes rooting.

PEST AND DISEASE PREVENTION: No serious pests or diseases.

COMMON PROBLEMS: Flowering and fall color are less dramatic in shade.

LANDSCAPE USE: Specimen tree.

OTHER COMMON NAMES: Sorrel tree.

Parrotia persica   Hamamelidaceae

PERSIAN PARROTIA

A wide-spreading, round-headed deciduous tree, Persian parrotia is often multitrunked with horizontal branching. Leaves turn orange, yellow, and scarlet in fall.

FLOWER COLOR AND SEASON: Inconspicuous, petal-less flowers with protruding red stamens from late winter to early spring.

HEIGHT AND SPREAD: To 40 feet (12 m) tall and 45 feet (13.5 m) wide.

BEST CLIMATE AND SITE: Zones 5–10. Tolerant of a variety of well-drained soil. Full sun for best leaf color.

CULTIVATION: Transplant balled-and-burlapped or container-grown plants in early spring.

PROPAGATION: Sow seed in fall. Graft in late winter or early spring on witch hazel (*Hamamelis* spp.). Take cuttings in midsummer.

PEST AND DISEASE PREVENTION: No serious pests or diseases.

COMMON PROBLEMS: Large trees are difficult to transplant, so they are best moved when small.

LANDSCAPE USE: Specimen tree; of interest for its fall foliage color and for its mottled bark.

Paulownia tomentosa   Bignoniaceae

ROYAL PAULOWNIA

Native to China, royal paulownia is a rapidly growing deciduous tree. The coarse, very large opposite leaves may be entire or lobed, and their undersides are covered with down.

FLOWER COLOR AND SEASON: Fragrant violet flowers borne in large pyramidal clusters in midspring.

HEIGHT AND SPREAD: To 40 feet (12 m) tall and as wide.

BEST CLIMATE AND SITE: Zones 5–9. Tolerant of a variety of well-drained soil. Full sun.

CULTIVATION: Transplant balled-and-burlapped or container-grown plants in early spring.

PROPAGATION: Sow seed indoors in early spring. Take root cuttings in winter.

PEST AND DISEASE PREVENTION: No serious pests or diseases.

COMMON PROBLEMS: Branches tend to be somewhat brittle. Flower buds may be killed by cold winter temperatures. Young plants may die back to the roots in cold climates.

LANDSCAPE USE: Specimen tree.

OTHER COMMON NAMES: Princess tree, empress tree.

Picea pungens   Pinaceae

COLORADO SPRUCE

Colorado spruce is a coniferous evergreen tree with horizontal branches and an overall pyramidal habit. The stiff needle-like leaves vary in color from green to silver-blue.

FLOWER COLOR AND SEASON: Reddish brown male and female flowers in late spring; followed by 5–7-inch (12.5–17.5 cm) hanging cones.

HEIGHT AND SPREAD: To 150 feet (45 m) tall and 60 feet (18 m) wide.

BEST CLIMATE AND SITE: Zones 2–7. Moist, humus-rich, well-drained soil. Full sun. Grows best in cool climates.

CULTIVATION: Transplant balled-and-burlapped plants in early spring.

PROPAGATION: Sow seed when ripe in fall or spring. Take cuttings in fall. Graft in spring.

PEST AND DISEASE PREVENTION: Take care not to injure plants with sharp gardening tools; such wounds are common entry points for pests and diseases. Mulch with organic matter to keep soil moist.

COMMON PROBLEMS: Intolerant of heat, drought, and air pollution.

LANDSCAPE USE: Specimen tree; screen plantings.

CULTIVARS: 'Glauca' (Colorado blue spruce) has bluish foliage. 'Thompsen' is a pyramidal form with whitish foliage.

OTHER SPECIES:

P. abies, Norway spruce, is a fast-growing tree. It is frequently used as a filler or screen. 'Conica' is a dense compact conical form to 25 feet (7.5 m).

Pinus mugo   Pinaceae

SWISS MOUNTAIN PINE

Swiss mountain pine is a coniferous evergreen with stiff needle-like leaves. The species can grow to be a small tree; many of its cultivars are more compact.

FLOWER COLOR AND SEASON: Insignificant yellow male and reddish female flowers in late spring; followed by tan or brown cones.

HEIGHT AND SPREAD: To 20 feet (6 m) tall and slightly wider.

BEST CLIMATE AND SITE: Zones 2–7. Humus-rich, moist, well-drained soil. Full sun.

CULTIVATION: Transplant balled-and-burlapped plants in spring. To promote more compact growth, trim new shoots back by half in spring.

PROPAGATION: Sow seed when ripe in fall or spring. Graft in late winter and early spring.

PEST AND DISEASE PREVENTION: Plants grown in healthy, fertile soil with adequate moisture tolerate insect attack better than stressed plants.

COMMON PROBLEMS: Nomenclature of *P. mugo* is confusing; plants you expect to remain 5 feet (1.5 m) tall may grow to 15 feet (4.5 m).

LANDSCAPE USE: Foundation plants; hedges.

OTHER SPECIES:

P. aristata, bristle-cone pine, is a slow-growing tree with short bluish green needles. It is very drought-tolerant. Zones 5–9. 'Compacta' is a dense globular form.

P. strobus, eastern white pine, is a tall tree with long needles. Plant in masses for screens or alone as a specimen tree. Zones 3–7.

Platanus occidentalis   Platanaceae

AMERICAN PLANETREE

American planetree, also known as sycamore, is native to eastern North America. This moisture-loving tree has coarse dark green leaves and mottled white bark.

FLOWER COLOR AND SEASON: Inconspicuous cream flowers in spring; followed by ball-shaped fruit.

HEIGHT AND SPREAD: To 90 feet (27 m) tall and 65 feet (19.5 m) wide.

BEST CLIMATE AND SITE: Zones 4–8. Adaptable to moist well-drained soil; grows to greatest size in rich, moist soil. Full sun. Tolerates air pollution.

CULTIVATION: Prune in winter if necessary.

PROPAGATION: Take hardwood cuttings in winter. Sow seed in spring.

PEST AND DISEASE PREVENTION: Avoid damaging the bark with sharp gardening tools; such wounds are prime entry sites for diseases. Clean up dropped leaves and twigs to remove overwintering sites for disease spores. Look for disease-resistant cultivars.

COMMON PROBLEMS: Drops leaves, twigs, and fruit, which may become unsightly.

LANDSCAPE USE: Street trees. Plant in borders of large properties.

OTHER COMMON NAMES: Plane, buttonwood, sycamore.

OTHER SPECIES:

P. x *acerifolia*, London planetree, has palmately lobed leaves to 10 inches (25 cm) wide and grows in wide-spreading form. 'Bloodgood' and 'Liberty' are very disease-resistant.

Populus deltoides   Salicaceae

EASTERN COTTONWOOD

Eastern cottonwood is a fast-growing deciduous tree with large leaves. It is planted primarily for its rapid growth and ability to survive where few other trees can.

FLOWER COLOR AND SEASON: Inconspicuous greenish catkins from mid- to late spring.

HEIGHT AND SPREAD: To 90 feet (27 m) tall and 70 feet (21 m) wide.

BEST CLIMATE AND SITE: Zones 2–8. Tolerant of a variety of soil conditions, even poor, dry ones, but prefers deep, moist, well-drained soil.

CULTIVATION: Plant in fall or spring. Prune in summer or fall; bleeds if pruned at other times.

PROPAGATION: Take cuttings in late summer or winter. Sow seed in summer.

PEST AND DISEASE PREVENTION: Keep soil evenly moist with organic mulch. Healthy plants will resist pests and diseases far better than stressed plants.

COMMON PROBLEMS: Weak-wooded and short-lived. Questing roots can spread into and clog drains and sewers.

LANDSCAPE USE: Screens; mass plantings.

OTHER COMMON NAMES: Poplar.

OTHER SPECIES:

P. alba, white poplar, has whitish bark and white undersides to the leaves. 'Richardii' has yellow upper leaf surfaces.

P. nigra 'Italica', Lombardy poplar, is a narrow columnar grower to 90 feet (27 m) tall.

Prunus serrulata   Rosaceae

FLOWERING CHERRY

Japanese flowering cherry is a rounded deciduous tree with an eye-catching display of spring flowers. The new leaves are often reddish brown; they mature to deep green.

FLOWER COLOR AND SEASON: Clustered white or pink flowers, single, semidouble, or double in form, in midspring.

HEIGHT AND SPREAD: To 25 feet (7.5 m) tall and nearly as wide.

BEST CLIMATE AND SITE: Zones 5–8. Deep, humus-rich, well-drained, moist soil. Full sun.

CULTIVATION: Transplant container-grown or balled-and-burlapped plants in spring. Prune after flowering.

PROPAGATION: Sow seed in fall. Take cuttings in summer or fall. Graft in late winter and early spring.

PEST AND DISEASE PREVENTION: Avoid overfeeding, which can stimulate succulent growth that is susceptible to pests and diseases. Also avoid planting in poorly drained soil.

COMMON PROBLEMS: Plants tend to be short-lived.

LANDSCAPE USE: Specimen tree; mass plantings.

CULTIVARS: 'Kwanzan' ('Sekiyama') has bronze foliage and double deep pink flowers. 'Shirotae' ('Mt. Fuji') has semidouble white flowers. 'Ukon' has bronze new foliage and pale yellow flowers.

OTHER SPECIES:

P. subhirtella, Higan cherry, is a bushy plant with small leaves of exceptionally fine texture. 'Autumnalis' has semidouble pink flowers usually repeated in fall.

DOUGLAS FIR

Native to western North America, Douglas fir is an imposing narrow-leaved coniferous evergreen with soft needles. It grows rapidly in pyramidal form.

FLOWER COLOR AND SEASON: Yellow male and greenish pink female flowers in late spring; followed by hanging red-brown cones.

HEIGHT AND SPREAD: To 200 feet (60 m) tall and 80 feet (24 m) wide.

BEST CLIMATE AND SITE: Zones 4–7. Tolerant of a variety of soil conditions but prefers moist, well-drained, slightly acid soil. Prefers cool, moist climates.

CULTIVATION: Transplant balled-and-burlapped plants in fall and spring. Rarely needs pruning.

PROPAGATION: Sow seed in fall.

PEST AND DISEASE PREVENTION: Vigorous, well-nourished plants have a natural ability to resist pests and diseases. Mulch with organic matter to keep soil moist.

COMMON PROBLEMS: Readily injured by strong wind or drought.

LANDSCAPE USE: Specimen tree for large properties.

CULTIVARS: 'Columnare' has a narrowly columnar form. 'Compacta' has a compact conical form with short needles.

CALLERY PEAR

Callery pear is a pyramidal to round-headed deciduous tree grown primarily for its spring flower display. Its rounded glossy dark green leaves turn purplish or reddish in fall.

FLOWER COLOR AND SEASON: White flowers from early to midspring; followed by roundish green fruit.

HEIGHT AND SPREAD: To 30 feet (9 m) tall and 18 feet (5.4 m) wide.

BEST CLIMATE AND SITE: Zones 5–9. Deep, moist, humus-rich, well-drained soil. Full sun.

CULTIVATION: Transplant container-grown or balled-and-burlapped plants in late winter while they are still dormant. Prune in winter or early spring.

PROPAGATION: Sow seed in fall. Graft in late winter and early spring.

PEST AND DISEASE PREVENTION: Avoid injury with sharp gardening tools; these wounds provide easy access for pests and diseases. Look for disease-resistant cultivars.

COMMON PROBLEMS: Tends to form narrow branch angles that are prone to splitting.

LANDSCAPE USE: Specimen tree.

CULTIVARS: 'Aristocrat' has darker foliage and better fall color. 'Bradford' is more vigorous than the species, growing to 50 feet (15 m) tall and 30 feet (9 m) wide.

OTHER SPECIES:

P. salicifolia, willow-leaved pear, has silvery narrow leaves. It is very prone to fire blight. 'Pendula' has weeping branches. Zones 4–8.

OAK

Q. rubra, *red oak, is an adaptable, fast-growing tree with dark green leaves that may turn red in fall. Unlike some other species, red oak is not difficult to transplant.*

Q. virginiana, *live oak, is a massive, spreading, usually evergreen tree with elongated oval dark green leaves. The older leaves drop in spring when the new foliage emerges.*

FLOWER COLOR AND SEASON: Inconspicuous greenish catkins in midspring; followed by roundish fruit (acorns).

HEIGHT AND SPREAD: *Q. acutissima:* to 45 feet (13.5 m) tall and as wide; *Q. alba:* to 80 feet (24 m) tall and nearly as wide; *Q. palustris:* to 45 feet (13.5 m) tall and 35 feet (10.5 m) wide; *Q. phellos:* to 50 feet (15 m) tall and 35 feet (10.5 m) wide; *Q. robur:* to 100 feet (30 m) tall and 80 feet (24 m) wide; *Q. rubra:* to 70 feet (21 m) tall and as wide; *Q. virginiana:* to 60 feet (18 m) tall and 100 feet (30 m) wide.

BEST CLIMATE AND SITE: *Q. acutissima:* Zones 6–8; *Q. alba, Q. palustris,* and *Q. rubra:* Zones 4–8; *Q. phellos:* Zones 6–9; *Q. virginiana:* Zones 7–10. Tolerant of a variety of soil conditions but thrives in moist, humus-rich, well-drained soil. Full sun.

CULTIVATION: Transplant young balled-and-burlapped plants in fall and spring. Prune in winter only as necessary to shape the tree.

PROPAGATION: Graft in late winter and early spring. Sow seed in fall.

PEST AND DISEASE PREVENTION: Tie burlap bands around main trunks to trap gypsy moth larvae; remove and destroy the caterpillars as they accumulate. Prune only in winter to avoid spreading oak wilt, which causes leaves to curl, turn brown,

and droop. Build up soil organic matter content with mulch and correct nutrient imbalances to ensure healthy plants with greater vigor to fight pest invasions.

COMMON PROBLEMS: Many species difficult to transplant.

LANDSCAPE USE: Specimen tree; shade trees for large properties. *Q. palustris* is an excellent street tree.

SPECIES:

Q. acutissima, sawtooth oak, is a wide-spreading deciduous tree with glossy toothed leaves.

Q. alba, white oak, is a slow-growing deciduous tree with spreading branches. The deeply cut, round-lobed leaves turn purplish red in fall.

Q. palustris, pin oak, is a pyramidal deciduous tree with deeply lobed leaves.

Q. phellos, willow oak, is a deciduous tree with narrow leaves that turn yellow in fall.

Q. robur, English oak, is a majestic broad-headed deciduous tree. The oblong leaves have rounded lobes and show no significant fall color. 'Fastigiata' is a very upright, columnar form.

Q. rubra, red oak, is a round-topped deciduous tree with shiny, dark green lobed leaves.

Q. virginiana, live oak, is evergreen in the warmer parts of its range, deciduous in the colder parts.

Robinia pseudoacacia   Leguminosae

BLACK LOCUST

A thorny deciduous tree, black locust has an open, upright habit and pinnately compound leaves. The cultivar 'Frisia' has bright yellow foliage all season long.

FLOWER COLOR AND SEASON: White or pink pea-like flowers borne in long pendulous clusters in early summer; followed by long brown pods.

HEIGHT AND SPREAD: To 75 feet (22.5 m) tall and 45 feet (13.5 m) wide.

BEST CLIMATE AND SITE: Zones 3–8. Tolerant of a variety of soil conditions but prefers slightly alkaline soil. Full sun to partial shade.

CULTIVATION: Plant in winter or early spring. Prune in late summer or fall only if necessary to shape the tree; bleeds if pruned in winter or spring.

PROPAGATION: Graft in spring. Sow seed when ripe in fall. Remove rooted suckers from the parent plant in winter.

PEST AND DISEASE PREVENTION: Mulch with organic matter to keep the soil evenly moist. Healthy, vigorous plants are most resistant to borers and other pests.

COMMON PROBLEMS: Tends to produce many new shoots (suckers) at the base. Thorns can be hazardous and plant parts toxic.

LANDSCAPE USE: Mass plantings for difficult sites where other trees won't thrive.

CULTIVARS: 'Burgundy' has dark pink flowers. 'Erecta' has a columnar habit. 'Semperflorens' blooms intermittently all summer.

Salix babylonica   Salicaceae

WEEPING WILLOW

Weeping willow is a moisture-loving deciduous tree with long narrow leaves. It has a gracefully weeping habit with branches that frequently touch the ground.

FLOWER COLOR AND SEASON: Inconspicuous greenish catkins from late spring to early summer.

HEIGHT AND SPREAD: To 40 feet (12 m) tall and slightly wider.

BEST CLIMATE AND SITE: Zones 6–10. Moist, well-drained, humus-rich soil. Full sun.

CULTIVATION: Transplant in fall and early spring. Prune in summer or fall; may bleed if pruned in winter or spring.

PROPAGATION: Take cuttings anytime.

PEST AND DISEASE PREVENTION: Mulch with organic matter to keep soil evenly moist. Avoid injury with gardening tools; such wounds are a common entry point for pests and diseases. If caterpillars attack, spray small plants with BT.

COMMON PROBLEMS: Weak-wooded. Leaves, twigs, and branches frequently drop. Do not plant too close to the house as the roots will clog drains.

LANDSCAPE USE: Specimen tree; useful bank-binding plants when grown near streams.

OTHER SPECIES:

S. alba, white willow, is native to Europe, northern Africa, and western Asia. It is a tree of loose, open upright growth. 'Chermesina' has bright red young stems. 'Sericea' has silvery white leaves. 'Tristis' (golden weeping willow) is a weeping form with yellow young stems. Zones 2–7.

| *Sophora japonica* Leguminosae | *Sorbus aucuparia* Rosaceae |

JAPANESE PAGODA TREE

EUROPEAN MOUNTAIN ASH

Japanese pagoda tree is a deciduous tree from the Orient. It grows to a round-headed form and has alternate, compound leaves. It is one of the last of the large trees to bloom.

European mountain ash is a deciduous tree with compound leaves that turn red in fall. The white spring flowers are followed by clusters of showy orange-red fruit.

FLOWER COLOR AND SEASON: Profuse creamy white mildly fragrant flowers in large 12 by 12-inch (30 by 30 cm) pendant terminal clusters in late summer and early fall; followed by brown pods that persist most of the winter.

HEIGHT AND SPREAD: To 65 feet (19.5 m) tall and 40 feet (12 m) wide.

BEST CLIMATE AND SITE: Zones 4–8. Adaptable to moist, well-drained soil. Full sun to light shade. Widely tolerant of city conditions, heat, and drought.

CULTIVATION: Transplant young balled-and-burlapped or container-grown plants in fall or early spring. Prune in fall only if necessary to shape the tree.

PROPAGATION: Sow seed when ripe in fall.

PEST AND DISEASE PREVENTION: No serious pests or diseases.

COMMON PROBLEMS: Species tends to grow in a rather loose, open form.

LANDSCAPE USE: Specimen tree; street trees.

CULTIVARS: 'Fastigiata' is an upright grower. 'Pendula' is a densely rounded tree with pendulous branches. 'Regent' is a fast grower with an upright habit and deeper leaf color.

FLOWER COLOR AND SEASON: Clustered small white flowers in late spring; followed by bright orange-red fruit.

HEIGHT AND SPREAD: To 35 feet (10.5 m) tall and nearly as wide.

BEST CLIMATE AND SITE: Zones 2–7. Tolerant of a variety of well-drained, soil conditions. Full sun to partial shade. Grows best in cooler climates.

CULTIVATION: Transplant balled-and-burlapped or container-grown plants in fall or spring.

PROPAGATION: Graft in late winter and early spring. Sow seed in spring.

PEST AND DISEASE PREVENTION: Avoid overfeeding, which can stimulate young succulent growth that is susceptible to rusts and fire blight. Keep soil moist with organic mulch.

COMMON PROBLEMS: Short-lived in alkaline or dry soil.

LANDSCAPE USE: Specimen tree; shade trees.

OTHER COMMON NAMES: Rowan tree.

CULTIVARS: 'Edulis' bears large fruit, often used for preserves. 'Fastigiata' is a very upright, columnar form. 'Pendula' has pendulous branches. 'Xanthocarpa' has yellow fruit.

JAPANESE STEWARTIA

A deciduous tree of pyramidal habit, Japanese stewartia has alternate leaves and interesting red flaking bark. The foliage exhibits good purplish fall color.

FLOWER COLOR AND SEASON: White camellia-like flowers from early to midsummer.

HEIGHT AND SPREAD: To 50 feet (15 m) tall and 35 feet (10.5 m) wide.

BEST CLIMATE AND SITE: Zones 5–9. Deep, moist, humus-rich, well-drained, lime-free soil. Sun to partial shade.

CULTIVATION: Transplant small container-grown or balled-and-burlapped plants in early spring. Pruning is rarely necessary.

PROPAGATION: Take 3–4-inch (7.5–10 cm) long cuttings with a heel of older wood in late spring or early summer. Bottom heat may encourage rooting. Sow seed in fall; may take 2 years to germinate.

PEST AND DISEASE PREVENTION: No serious pests or diseases.

COMMON PROBLEMS: Few nurseries offer Japanese stewartia, so it can be difficult to obtain. But it is worth the effort!

LANDSCAPE USE: Specimen tree.

JAPANESE SNOWBELL

Japanese snowbell is a showy deciduous tree with a horizontal branching structure. The bell-shaped white flowers bloom profusely on the undersides of the branches.

FLOWER COLOR AND SEASON: Pendulous white flowers from late spring to early summer.

HEIGHT AND SPREAD: To 30 feet (9 m) tall and nearly as wide.

BEST CLIMATE AND SITE: Zones 5–9. Moist, humus-rich, well-drained, acid soil. Full sun to light shade. Tolerates city conditions; shelter from strong winds.

CULTIVATION: Transplant container-grown or balled-and-burlapped plants in early spring. Prune in summer only if necessary to shape the plant.

PROPAGATION: Take cuttings in summer. Sow seed in summer; may take 2 years to germinate.

PEST AND DISEASE PREVENTION: No serious pests or diseases. Keep soil moist by mulching with organic matter.

COMMON PROBLEMS: Plants grow poorly in dry or alkaline soil.

LANDSCAPE USE: Handsome small trees, ideal as a specimen near a patio; shade trees.

OTHER SPECIES:

S. obassia, fragrant snowbell, bears its flowers in long clusters. It grows to 20 feet (6 m) tall and 15 feet (4.5 m) wide. Zones 6–9.

Taxodium distichum	Taxodiaceae	*Thuja occidentalis*	Cupressaceae

BALD CYPRESS

AMERICAN ARBORVITAE

Bald cypress is a deciduous tree native to the swampy portions of the southeastern United States. The leaves are bright green and needle-like, turning rich brown in fall.

FLOWER COLOR AND SEASON: Inconspicuous greenish flowers in early spring.

HEIGHT AND SPREAD: To 125 feet (37.5 m) tall and 60 feet (18 m) wide.

BEST CLIMATE AND SITE: Zones 4–9. Prefers moist situation—grows and thrives even in standing water. Full sun.

CULTIVATION: Transplant balled-and-burlapped plants in fall or spring.

PROPAGATION: Graft in late winter and early spring. Take cuttings in early summer. Sow seed in fall.

PEST AND DISEASE PREVENTION: No serious pests or diseases.

COMMON PROBLEMS: Plants grown in alkaline soils can show severe chlorosis (yellowing) of the leaves.

LANDSCAPE USE: Waterside plantings on large properties.

CULTIVARS: 'Pendens' is a pyramidal form with horizontal branches drooping at the tips. 'Shawnee Brave' has a very narrow pyramidal habit.

American arborvitae is a large upright pyramidal evergreen tree with scale-like dark green or golden green leaves borne in flattened fans. The leaves are aromatic when crushed.

FLOWER COLOR AND SEASON: Inconspicuous reddish male and yellowish brown female flowers in midspring; followed by small dried capsules.

HEIGHT AND SPREAD: To 60 feet (18 m) tall and 20 feet (6 m) wide.

BEST CLIMATE AND SITE: Zones 2–7. Best where atmospheric moisture is high. Tolerant of a variety of soil conditions but prefers deep, loamy, humus-rich soil. Full sun.

CULTIVATION: Transplant balled-and-burlapped plants preferably in spring. Prune in early spring if necessary.

PROPAGATION: Sow seed in fall or spring. Take cuttings in late summer.

PEST AND DISEASE PREVENTION: Mulch to keep the soil evenly moist. Bagworms may attack, producing soft cone-like cocoons; use a knife to carefully cut the cocoons from the branches.

COMMON PROBLEMS: Subject to sun scorch when exposed to bright afternoon winter sun and wind.

LANDSCAPE USE: Screens; hedges; foundation plantings; accent plants.

OTHER SPECIES:

T. orientalis, Oriental arborvitae, grows as a tree or upright shrub. 'Aurea' is a low globose form with yellow foliage. 'Blue Spire' is a pyramidal form with bluish foliage.

Tilia x *europaea*   Tiliaceae

EUROPEAN LINDEN

European linden is a tall, fast-growing deciduous tree with heart-shaped leaves. The creamy white summer flowers are exceptionally fragrant and attractive to bees.

FLOWER COLOR AND SEASON: Fragrant creamy white flowers in drooping clusters in early summer.

HEIGHT AND SPREAD: To 100 feet (30 m) tall and 60 feet (18 m) wide.

BEST CLIMATE AND SITE: Zones 3–7. Tolerant of a wide variety of soil conditions but thrives in deep, moist, humus-rich, well-drained soil. Full sun. Adaptable to city conditions.

CULTIVATION: Plant in winter or early spring. Thin out branches in late summer when overcrowded.

PROPAGATION: Graft in late winter and early spring. Sow seed in fall.

PEST AND DISEASE PREVENTION: Mulch with organic matter to keep soil evenly moist. Healthy plants are more resistant to pests and diseases. Clean up dropped leaves to remove overwintering sites for pests and diseases.

COMMON PROBLEMS: Leaves can brown and become unsightly during summer droughts.

LANDSCAPE USE: Specimen tree; street trees; hedges.

OTHER SPECIES:

T. americana, basswood, has a pyramidal habit when young but becomes rounded with age. 'Fastigiata' is a dense pyramidal form.

T. cordata, little-leaved linden, has a broadly columnar form. 'Greenspire' has a straight trunk with radial branches.

Tsuga canadensis   Pinaceae

CANADA HEMLOCK

Canada hemlock is a tall coniferous evergreen tree with small soft needles and gracefully drooping branches. It grows in a loosely pyramidal form.

FLOWER COLOR AND SEASON: Yellow male and greenish female flowers in late spring; followed by small pale brown cones.

HEIGHT AND SPREAD: To 100 feet (30 m) tall and 60 feet (18 m) wide.

BEST CLIMATE AND SITE: Zones 4–7. Deep, moist, well-drained soil. Full sun to light shade. Grows best in cool, moist locations.

CULTIVATION: Plant in early spring. Water during periods of drought. No pruning is necessary except to shape the trees when young. Prune in spring.

PROPAGATION: Sow seed in fall. Take cuttings in late summer. Graft in late winter and early spring.

PEST AND DISEASE PREVENTION: Mulch with organic matter to keep soil evenly moist. Take care not to injure with lawn mower or sharp gardening tools; injured plants are more susceptible to pests.

COMMON PROBLEMS: Plants become very leggy in shade. Scales and wooly adelgids can seriously weaken plants in some areas.

LANDSCAPE USE: Specimen tree; screens; hedges.

CULTIVARS: 'Pendula' (sargent hemlock) has a markedly pendulous habit and is twice as wide as it is tall.

OTHER SPECIES:

T. caroliniana, Carolina hemlock, has smaller whorled needles that give it a denser look.

Ulmus parvifolia   Ulmaceae

CHINESE ELM

Chinese elm is a round-topped usually deciduous tree that is semi-evergreen in the warmer portions of its range. Its bark peels off in irregular contrasting patches.

FLOWER COLOR AND SEASON: Inconspicuous reddish flowers in fall.

HEIGHT AND SPREAD: To 50 feet (15 m) tall and 40 feet (12 m) wide.

BEST CLIMATE AND SITE: Zones 5–9. Moist, humus-rich, well-drained soil. Full sun.

CULTIVATION: Plant in winter or early spring. Prune in fall.

PROPAGATION: Sow seed when ripe. Graft in spring.

PEST AND DISEASE PREVENTION: Keep soil moist with organic mulch. Maintain vigor by feeding and watering copiously. Vigorous trees are less susceptible to pests and diseases.

COMMON PROBLEMS: Usually trouble-free.

LANDSCAPE USE: Specimen tree; shade trees; street trees.

CULTIVARS: 'Drake' has more upright branches than the species. 'Sempervirens' has broadly arching or weeping branches with smaller leaves than the species. 'True Green' has small glossy leaves and is more evergreen and less hardy than the species.

Zelkova serrata   Ulmaceae

JAPANESE ZELKOVA

Japanese zelkova is a deciduous tree from Japan, closely related to the elms. Its habit is rounded with numerous ascending branches; the leaves turn yellow or russet in fall.

FLOWER COLOR AND SEASON: Inconspicuous greenish flowers in early spring.

HEIGHT AND SPREAD: To 90 feet (27 m) tall and nearly as wide.

BEST CLIMATE AND SITE: Zones 5–8. Tolerant of a variety of soil conditions and air pollution. Full sun to light shade.

CULTIVATION: Transplant balled-and-burlapped or container-grown plants in fall or spring. No pruning is necessary except to shape the trees by thinning crowded branches in late summer.

PROPAGATION: Sow seed in fall. Take cuttings in summer.

PEST AND DISEASE PREVENTION: No serious pests or diseases.

COMMON PROBLEMS: Young plants are subject to frost injury.

LANDSCAPE USE: Specimen tree; street trees; screens.

CULTIVARS: 'Village Green' is a fast-growing, vigorous form that is hardier than the species and has reddish fall color.

Abelia x *grandiflora*   Caprifoliaceae

GLOSSY ABELIA

Glossy abelia is a dense, semi-evergreen shrub with dark green opposite leaves that turn bronze or purple in fall. The delicate flowers are lightly fragrant.

FLOWER COLOR AND SEASON: Pinkish purple or white tubular flowers borne in loose, terminal clusters in late spring to early summer.

HEIGHT AND SPREAD: To 6 feet (1.8 m) tall and as wide.

BEST CLIMATE AND SITE: Zones 6–10. Deep, moist, well-drained, humus-rich soil. Full sun.

CULTIVATION: Plant in spring or winter. Grow in a protected site in the colder portion of its range. Prune in late winter or early spring to remove winter-damaged wood.

PROPAGATION: Take softwood cuttings in early summer, hardwood cuttings in fall.

PEST AND DISEASE PREVENTION: No serious pests or diseases.

COMMON PROBLEMS: Usually trouble-free.

LANDSCAPE USE: Informal hedges; foundation plantings; shrub borders.

CULTIVARS: 'Sherwood' is a compact form only 3 feet (90 cm) tall.

Aesculus parviflora   Hippocastanaceae   *Aronia arbutifolia*   Rosaceae

BOTTLEBRUSH BUCKEYE

RED CHOKEBERRY

Bottlebrush buckeye is a deciduous shrub, occasionally growing as a single-trunked small tree. Its compound leaves consist of five to seven leaflets, each 3–9 inches (7.5–23 cm) long.

Red chokeberry is a vigorous deciduous shrub planted for its spectacular display of brilliant red fruit in fall and winter. The alternate leaves are narrowly oval and dull green.

FLOWER COLOR AND SEASON: Upright panicles of white flowers with pink stamens and red anthers in midsummer; followed by spiny fruit.

HEIGHT AND SPREAD: 10–12 feet (3–3.6 m) tall and nearly as wide.

BEST CLIMATE AND SITE: Zones 4–8. Deep, moist, humus-rich soil. Full sun to light shade.

CULTIVATION: Transplant container-grown or balled-and-burlapped plants in early spring.

PROPAGATION: Sow seed in fall. Layer established plants in spring.

PEST AND DISEASE PREVENTION: Provide good air circulation to avoid fungal diseases such as leaf blotch and canker. Healthy plants are better able to resist pests and diseases.

COMMON PROBLEMS: Spreads freely by suckers. Japanese beetles may attack leaves. To control, knock beetles into a bucket of soapy water.

LANDSCAPE USE: Specimen shrubs; shrub borders. Especially valued as a midsummer source of color.

CULTIVARS: 'Rogers' is a late-blooming form with very long inflorescences.

VARIETIES: *A. parviflora* var. *serotina* is a late-blooming form with larger flowers.

FLOWER COLOR AND SEASON: White flowers, sometimes tinged with pink, borne in loose clusters in late spring; followed by conspicuous red fruit.

HEIGHT AND SPREAD: To 8 feet (2.4 m) tall and as wide.

BEST CLIMATE AND SITE: Zones 4–8. Average, well-drained soil. Full sun to light shade. Adapts to dry or wet conditions.

CULTIVATION: Plant in spring. Best fruit production in full sun. Seldom requires pruning.

PROPAGATION: Take cuttings in early summer. Divide in early spring or fall. Remove seed from its fleshy coating and sow in fall.

PEST AND DISEASE PREVENTION: Choose a site with good air circulation. Clean up all dropped leaves to remove overwintering sites for disease spores. Prune off canes damaged by borers and seal ends with paraffin wax to prevent recurrence.

COMMON PROBLEMS: Plants tend to become leggy. Prune after flowering if necessary to promote a bushier habit. Also produces suckers.

LANDSCAPE USE: Valued for its fall fruit color. Most effective in mass plantings.

CULTIVARS: 'Brilliantissima' bears glossy darker red fruit. 'Erecta' has a narrow columnar habit.

Aucuba japonica   Cornaceae

JAPANESE AUCUBA

Japanese aucuba is a shade-loving evergreen shrub with opposite glossy green leaves. The variegated cultivars are often grown as houseplants but grow equally well outdoors.

FLOWER COLOR AND SEASON: Small purple flowers in terminal clusters in late winter to early spring; followed by bright scarlet fruit on female plants.

HEIGHT AND SPREAD: To 10 feet (3 m) tall and as wide.

BEST CLIMATE AND SITE: Zones 6–10. Deep, moist, well-drained soil. Tolerates dense shade, air pollution, and competition from tree roots.

CULTIVATION: Plant in winter or spring. Male and female flowers are borne on separate plants. You'll need to buy at least one male plant if you want fruit on the females. Seldom needs pruning.

PROPAGATION: Take semihardwood cuttings in late spring.

PEST AND DISEASE PREVENTION: No serious pests or diseases.

COMMON PROBLEMS: In colder areas subject to leaf browning when exposed to wind or afternoon winter sun.

LANDSCAPE USE: Shrub borders; foundation plantings; containers; under trees.

OTHER COMMON NAMES: Japanese laurel.

CULTIVARS: 'Crassifolia' is male with large green leathery leaves. 'Crotonifolia' may be either male or female with large leaves speckled with yellow. 'Variegata' is female with leaves blotched creamy yellow.

Berberis thunbergii   Berberidaceae

JAPANESE BARBERRY

Japanese barberry is a dense, very thorny shrub with small leaves that, while deciduous, often turn rich red or purple and remain on the plant well into winter.

FLOWER COLOR AND SEASON: Small yellow flowers in late spring; followed by bright red persistent fruit.

HEIGHT AND SPREAD: To 8 feet (2.4 m) tall and 15 feet (4.5 m) wide.

BEST CLIMATE AND SITE: Zones 4–10. Deep, moist, well-drained soil. Full sun to almost full shade.

CULTIVATION: Plant in spring. Prune if necessary to remove overcrowded shoots after flowering or in winter after fruiting.

PROPAGATION: Take cuttings in late spring. Remove seed from its fleshy coating and sow in fall.

PEST AND DISEASE PREVENTION: No serious pests or diseases.

COMMON PROBLEMS: Does poorly in excessively wet soils. Spiny stems often trap leaves and other debris within the plant, giving it an untidy appearance.

LANDSCAPE USE: Informal hedges; foundation plantings; shrub borders. Readily lends itself to pruning as a formal hedge.

CULTIVARS: 'Aurea' has yellow leaves. 'Crimson Pygmy' is a dwarf form with red-purple foliage. 'Rose Glow' has purple leaves.

| *Buddleia davidii* | Loganiaceae | *Buxus sempervirens* | Buxaceae |

ORANGE-EYE BUTTERFLY BUSH

COMMON BOXWOOD

Orange-eye butterfly bush is a deciduous shrub, native to China, with long, narrow opposite leaves. It tends to die back to the roots in the colder portions of its range.

Common boxwood is a spreading shrub with small glossy dark green leaves. Its dense branching structure and slow growth make it popular for use in hedges and topiaries.

FLOWER COLOR AND SEASON: White, pink, red, purple, violet, or pale purple flowers borne in upright, terminal spikes in midsummer to early fall.

HEIGHT AND SPREAD: To 15 feet (4.5 m) tall and as wide.

BEST CLIMATE AND SITE: Zones 5–10. Deep, moist, well-drained, humus-rich soil. Full sun.

CULTIVATION: Plant in spring. Cut back severely in late winter or early spring.

PROPAGATION: Take cuttings in early summer or early fall. Sow seed in spring or fall.

PEST AND DISEASE PREVENTION: No serious pests or diseases.

COMMON PROBLEMS: In the northern portion of its range treat *B. davidii* and its cultivars as herbaceous perennials by cutting the stems to the ground and covering them with mulch.

LANDSCAPE USE: Best used toward the back of flower borders. Also great for shrub borders and informal hedges. Highly attractive to butterflies.

CULTIVARS: 'Black Knight' has deep purple flowers. 'Charming Summer' bears light lavender pink flowers. 'Nanho Purple' has red-purple flowers and a dwarf, spreading habit. 'Royal Red' bears wine-red flowers. 'White Profusion' has white flowers.

FLOWER COLOR AND SEASON: Inconspicuous pale green flowers in early spring.

HEIGHT AND SPREAD: To 20 feet (6 m) tall and slightly wider.

BEST CLIMATE AND SITE: Zones 6–10. Deep, moist, well-drained soil. Full sun to partial shade.

CULTIVATION: Transplant balled-and-burlapped or container-grown plants in spring. Use a compost or bark mulch around the base of the plants. This will help keep the shallow roots cool and moist and reduce the need for cultivation.

PROPAGATION: Take cuttings in summer.

PEST AND DISEASE PREVENTION: Leafminer larvae can burrow inside leaves and produce tan patches. Remove and destroy affected leaves to prevent adult flies from multiplying.

COMMON PROBLEMS: Leaves often turn brown if exposed to cold, dry winter winds. Spray foliage with an antidessicant in fall to prevent. Prune out damaged stems.

LANDSCAPE USE: Informal hedges; foundation plantings; screen plantings; topiary. Lends itself well to pruning.

CULTIVARS: 'Argentea' has leaves bordered with white. 'Aureo-variegata' has leaves variegated with yellow. 'Pendula' is a tree form with pendant branches. 'Suffruticosa' is a dwarf form.

Callicarpa bodinieri   Verbenaceae

BODINIER BEAUTYBERRY

Bodinier beautyberry is a deciduous shrub with lilac purple summer flowers and bright purple berries. Its narrowly oval, opposite leaves turn yellow in fall.

FLOWER COLOR AND SEASON: Lilac-colored blooms borne in rounded, dense clusters in early summer; followed by lavender or rich purple fruit. The conspicuous fruit persists long after the leaves drop.

HEIGHT & SPREAD: To 8 feet (2.4 m) tall but not as wide.

BEST CLIMATE AND SITE: Zones 5–9. Deep, moist, well-drained soil. Full sun.

CULTIVATION: Plant in spring. Cut back severely in late winter or early spring; plants bloom and fruit on new wood. Plant several together for best fruiting.

PROPAGATION: Remove seed from its fleshy covering and sow in fall or late winter. Take softwood cutting in spring or summer.

PEST AND DISEASE PREVENTION: No serious pests or diseases.

COMMON PROBLEMS: Will not thrive in poorly drained soils.

LANDSCAPE USE: Shrub borders, mass plantings.

CULTIVARS: 'Profusion' bears very abundant clusters of violet berries.

Calycanthus floridus   Calycanthaceae

CAROLINA ALLSPICE

Deciduous Carolina allspice bears reddish or yellow flowers and glossy green leaves that turn bronze or purple in fall. It is native to the southeastern United States.

FLOWER COLOR AND SEASON: Very fragrant, strap-shaped reddish purple petals, tinged with brown, in early summer.

HEIGHT AND SPREAD: 6–8 feet (1.8–2.4 m) tall and nearly as wide.

BEST CLIMATE AND SITE: Zones 4–9. Humus-rich, well-drained but moisture-retentive soil. Full sun to light shade. Tends to be much shorter when grown in full sun.

CULTIVATION: Plant in spring. Prune after flowering.

PROPAGATION: Take cuttings in early summer. Layer in fall. Sow seed in fall. Remove rooted suckers in spring.

PEST AND DISEASE PREVENTION: No serious pests or diseases.

COMMON PROBLEMS: Fragrance varies among plants; smell before you buy.

LANDSCAPE USE: Shrub borders; plant near outdoor living areas for fragrance.

OTHER COMMON NAMES: Carolina sweet shrub, common sweet shrub, pineapple shrub, strawberry shrub.

CULTIVARS: 'Athens' is a yellow-flowered form.

Camellia japonica   Theaceae

COMMON CAMELLIA

Common camellia is an evergreen shrub or tree with deep green glossy leaves. It is commonly planted in warm climates for the colorful winter and early-spring flowers.

FLOWER COLOR AND SEASON: Single, semidouble, or fully double flowers in shades of white, pink, or red in late winter to early spring.
HEIGHT AND SPREAD: 20–25 feet (6–7.5 m) tall and nearly as wide.
BEST CLIMATE AND SITE: Zones 7–10 or in slightly colder areas if protected from winter sun and winds. Peaty, lime-free, humus-rich soil. Partial shade.
CULTIVATION: Transplant container-grown or balled-and-burlapped plants in winter or early spring. Apply adequate water to keep soil evenly moist during summer and winter. Mulch to keep roots cool and moist and to prevent weed problems.
PROPAGATION: Take cuttings of current season's growth in late summer.
PEST AND DISEASE PREVENTION: Flower blight can cause brown spots on petals. Avoid problems by buying only bareroot plants; also pick off and destroy any flower buds before planting. If the disease strikes, remove and destroy all infected buds and flowers, and apply a fresh layer of mulch around the base of the plant. Prune off and destroy parts of the plant infested by scales or mealybugs.
COMMON PROBLEMS: Flower buds can be damaged by untimely frosts.
LANDSCAPE USE: Specimen shrub; shrub borders; informal hedges.

Caryopteris x *clandonensis*   Verbenaceae

BLUEBEARD

Bluebeard is a deciduous subshrub of hybrid origin with blue flowers and dull green leaves. In the colder portions of its range it dies back to the roots each winter.

FLOWER COLOR AND SEASON: Blue flowers borne in dense spikes in mid- to late summer.
HEIGHT AND SPREAD: To 4 feet (1.2 m) tall and as wide.
BEST CLIMATE AND SITE: Zones 5–9. Moist, well-drained, loamy soil. Full sun and a sheltered position, such as near a sunny wall, in colder zones.
CULTIVATION: Plant in late winter or spring. Cut back nearly to the ground in late winter since flowers grow on new wood.
PROPAGATION: Take cuttings in early summer. Divide in spring.
PEST AND DISEASE PREVENTION: No serious pests or diseases.
COMMON PROBLEMS: Usually trouble-free.
LANDSCAPE USE: Informal hedges; shrub borders; perennial borders.
CULTIVARS: 'Dark Knight' is a compact grower with darker foliage and deep blue flowers. 'Ferndown' has dark blue flowers. 'Heavenly Blue' has light blue flowers.

Chaenomeles speciosa   Rosaceae

FLOWERING QUINCE

Native to China, flowering quince is a spreading deciduous shrub with spiny branches. Its oval, alternate leaves are glossy deep green above, paler below.

FLOWER COLOR AND SEASON: Clusters of showy red flowers; followed by pear-shaped yellow-green fruit. Flowers bloom in late winter (in warm or protected areas) or in late spring to early summer. Sometimes will rebloom lightly in fall.

HEIGHT AND SPREAD: To 10 feet (3 m) tall and 20 feet (6 m) wide.

BEST CLIMATE AND SITE: Zones 4–10. Deep, moist, humus-rich, well-drained soil. Full sun.

CULTIVATION: Plant in fall or spring. Regular renewal pruning will promote more lavish bloom.

PROPAGATION: Take cuttings in late summer. Layer in spring.

PEST AND DISEASE PREVENTION: Subject to scales and aphids. Avoid overfeeding, which causes succulent growth that attracts pests. To control scales, prune and destroy infested parts; spray remaining stems with horticultural oil. Control aphids by spraying with insecticidal soap.

COMMON PROBLEMS: Leaves can turn yellow when plants are grown on alkaline soils.

LANDSCAPE USE: Shrub borders; specimen shrubs; informal hedges.

CULTIVARS: 'Falconnet Charlet' has double salmon-pink flowers. 'Nivalis' has pure white flowers. 'Rubra Grandiflora' bears very large crimson flowers and has a low, spreading habit.

Clethra alnifolia   Clethraceae

SUMMER-SWEET

Native to the southeastern United States, summer-sweet is a deciduous shrub valued primarily for its fragrant flower spikes. The leaves turn bright yellow or orange in fall.

FLOWER COLOR AND SEASON: White, very fragrant flowers borne in long, narrow upright clusters in mid- to late summer.

HEIGHT AND SPREAD: 5–8 feet (1.5–2.4 m) tall and as wide.

BEST CLIMATE AND SITE: Zones 5–9. Well-drained, loamy soil. Full sun.

CULTIVATION: Plant in spring. Prune in late winter.

PROPAGATION: Take cuttings in midsummer. Sow seed in late fall.

PEST AND DISEASE PREVENTION: No serious pests or diseases.

COMMON PROBLEMS: Sometimes slow to become established.

LANDSCAPE USE: Hedges; shrub borders.

CULTIVARS: 'Rosea' has deep pink buds opening to soft-pink flowers.

OTHER SPECIES:

    C. acuminata, cinnamon clethra, has nodding flower clusters and cinnamon brown bark. Zones 5–9.

Cornus sericea (C. stolonifera)   Cornaceae

RED-OSIER DOGWOOD

Red-osier dogwood is an opposite-leaved deciduous shrub with colorful red bark. Native to the eastern United States, it spreads rapidly by creeping underground stems.

FLOWER COLOR AND SEASON: White flowers in late spring; followed by white berries.

HEIGHT AND SPREAD: To 7 feet (2.1 m) tall and nearly as wide.

BEST CLIMATE AND SITE: Zones 2–7. Deep, moist, well-drained soil. Full sun to full shade.

CULTIVATION: Plant in spring. For best stem color, prune to ground level in early spring.

PROPAGATION: Take cuttings in late fall. Remove suckers in fall. Layer in fall.

PEST AND DISEASE PREVENTION: No serious pests or diseases.

COMMON PROBLEMS: Grows poorly in dry, alkaline soils. Mulch regularly with organic matter to keep the soil evenly moist.

LANDSCAPE USE: Shrub borders; woodland or swamp plantings. Primarily valued for winter color.

CULTIVARS: 'Flaviramea' has yellow stems. 'Isanti' is a dwarf, compact form with bright red stems. 'Nitida' has green stems.

Corylopsis spicata   Hamamelidaceae

SPIKE WINTER HAZEL

Spike winter hazel is a compact deciduous shrub of particular interest for its early flowering period. The fragrant yellow flowers bloom before the new leaves emerge.

FLOWER COLOR AND SEASON: Drooping clusters of fragrant yellow flowers in late winter to early spring.

HEIGHT AND SPREAD: To 6 feet (1.8 m) tall and slightly wider.

BEST CLIMATE AND SITE: Zones 5–9. Moist, well-drained, slightly acid soil. Full sun to partial shade.

CULTIVATION: Transplant container-grown or balled-and-burlapped plants in fall or spring.

PROPAGATION: Take softwood cuttings in summer. Leave the cuttings undisturbed until growth begins the following spring; then transplant to a nursery bed or individual containers. Layer in fall.

PEST AND DISEASE PREVENTION: No serious pests or diseases.

COMMON PROBLEMS: Flower buds can be injured by late spring frosts.

LANDSCAPE USE: Woodland plantings; shrub borders. Best displayed against a background of evergreens.

OTHER SPECIES:

C. glabrescens, fragrant winter hazel, blooms in early to midspring. It grows to 15 feet (4.5 m) tall and 10 feet (3 m) wide. Zones 5–9.

Cotoneaster horizontalis   Rosaceae

ROCKSPRAY COTONEASTER

Rockspray cotoneaster is a spreading deciduous shrub with bright red fruit and dark green glossy leaves that turn orange or red in fall and persist well into winter.

FLOWER COLOR AND SEASON: Pink flowers in mid- to late spring; followed by bright coral red fruit.

HEIGHT AND SPREAD: To 3 feet (90 cm) tall and 6 feet (1.8 m) wide.

BEST CLIMATE AND SITE: Zones 4–9. Moist, deep, well-drained soil. Full sun.

CULTIVATION: Transplant container-grown plants in fall or early spring.

PROPAGATION: Take cuttings in early summer. Sow seed in spring. Layer in fall.

PEST AND DISEASE PREVENTION: Take care not to damage the plant with sharp garden tools; these wounds are common entry points for pests and diseases such as fire blight and borers. Lace bugs and spider mites can cause yellow or white speckling on leaves. Spray leaves, especially the undersides, with insecticidal soap.

COMMON PROBLEMS: Because of rather sparse root systems, plants are often slow to establish. Mulch with organic matter to keep the soil evenly moist, especially while the shrubs are young.

LANDSCAPE USE: Groundcovers; rock gardens.

CULTIVARS: 'Little Gem' is a dwarf, mound-shaped form. 'Variegatus' has leaves edged with white, turning pink in fall.

Daphne cneorum   Thymeleaceae

ROSE DAPHNE

Rose daphne is a low-growing evergreen shrub with narrow, strap-shaped leaves and exceptionally fragrant spring flowers. It is native to central and eastern Europe.

FLOWER COLOR AND SEASON: Dense terminal heads of fragrant pink flowers in late spring, sometimes repeating in fall.

HEIGHT AND SPREAD: To 1 foot (30 cm) tall and 3 feet (90 cm) wide.

BEST CLIMATE AND SITE: Zones 4–9. Moist, well-drained, neutral or slightly alkaline soil. Full sun with protection from winter winds.

CULTIVATION: Transplant container-grown plants in early fall or early spring.

PROPAGATION: Layer in fall. Take cuttings in late summer.

PEST AND DISEASE PREVENTION: Few serious pests or diseases. Rose daphne does not like strong fertilizers. A leafy mulch applied in early spring will supply adequate nutrients.

COMMON PROBLEMS: Plants are often slow to establish.

LANDSCAPE USE: Foundation shrubs; front of shrub borders.

CULTIVARS: 'Alba' has white flowers. 'Eximia' is larger in leaf and flower.

OTHER SPECIES:

D. odora, winter daphne, has purple-and-white flowers and dark green oval leaves. 'Alba' has white flowers. 'Aureo-Marginata' is hardier than the species, with yellow-edged leaves. Zones 7–10.

| *Deutzia gracilis* Saxifragaceae | *Enkianthus campanulatus* Ericaceae |

SLENDER DEUTZIA

REDVEIN ENKIANTHUS

Slender deutzia is a deciduous shrub with long, lance-shaped leaves and clusters of white blooms in spring. Deutzias are excellent choices for flowering shrub borders.

FLOWER COLOR AND SEASON: Clusters of white flowers in late spring.

HEIGHT AND SPREAD: To 6 feet (1.8 m) tall and nearly as wide.

BEST CLIMATE AND SITE: Zones 4–9. Deep, moist, well-drained soil. Full sun.

CULTIVATION: Plant in spring. After flowering, thin out drastically by cutting away weak and old wood, but leave the young shoots alone as these will bear the best blooms.

PROPAGATION: Sow seed in fall. Take softwood cuttings in summer.

PEST AND DISEASE PREVENTION: Few serious pests or diseases.

COMMON PROBLEMS: Lack of pruning will result in few flowers.

LANDSCAPE USE: Specimen shrub; shrub borders.

CULTIVARS: 'Aurea' has yellow leaves. 'Marmorata' has leaves spotted with yellow.

OTHER SPECIES:

D. scabra, fuzzy deutzia, has oval or heart-shaped leaves and brown peeling bark. Its white early-summer flowers are often tinged with pink. 'Candidissima' bears double white flowers. Zones 5–9.

Native to Japan, redvein enkianthus is a tall deciduous shrub with oval, whorled leaves clustered at the ends of the branch-lets. The leaves turn brilliant scarlet in fall.

FLOWER COLOR AND SEASON: Drooping clusters of creamy yellow flowers, lightly tinged with red, in late spring.

HEIGHT AND SPREAD: To 12 feet (3.6 m) tall and not as wide.

BEST CLIMATE AND SITE: Zones 4–8. Deep, moist, humus-rich, well-drained, acid soil. Full sun to dense shade.

CULTIVATION: Plant in spring. Expose to western sun for best fall color. No pruning necessary.

PROPAGATION: Take cuttings in late spring. Sow seed in early spring. Layer in fall.

PEST AND DISEASE PREVENTION: No serious pests or diseases.

COMMON PROBLEMS: Will not flourish in dry or alkaline soils. Mulch with compost to keep the soil evenly moist.

LANDSCAPE USE: Foundation plantings; shrub borders; woodland plantings.

CULTIVARS: 'Albiflorus' has pure white flowers. 'Red Bells' has red flowers.

Erica cinerea   Ericaceae

TWISTED HEATH

Twisted heath is an evergreen shrub with small bell-shaped flowers and tiny needle-like leaves on stiff, much-divided branches. It is excellent for use as a groundcover.

FLOWER COLOR AND SEASON: White, pinkish red, or purplish flowers in early to late summer.

HEIGHT AND SPREAD: To 18 inches (45 cm) tall and 4 feet (1.2 m) wide.

BEST CLIMATE AND SITE: Zones 5–7. Acid, moist, peaty soil, preferably low in fertility. Full sun to light shade. Best where nights are cool and moist.

CULTIVATION: Plant in fall or spring. Prune lightly after flowering. Do not fertilize. Shelter plants from sweeping winds, and keep watered during dry periods.

PROPAGATION: Sow seed or take cuttings in spring. Layer in summer.

PEST AND DISEASE PREVENTION: No serious pests or diseases.

COMMON PROBLEMS: Will not flourish where summers are extremely hot and winters extremely cold. Intolerant of drought; mulch to keep the soil evenly moist. High soil fertility can cause loose, open growth.

LANDSCAPE USE: Best used in masses as groundcovers.

OTHER SPECIES:

E. carnea, spring heath, has white, pinkish red, or purplish flowers in winter to midspring. It grows to 1 foot (30 cm) tall and 2 feet (60 cm) wide. 'Springwood Pink' has light pink flowers and a trailing habit. Zones 5–7.

Eriobotrya japonica   Rosaceae

LOQUAT

Loquat is an evergreen bush or tree of rounded form native to China and Japan. Its leaves are dark glossy green above; the undersurfaces are covered with brownish hair.

FLOWER COLOR AND SEASON: Fragrant white flowers borne in long clusters in fall; followed by edible, pear-shaped orange-yellow fruit.

HEIGHT AND SPREAD: To 20 feet (6 m) tall and as wide.

BEST CLIMATE AND SITE: Zones 8–11. Deep, moist, well-drained, humus-rich soil. Full sun to partial shade.

CULTIVATION: Plant in spring. Grow in a protected site, such as against a sunny wall, in the colder portion of its range.

PROPAGATION: Sow seed in spring. Take cuttings in late summer.

PEST AND DISEASE PREVENTION: No serious pests or diseases.

COMMON PROBLEMS: Requires long summer to ripen fruit.

LANDSCAPE USE: Specimen shrub; shrub borders. Valued for its excellent foliage and fruit.

CULTIVARS: 'Gold Nugget' has very dark green leaves and bears excellent and abundant fruit. 'Variegata' has leaves variegated with white.

| *Euonymus alata* | Celastraceae | *Forsythia* x *intermedia* | Oleaceae |

BURNING BUSH

BORDER FORSYTHIA

Native to China and Japan, burning bush is a deciduous shrub with dark green leaves that turn rich rosy scarlet in fall. The mature branches develop curious corky flanges or wings.

FLOWER COLOR AND SEASON: Inconspicuous greenish white flowers in mid- to late spring; followed by purplish fruit.

HEIGHT AND SPREAD: 10–15 feet (3–4.5 m) tall and nearly as wide.

BEST CLIMATE AND SITE: Zones 3–9. Virtually any well-drained soil. Full sun to partial shade.

CULTIVATION: Transplant balled-and-burlapped or container-grown plants in fall or spring. Prune in winter if you want to shape the plant; otherwise it seldom requires pruning.

PROPAGATION: Take cuttings during the growing season. Remove seed from its fleshy coating and sow in fall.

PEST AND DISEASE PREVENTION: Prune and destroy parts infested by scales, which cause leaves to yellow and drop.

COMMON PROBLEMS: Not tolerant of very wet or very dry soil.

LANDSCAPE USE: Specimen shrub; shrub borders; informal hedges.

OTHER COMMON NAMES: Winged euonymus.

CULTIVARS: 'Compacta' is a low-growing, dense plant.

Border forsythia is a deciduous shrub with clusters of yellow flowers that bloom in spring before the leaves emerge. The foliage may turn an attractive reddish purple in fall.

FLOWER COLOR AND SEASON: Bright yellow flowers in early to midspring.

HEIGHT AND SPREAD: To 8 feet (2.4 m) tall and nearly as wide.

BEST CLIMATE AND SITE: Zones 5–9. Deep, moist, well-drained soil; tolerates lime and air pollution. Full sun.

CULTIVATION: Plant in spring. Remove older weak-growing or dead wood after flowering. The bushes will then have the whole summer to produce fresh growth on which next year's flowers will be borne.

PROPAGATION: Take softwood cuttings in summer or hardwood cuttings in late fall. Layer in fall. Remove suckers in fall.

PEST AND DISEASE PREVENTION: No serious pests or diseases.

COMMON PROBLEMS: In severe climates, late frosts can damage flowers.

LANDSCAPE USE: Specimen shrub; informal hedges. Plant in masses against an evergreen background.

CULTIVARS: 'Lynwood' has yellow flowers along entire stems. 'Spring Glory' bears pale yellow flowers.

OTHER SPECIES:

F. suspensa, weeping forsythia, is a rambling shrub with yellow spring flowers, arching branches, and three-lobed leaves. It grows to 10 feet (3 m) tall. Zones 5–9.

| *Fothergilla gardenii* | Hamamelidaceae | *Fuchsia* x *hybrida* | Onagraceae |

DWARF FOTHERGILLA

Native to the southeastern United States, dwarf fothergilla is a low-growing deciduous shrub with fragrant white flowers in spring and dramatic yellow or orange fall color.

FLOWER COLOR AND SEASON: Fragrant white flowers borne in spikes in mid- to late spring.

HEIGHT AND SPREAD: To 3 feet (90 cm) tall and as wide.

BEST CLIMATE AND SITE: Zones 5–9. Deep, moist, humus-rich, well-drained soil. Full sun to partial shade.

CULTIVATION: Transplant container-grown or balled-and-burlapped plants in late winter or early spring.

PROPAGATION: Sow seed in summer. Take cuttings in summer and leave rooted cuttings undisturbed until the following year. Layer in fall.

PEST AND DISEASE PREVENTION: No serious pests or diseases.

COMMON PROBLEMS: Will not thrive in wet or alkaline soils.

LANDSCAPE USE: Shrub borders; woodland plantings.

CULTIVARS: 'Blue Mist' has frosty blue foliage that turns yellow and red in fall.

OTHER SPECIES:
F. *major* is a larger pyramidal or rounded plant, growing to 9 feet (2.7 m) tall and as wide. Zones 5–9.

COMMON FUCHSIA

Largely derived from South American species, common fuchsias are alternate-leaved deciduous shrubs of upright or spreading habit. Their leaves are often tinged with purple.

FLOWER COLOR AND SEASON: Pendant flowers, usually with contrasting corollas, in combinations too numerous to name. Possible colors include white, yellow, pink, red, and purple. Bloom in early summer to fall.

HEIGHT AND SPREAD: To 6 feet (1.8 m) tall and as wide.

BEST CLIMATE AND SITE: Zones 9–11. Deep, moist, humus-rich, well-drained soil. Partial shade.

CULTIVATION: Plant in winter or spring. Prune in early spring. Do not allow to dry out, particularly when grown in baskets.

PROPAGATION: Take cuttings in fall and early winter.

PEST AND DISEASE PREVENTION: Sprinkle foliage with water during hot, dry weather to discourage spider mites. If spider mites or whiteflies are a problem, spray the undersides of the leaves with insecticidal soap.

COMMON PROBLEMS: May die to the ground in winter, but will bloom on new wood produced in spring.

LANDSCAPE USE: Where hardy, shrub borders and informal hedges. Upright types can be trained to standard form. Widely used as hanging basket plants where not hardy.

CULTIVARS: 'Riccartonii' is small-flowered and hardier than most. 'Swingtime' has double flowers with red calyx and white corolla.

Gardenia jasminoides   Rubiaceae

COMMON GARDENIA

Native to China, common gardenia is an evergreen shrub
with very glossy, thick leathery leaves. Its creamy white, waxy
summer flowers are intensely fragrant.

FLOWER COLOR AND SEASON: Very fragrant single,
    semidouble, or double white flowers in early to
    midsummer.

HEIGHT AND SPREAD: To 6 feet (1.8 m) tall and as
    wide.

BEST CLIMATE AND SITE: Zones 8–10. Peaty, humus-
    rich, moisture-retentive, acid soil. Partial shade;
    protect from hot afternoon sun.

CULTIVATION: Transplant in spring. Cut untidy plants
    well back in early spring.

PROPAGATION: Take cuttings in summer.

PEST AND DISEASE PREVENTION: Avoid damaging
    plants with gardening tools; these wounds are a
    common entry point for pests and diseases such as
    mealybugs and stem canker. If mealybugs, aphids,
    or whiteflies attack, spray with insecticidal soap.

COMMON PROBLEMS: Sensitive to dry soil; mulch to
    help retain moisture.

LANDSCAPE USE: Where hardy, foundation shrubs or
    specimen plants; elsewhere, a greenhouse plant.
    Also grows well in containers.

OTHER COMMON NAMES: Cape jasmine.

CULTIVARS: 'Mystery' is a bushy plant with large,
    double flowers. 'Radicans' is low-growing and has
    small flowers. 'Radicans Variegata' is low-growing
    with leaves edged in creamy white. 'Veitchii' is a
    free-flowering plant of compact, upright habit.

Hamamelis mollis   Hamamelidaceae

CHINESE WITCH HAZEL

Chinese witch hazel is a deciduous shrub or tree with heart-
shaped leaves and zigzag branches that are downy when young.
The yellow winter flowers have strap-shaped petals.

FLOWER COLOR AND SEASON: Fragrant yellow flow-
    ers in winter.

HEIGHT AND SPREAD: To 25 feet (7.5 m) tall and
    nearly as wide.

BEST CLIMATE AND SITE: Zones 5–9. Light, moist,
    well-drained, humus-rich soil. Full sun.

CULTIVATION: Transplant container-grown or balled-
    and-burlapped plants in fall or spring. For best
    habit train to single stem by removing low-grow-
    ing side branches.

PROPAGATION: Layer in late summer. Graft in spring.
    Sow seed outdoors in summer; may take up to
    2 years to germinate.

PEST AND DISEASE PREVENTION: No serious pests or
    diseases.

COMMON PROBLEMS: Intolerant of dry soils.

LANDSCAPE USE: Specimen plant; shrub borders; wood-
    land plantings; city gardens.

OTHER SPECIES:

H. x intermedia is of hybrid origin and has variously
    colored fragrant spring flowers. 'Arnold Promise'
    is free-flowering, with yellow flowers and good
    reddish fall color. 'Feuerzauber' has copper red
    flowers. Zones 5–9.

H. virginiana, common witch hazel, is a fall-bloom-
    ing shrub to 10 feet (3 m) tall. Zones 5–9.

| Hibiscus syriacus | Malvaceae | Hydrangea spp. | Hydrangeaceae |

ROSE-OF-SHARON

HYDRANGEA

Rose-of-Sharon is a late-blooming deciduous shrub with up-right branches and a bushy habit. The showy hibiscus-like single or double flowers bloom in a range of colors.

Hydrangeas are deciduous shrubs with opposite, broad leaves and showy summer flowers. H. macrophylla, *big-leaved hydrangea, has blue or pink flowers, depending on soil pH.*

FLOWER COLOR AND SEASON: 2½–4-inch (6–10 cm) trumpet-shaped flowers in white, pink, red, lavender, or purple in late summer to early fall.

HEIGHT AND SPREAD: To 15 feet (4.5 m) tall and 10 feet (3 m) wide.

BEST CLIMATE AND SITE: Zones 5–9. Deep, moist, well-drained soil. Full sun.

CULTIVATION: Plant in spring or fall. Prune in winter by removing at least two-thirds of the previous season's growth.

PROPAGATION: Take cuttings during summer. Layer in spring. Graft in late winter and early spring.

PEST AND DISEASE PREVENTION: If aphids or whiteflies attack leaves, spray with insecticidal soap. Control Japanese beetles by knocking them into a bucket of soapy water.

COMMON PROBLEMS: Lack of pruning will result in small flowers. Young, vigorous plants can be winter-killed. Protect from wind and do not fertilize after midsummer. Self-sown seedlings can be a problem; choose cultivars such as 'Diana' and 'Helene' that set little if any seed.

LANDSCAPE USE: Specimen plant; shrub borders.

CULTIVARS: 'Blue Bird' has blue flowers. 'Diana' has pure white flowers. 'Helene' has white flowers with red throats. 'Pink Giant' has large pink flowers.

FLOWER COLOR AND SEASON: *H. macrophylla:* blue or pink flowers (blue in acid soils, pink in alkaline) borne in large, flat clusters up to 10 inches (25 cm) across in midsummer. *H. paniculata:* white flowers in immense pyramidal clusters in midsummer to early fall. *H. quercifolia:* white flowers borne in erect, pyramidal clusters in early to late summer. Flower clusters contain both fertile and sterile flowers; the latter are more showy.

HEIGHT AND SPREAD: *H. macrophylla:* to 10 feet (3 m) tall and as wide; *H. paniculata:* to 20 feet (6 m) tall but not as wide; *H. quercifolia:* to 10 feet (3 m) tall and as wide.

BEST CLIMATE AND SITE: *H. macrophylla:* Zones 6–9; *H. paniculata:* Zones 4–8; *H. quercifolia:* Zones 5–8. Deep, moist, well-drained soil. Partial shade; protect from hot afternoon sun.

CULTIVATION: Plant during fall or spring. Keep well watered during summer. *H. macrophylla:* cut back by half after flowering; *H. paniculata:* prune heavily in winter; *H. quercifolia:* prune lightly after flowering for more compact growth.

PROPAGATION: *H. macrophylla:* take cuttings anytime during the growing season; *H. paniculata:* take cuttings in summer; *H. quercifolia:* layer in spring or sow seed in fall.

PEST AND DISEASE PREVENTION: No serious pests or

HOLLY

H. paniculata 'Grandiflora', commonly known as peegee hydrangea, has almost all sterile flowers, creating huge inflorescences. It sometimes grows in a tree-like form.

Hollies are alternate-leaved evergreen or deciduous shrubs and trees. I. opaca, American holly, is an evergreen tree or shrub with dull green spiny leaves and red fruit in winter.

diseases. Mulch with organic matter to keep the soil evenly moist.

COMMON PROBLEMS: Buds or stems may be damaged in cold-winter areas. Plants will usually resprout from the roots but will generally not flower until the following year.

LANDSCAPE USE: Specimen shrub; shrub borders.

    H. paniculata is an extremely coarse plant, rather out of keeping with many small gardens.

SPECIES:

    H. macrophylla, big-leaved hydrangea, has broad, thick leaves. 'Nikko Blue' has a rich blue flower color retained over a wide range of soil pH. 'Mariesii' bears flowers that are nearly always pink (mauve-pink in acid soils).

    H. paniculata, panicle hydrangea, has elliptical dark green leaves. It is native to China and Japan. 'Praecox' has smaller flowers but blooms almost 6 weeks earlier than 'Grandiflora'.

    H. quercifolia, oak-leaved hydrangea, is native to the southeastern United States and has large scalloped leaves, resembling those of oaks, that turn rich red in fall. 'Snow Queen' is notable for the number and size of its flower clusters and its rich, deep red-purple fall color. 'Snowflake' appears double-flowered.

FLOWER COLOR AND SEASON: Inconspicuous white flowers in late spring to early summer; followed by red or occasionally yellow fruit on female plants.

HEIGHT AND SPREAD: *I. aquifolium:* to 60 feet (18 m) tall and nearly as wide; *I. cornuta:* to 8 feet (2.4 m) tall and as wide; *I. crenata:* to 20 feet (6 m) tall and nearly as wide; *I. opaca:* to 40 feet (12 m) tall and nearly as wide; *I. verticillata:* to 8 feet (2.4 m) tall and as wide.

BEST CLIMATE AND SITE: Zones 5–8. Deep, moist, well-drained soil. Full sun to light shade.

CULTIVATION: Transplant container-grown or balled-and-burlapped plants in fall or spring. Hollies are dioecious, which means that the male and female flowers are borne on separate plants. You'll need at least one male for every five female plants of the same species to get berries on the females. Prune in late spring if necessary. Mulch to keep soil moist.

PROPAGATION: Layer in summer. Take cuttings of evergreen types anytime, deciduous types in midsummer. Remove seed from fleshy covering and sow in fall; may take 18 months to germinate.

PEST AND DISEASE PREVENTION: Leafminers are a major problem, especially on *I. opaca.* Leafminer larvae burrow inside leaves and produce brown or tan patches. Remove and destroy affected leaves. For scales, spray with horticultural oil.

HOLLY—CONTINUED

The brilliant red berries of I. verticillata, *winterberry, are a natural choice for brightening up the winter garden. This deciduous holly thrives in moist, acid soil.*

COMMON PROBLEMS: Leaves may turn yellow due to lack of nitrogen; fertilize regularly to keep plants green and vigorous.

LANDSCAPE USE: Specimen tree or shrub; foundation plantings, hedges.

SPECIES:

I. aquifolium, English holly, is an evergreen tree or large shrub with very glossy spiny leaves. 'Argenteo-marginata' has dark green leaves edged with creamy white. 'Balkans' is one of the hardiest cultivars of the species with glossy green leaves. 'Gold Coast' has dark green leaves with golden yellow margins.

I. cornuta, Chinese holly, has spiny evergreen leaves. 'Burfordii' is a heavy fruiter with glossy dark green leaves that are spineless except for the tips.

I. crenata, Japanese holly, is a dense, twiggy evergreen with small elliptical, spine-free leaves. 'Convexa' has a dense vase-shaped form and is very hardy. 'Helleri' has a compact globose form.

I. opaca, American holly, has dull, spiny evergreen leaves. 'Merry Christmas' has darker leaves and bright red fruit.

I. verticillata, winterberry, is native to eastern North America and is a deciduous shrub that tolerates swampy conditions. 'Christmas Cheer' is a heavy producer of red fruit.

Itea virginica — Saxifragaceae

VIRGINIA SWEETSPIRE

Virginia sweetspire is a summer-blooming deciduous shrub native to the eastern United States. Its alternate leaves are narrowly oval, turning brilliant red in fall.

FLOWER COLOR AND SEASON: Creamy white fragrant flowers borne in dense, narrow terminal clusters in early summer.

HEIGHT AND SPREAD: To 5 feet (1.5 m) tall but not as wide.

BEST CLIMATE AND SITE: Zones 5–9. Deep, humus-rich, constantly moist soil. Full sun to partial shade.

CULTIVATION: Plant in spring. Rarely requires pruning.

PROPAGATION: Take cuttings in early summer. Divide or remove rooted suckers in spring.

PEST AND DISEASE PREVENTION: No serious pests or diseases. Avoid growing in dry, alkaline soil.

COMMON PROBLEMS: Does poorly in dry soil.

LANDSCAPE USE: Woodland plantings; shrub borders. Valued for its fragrance and fall color.

CULTIVARS: 'Henry's Garnet' has reddish purple fall color and long flower clusters.

JUNIPER

Junipers are evergreen shrubs or trees. Their leaves are needle-like when young, flat and scale-like when mature. J. communis, common juniper, keeps its immature foliage.

FLOWER COLOR AND SEASON: Inconspicuous spring flowers, yellow on the male, greenish on the female; followed by small blue fruit on the female.

HEIGHT AND SPREAD: *J. chinensis* and *J. communis:* to 60 feet (18 m) tall varying widely with the cultivar; *J. horizontalis:* to 12 inches (30 cm) tall and 8 feet (2.4 m) wide; *J. sabina:* to 10 feet (3 m) tall and slightly wider.

BEST CLIMATE AND SITE: *J. communis* and *J. horizontalis:* Zones 3–7; *J. chinensis* and *J. sabina:* Zones 4–8. Widely tolerant of different soil conditions—even dry. Full sun to light shade.

CULTIVATION: Transplant container-grown or balled-and-burlapped plants in late winter or spring. No pruning is necessary.

PROPAGATION: Take cuttings in late summer, fall, or winter. Layer low-growing types in summer. Remove seed from its fleshy covering and sow in fall.

PEST AND DISEASE PREVENTION: Handpick and destroy bagworms, which spin silken bags that are studded with needles and resemble pine cones. Plant as groundcover to encourage predators of mites, or spray leaves with insecticidal soap. Prune and destroy plant parts infested with scales.

COMMON PROBLEMS: Several species are alternate hosts to cedar-apple rust. Avoid planting junipers near apple trees.

J. horizontalis 'Blue Chip' is a low-growing cultivar that makes an excellent groundcover. Its striking silver-blue foliage may turn purplish in winter.

LANDSCAPE USE: Specimen shrub; foundation plants; groundcovers.

SPECIES:

J. chinensis, Chinese juniper, is native to Japan, China, and Mongolia and grows as a tree or shrub. 'Blue Vase' has a vase-shaped form and blue foliage. 'Hetzii' is a large upright spreader with bluish foliage. 'Mint Julep' is a compact fountain-like form with bright green foliage. 'Pfitzeriana' is a wide-spreading form with green foliage. The variety *sargentii* is a low-growing blight-resistant spreader with scale-like blue-green foliage.

J. communis 'Depressa' is a broad prostrate form with bluish foliage. 'Hibernica' is a very narrow upright form with bluish foliage.

J. horizontalis, creeping juniper, is a shrub with long, pendulous stems that turn purplish in fall. It is native to the northeastern United States. 'Blue Mat' has a prostrate habit and blue-green foliage. 'Glomerata' is very dwarf with green scale-like leaves that turn purple in fall. 'Mother Lode' has a prostrate habit and golden foliage. 'Plumosa' is wide-spreading with gray-green leaves that turn purple in fall.

J. sabina, savin juniper, is a European native with especially aromatic leaves. It grows as a spreading shrub. 'Blue Danube' has bluish green foliage.

Kalmia latifolia   Ericaceae   *Kerria japonica*   Rosaceae

MOUNTAIN LAUREL

JAPANESE KERRIA

Native to the eastern United States, mountain laurel is a robust evergreen shrub with alternate glossy green leaves. The showy late-spring flowers are held in terminal clusters.

FLOWER COLOR AND SEASON: White, pink, or rose flowers in late spring to early summer.

HEIGHT AND SPREAD: To 20 feet (6 m) tall and as wide.

BEST CLIMATE AND SITE: Zones 4–7. Moisture-retentive, humus-rich, peaty soil. Full sun to partial shade.

CULTIVATION: Transplant container-grown or balled-and-burlapped plants in spring or fall. Mulch to keep shallow roots cool and to control weeds. No pruning is required.

PROPAGATION: Layer in fall. Sow seed in early spring. Take cuttings in late summer.

PEST AND DISEASE PREVENTION: Avoid damaging plants with sharp gardening tools; these wounds are common entry points for pests such as borers. Lace bugs can cause yellow speckling on leaves; spray foliage (especially the undersides of the leaves) with insecticidal soap to control.

COMMON PROBLEMS: Grows poorly in dry or alkaline soil.

LANDSCAPE USE: Foundation shrubs; shrub borders; woodland plantings.

CULTIVARS: 'Bullseye' bears white flowers banded with red. 'Elf' is a very dwarf form with pink buds that open to near white flowers. 'Ostbo Red' has red buds that open to light pink flowers.

Japanese kerria is a bushy deciduous shrub with slender green branches that hold their color year-round. The cultivar 'Pleniflora' has double yellow spring flowers.

FLOWER COLOR AND SEASON: Golden yellow five-petaled flowers in mid- to late spring.

HEIGHT AND SPREAD: To 6 feet (1.8 m) tall and as wide.

BEST CLIMATE AND SITE: Zones 4–8. Deep, moist, humus-rich, well-drained soil. Full sun to partial shade.

CULTIVATION: Plant in early spring. Thin out old stems after flowering. Mulch with compost or aged manure after pruning.

PROPAGATION: Take cuttings in summer or fall. Divide clumps in fall.

PEST AND DISEASE PREVENTION: No serious pests or diseases.

COMMON PROBLEMS: Slow to establish.

LANDSCAPE USE: Specimen shrub; shrub borders.

CULTIVARS: 'Pleniflora' has ball-shaped double flowers. 'Variegata' has single flowers and leaves deeply margined in white.

Lagerstroemia indica   Lythraceae

CRAPE MYRTLE

Crape myrtle is a summer-blooming deciduous shrub with gray peeling bark and privet-like leaves that are bronze in spring, deep green in summer, and yellow, orange, and red in fall.

FLOWER COLOR AND SEASON: Curiously crinkled white, pink, red, lavender, or purple flowers in terminal 6–9-inch (15–23 cm) clusters in mid- to late summer.

HEIGHT AND SPREAD: To 20 feet (6 m) tall and 12 feet (3.6 m) wide.

BEST CLIMATE AND SITE: Zones 7–10. Moist, deep, well-drained soil. Full sun.

CULTIVATION: Transplant container-grown or balled-and-burlapped plants in spring. Prune in early spring, shortening the previous year's shoots to half or one-third of their length.

PROPAGATION: Take cuttings in late spring or early summer.

PEST AND DISEASE PREVENTION: Allow sufficient air circulation between plants to deter mildew. Choose mildew-resistant cultivars.

COMMON PROBLEMS: Stems may die back to the ground in particularly cold winters; new flowering shoots will grow up from the roots.

LANDSCAPE USE: Specimen shrub; shrub borders; screens. Plants often have multiple trunks.

CULTIVARS: 'Catawba' has dark purple flowers and is mildew-resistant. 'Natchez' has white flowers and is mildew-resistant. 'Peppermint Lace' has deep rose flowers edged in white. 'Yumi' has lavender-pink flowers and is mildew-resistant.

Leucothoe fontanesiana   Ericaceae

DROOPING LEUCOTHOE

Native to the mountains of the eastern United States, drooping leucothoe is an evergreen shrub with arching branches and narrow dark green leaves that turn purplish in winter.

FLOWER COLOR AND SEASON: White flowers produced in 12–18 inch (30–45 cm) drooping clusters in midspring.

HEIGHT AND SPREAD: To 6 feet (1.8 m) tall and as wide.

BEST CLIMATE AND SITE: Zones 4–9. Moist, humus-rich, acid soil. Partial shade.

CULTIVATION: Transplant container-grown or balled-and-burlapped plants in spring. Mulch regularly with organic matter. Prune oldest stems to the ground after flowering.

PROPAGATION: Take cuttings in late spring or early summer. Layer, divide, or sow seed in spring.

PEST AND DISEASE PREVENTION: No serious pests or diseases.

COMMON PROBLEMS: Tends to be semideciduous in the colder portions of its range.

LANDSCAPE USE: Foundation plantings; shrub borders.

CULTIVARS: 'Nana' is a dwarf spreading form. 'Rainbow' has leaves variegated with pink, copper, and white.

| *Ligustrum japonicum* | Oleaceae | *Mahonia aquifolium* | Berberidaceae |

JAPANESE PRIVET

OREGON GRAPE

Japanese privet is an evergreen shrub with glossy leaves. Its dense growth and tolerance of heavy pruning make it a natural choice for hedges and topiaries.

FLOWER COLOR AND SEASON: Whitish ill-smelling flowers in small, terminal clusters in early summer; followed by black fruit.

HEIGHT AND SPREAD: To 12 feet (3.6 m) tall and nearly as wide.

BEST CLIMATE AND SITE: Zones 7–10. Moist, well-drained soil. Full sun to light shade.

CULTIVATION: Plant in fall, spring, or winter. Prune after flowering.

PROPAGATION: Take softwood cuttings anytime during growing season.

PEST AND DISEASE PREVENTION: Avoid poorly drained soil. Leafminers can cause brown tunnels in leaves; pick off and destroy damaged foliage. Control scales by pruning off severely infested parts and spraying the rest of the plant with horticultural oil.

COMMON PROBLEMS: The wide-spreading roots can impoverish the soil; avoid planting flower borders close to a privet hedge.

LANDSCAPE USE: Hedges.

CULTIVARS: 'Rotundifolium' is denser and lower-growing than the species.

OTHER SPECIES:
L. vulgare, common privet, is a vigorous semi-evergreen with narrow leaves. 'Lodense' is a very low-growing dense plant. Zones 4–9.

Oregon grape is a broad-leaved evergreen shrub with spiny, pinnately compound leaves. The prominent yellow flower clusters give way to showy blue fruit that resembles grapes.

FLOWER COLOR AND SEASON: Clustered bright yellow flowers in late spring to early summer; followed by grape-like blue fruit.

HEIGHT AND SPREAD: To 3 feet (90 cm) tall and as wide.

BEST CLIMATE AND SITE: Zones 5–9. Deep, moist, well-drained soil. Full sun to light shade.

CULTIVATION: Transplant container-grown or balled-and-burlapped plants in spring. After flowering cut a few of the oldest stems to the ground each year for more compact growth.

PROPAGATION: Take cuttings in late winter. Sow seed in late spring. Divide in fall.

PEST AND DISEASE PREVENTION: Alternate host to black stem rust; avoid planting where wheat is a major commercial crop.

COMMON PROBLEMS: In colder zones the leaves may be damaged if exposed to winter winds and afternoon sun.

LANDSCAPE USE: Specimen shrub; foundation plantings; shrub borders.

OTHER COMMON NAMES: Holly grape.

OTHER SPECIES:
M. bealei, leather-leaved mahonia, has leathery blue-green leaves and very fragrant flowers. It grows to 6 feet (1.8 m) tall and as wide. Zones 6–9.

Myrica pensylvanica   Myricaceae

BAYBERRY

Bayberry is a deciduous or semi-evergreen shrub with fragrant leaves. The wax-coated fruits are sometimes used in candle making; they also provide winter interest.

FLOWER COLOR AND SEASON: Insignificant greenish catkins in late spring; followed by clustered waxy white fruit.

HEIGHT AND SPREAD: To 9 feet (2.7 m) tall and as wide.

BEST CLIMATE AND SITE: Zones 2–7. Adapts to a wide range of soil conditions. Good tolerance to seaside conditions. Full sun to partial shade.

CULTIVATION: Transplant container-grown or balled-and-burlapped plants in spring. Prune lightly anytime to encourage compact growth; rejuvenate older plants by pruning heavily every 1–2 years.

PROPAGATION: Take cuttings in late spring. Layer in fall. Soak seed in hot water or rub it against a rough surface to remove the waxy coating, then sow in fall.

PEST AND DISEASE PREVENTION: No serious pests or diseases.

COMMON PROBLEMS: Leaves can become chlorotic (turn yellow) when grown in alkaline soils.

LANDSCAPE USE: Shrub borders; hedges; woodland plantings.

OTHER SPECIES:

M. cerifera, wax myrtle, is an evergreen native to the southeastern United States and grows as a tall shrub or tree. Zones 6–9.

Nandina domestica   Berberidaceae

HEAVENLY BAMBOO

Heavenly bamboo is an evergreen shrub with glossy green alternate, compound leaves that turn rich red in fall. Young foliage is often tinged with pink or bronze when unfurling.

FLOWER COLOR AND SEASON: White flowers are borne in large clusters in midsummer; followed by clustered red fruit that persists nearly all winter.

HEIGHT AND SPREAD: To 10 feet (3 m) tall and 6 feet (1.8 m) wide.

BEST CLIMATE AND SITE: Zones 6–10. Deep, moisture-retentive, well-drained soil. Full sun to dense shade.

CULTIVATION: Transplant container-grown plants in late winter or spring. Cut a few of the oldest stems to the ground each spring to encourage new growth.

PROPAGATION: Take cuttings in summer. Remove seed from its fleshy covering and sow in fall.

PEST AND DISEASE PREVENTION: No serious pests or diseases.

COMMON PROBLEMS: Plants may be damaged by low winter temperatures, especially in the colder parts of their range.

LANDSCAPE USE: Foundation plantings; hedges.

CULTIVARS: 'Alba' is white-fruited. 'Compacta' is a dwarf form. 'Harbour Dwarf' is a dwarf form with foliage that is tipped pink or bronze in spring and that turns orange or bronzy red in winter. 'Royal Princess' has very delicate fern-like foliage.

Nerium oleander Apocynaceae

OLEANDER

Native to the Mediterranean coast, oleander is a vigorous evergreen shrub with narrow, leathery dark green leaves that are opposite or whorled around the stalk.

FLOWER COLOR AND SEASON: Single or double flowers in various shades of white, yellow, pink, red, and purple sometimes measuring up to 3 inches (7.5 cm) across, in midspring to late summer.

HEIGHT AND SPREAD: To 20 feet (6 m) tall and 10 feet (3 m) wide.

BEST CLIMATE AND SITE: Zones 7–10. Widely tolerant of heat, drought, and seaside conditions. Full sun.

CULTIVATION: Plant in spring. Prune lightly after flowering to maintain thick bushy growth. Prune by half to rejuvenate old plants in winter.

PROPAGATION: Take cuttings anytime in growing season.

PEST AND DISEASE PREVENTION: Subject to scales, which turn plants yellow. Prune off infested plant parts.

COMMON PROBLEMS: All parts of the plant are toxic if eaten.

LANDSCAPE USE: Informal hedges; screen plantings; shrub borders; street plantings; containers.

CULTIVARS: 'Calypso' bears single cherry red flowers. 'Isle of Capri' has single light yellow flowers. 'Mrs. Reoding' has double salmon-pink flowers. 'Sister Agnes' has single white flowers.

Osmanthus fragrans Oleaceae

FRAGRANT OLIVE

Native to Asia, fragrant olive is an evergreen shrub with holly-like dark green opposite leaves. Clusters of sweetly scented white flowers bloom in spring and summer.

FLOWER COLOR AND SEASON: Very fragrant, small white tubular flowers in drooping clusters in early spring to early summer; followed by blue-black berries.

HEIGHT AND SPREAD: To 20 feet (6 m) tall and as wide.

BEST CLIMATE AND SITE: Zones 8–10. Deep, moist, well-drained soil. Full sun to light shade.

CULTIVATION: Plant in winter, fall, or spring. Cut back after flowering to maintain desired height and form.

PROPAGATION: Take cuttings in late summer. Layer in spring or summer.

PEST AND DISEASE PREVENTION: No serious pests or diseases.

COMMON PROBLEMS: Very frost-sensitive.

LANDSCAPE USE: Informal hedges; foundation plantings; shrub borders; containers.

OTHER COMMON NAMES: Sweet olive.

FORMS: *O. fragrans* f. *aurantiacus* has orange flowers.

| *Paeonia suffruticosa* | Paeoniaceae | *Philadelphus coronarius* | Saxifragaceae |

TREE PEONY

SWEET MOCK ORANGE

Unlike the more familiar garden peony, tree peony does not die back to the roots each winter. Instead, it forms a magnificent dense, opposite-leaved deciduous shrub with a spreading habit.

Native to southern Europe, sweet mock orange is a deciduous shrub with opposite leaves. The single or double white flowers bloom in late spring and are usually very fragrant.

FLOWER COLOR AND SEASON: Very large single or double flowers in white, pink, red, lavender, or yellow in mid- to late spring.

HEIGHT AND SPREAD: To 5 feet (1.5 m) tall and slightly wider.

BEST CLIMATE AND SITE: Zones 5–8. Deep, moist, well-drained, humus-rich soil. Full sun to partial shade.

CULTIVATION: Plant in spring or fall. Keep soil evenly moist in summer. Benefits from organic mulch. Do not cut back when foliage dies in winter, as you would an herbaceous peony. Just prune off any winter-damaged wood in spring.

PROPAGATION: Layer in spring. Graft on roots of herbaceous peonies in late summer.

PEST AND DISEASE PREVENTION: No serious pests or diseases.

COMMON PROBLEMS: Leaves and flowers can be damaged by late spring frosts.

LANDSCAPE USE: A magnificent specimen shrub—truly a garden gem.

CULTIVARS: Many are available; some are listed here. 'Age of Gold' bears golden yellow double flowers. 'Godaishu' has pure white semidouble flowers. 'Hana Kisoi' has deep shell pink semidouble flowers. 'Kamada Nishiki' has raspberry red double flowers. 'Tira' has light yellow single flowers.

FLOWER COLOR AND SEASON: Single or occasionally double white flowers, usually highly fragrant, in late spring.

HEIGHT AND SPREAD: To 8 feet (2.4 m) tall but not as wide.

BEST CLIMATE AND SITE: Zones 4–9. Tolerant of many soil conditions, even dry soil. Full sun to partial shade.

CULTIVATION: Plant in spring. Prune leggy plants immediately after flowering. Cut back by one-third and cut out old canes.

PROPAGATION: Take cuttings in summer. Remove a few rooted stems in spring or fall.

PEST AND DISEASE PREVENTION: No serious pests or diseases.

COMMON PROBLEMS: Provides little interest when not in flower.

LANDSCAPE USE: Shrub borders.

CULTIVARS: Many hybrids and cultivars are available. Some of the best are listed here. 'Belle Etoile' bears single flowers over 2 inches (5 cm) in diameter. 'Boule d' Argent' has double flowers that are 2 inches (5 cm) in diameter. 'Minnesota Snowflake' has double flowers that are 2 inches (5 cm) in diameter; it is exceptionally vigorous and winter-hardy. 'Virginal' bears double flowers that are 2 inches (5 cm) in diameter.

Photinia serrulata Rosaceae

CHINESE PHOTINIA

Chinese photinia is a large shrub or small tree widely used in warm climates for hedges and screens. Its lustrous evergreen leaves are red when they first appear in spring.

FLOWER COLOR AND SEASON: White flowers in small clusters in late spring; followed by bright red fruit.

HEIGHT AND SPREAD: To 30 feet (9 m) tall and 15 feet (4.5 m) wide.

BEST CLIMATE AND SITE: Zones 7–10. Virtually any well-drained soil. Full sun to light shade.

CULTIVATION: Transplant container-grown or balled-and-burlapped plants in spring. Prune lightly in summer to encourage dense growth and colorful new shoots.

PROPAGATION: Layer in spring or summer. Take cuttings anytime. Sow seed in fall.

PEST AND DISEASE PREVENTION: Avoid planting near pear trees, apple trees, cotoneasters, and other plants that are susceptible to fire blight.

COMMON PROBLEMS: Dry soil will slow growth. Keep soil moist by mulching with organic matter. Mildew may cause powdery white spots on leaves.

LANDSCAPE USE: Hedges; shrub borders.

OTHER SPECIES:

P. villosa, Oriental photinia, is native to China, Korea, and Japan. This glossy-leaved deciduous shrub has alternate leaves that turn fine bronzy red in fall. Zones 4–9.

Pieris japonica Ericaceae

JAPANESE PIERIS

Japanese pieris is an evergreen shrub with dark green leaves that are often bronze or reddish when young. The pendulous clusters of flowers buds are conspicuous all winter.

FLOWER COLOR AND SEASON: Fragrant white flowers in midspring.

HEIGHT AND SPREAD: To 8 feet (2.4 m) tall and as wide.

BEST CLIMATE AND SITE: Zones 4–9. Moist, humus-rich, well-drained, acid soil. Full sun to light shade.

CULTIVATION: Transplant container-grown or balled-and-burlapped plants in spring. Prune after flowering to remove dead wood.

PROPAGATION: Layer in spring or summer. Take cuttings in summer. Sow seed in fall or early spring.

PEST AND DISEASE PREVENTION: Lace bugs frequently attack, causing yellow leaves. To control, spray leaves (especially the undersides) with insecticidal soap.

COMMON PROBLEMS: Cannot tolerate poorly drained soil.

LANDSCAPE USE: Specimen shrub; shrub borders; foundation plantings.

CULTIVARS: 'Dorothy Wycoff' is a compact grower with deep red buds that open to pink. 'Red Mill' is exceptionally hardy. 'Valley Valentine' bears very long-lasting deep pink flowers. 'Variegata' has white-edged leaves. 'White Cascade' has pure white flowers.

| *Potentilla fruticosa* | Rosaceae | *Pyracantha coccinea* | Rosaceae |

SHRUBBY CINQUEFOIL

SCARLET FIRETHORN

Shrubby cinquefoil is a compact deciduous shrub with compound leaves. The flowers are usually yellow, but cultivars with red, pink, orange, or white flowers are also available.

Scarlet firethorn is grown for its masses of orange-red berries that last through fall. This shrub is evergreen in the warmer portions of its range, deciduous in colder portions.

FLOWER COLOR AND SEASON: Yellow five-petaled flowers in early summer to early fall.

HEIGHT AND SPREAD: To 4 feet (1.2 m) tall and as wide.

BEST CLIMATE AND SITE: Zones 2–8. Tolerant of many soil conditions including alkaline soil. Full sun to very light shade.

CULTIVATION: Transplant in spring. Prune during winter for a thicker habit. Cut all stems back by one-third or remove a few of the oldest stems at ground level.

PROPAGATION: Take cuttings in summer. Sow seed in fall.

PEST AND DISEASE PREVENTION: No serious pests or diseases.

COMMON PROBLEMS: Will not thrive in dense shade.

LANDSCAPE USE: Informal hedges; shrub borders; edgings.

CULTIVARS: 'Coronation Triumph' is a vigorous form with soft green foliage and many bright yellow flowers. 'Katherine Dykes' has pale yellow flowers and silvery green foliage. 'Mount Everest' has large white flowers. 'Tangerine' has orange flowers (when grown in light shade).

FLOWER COLOR AND SEASON: White flowers in flat clusters from late spring to early summer; followed by persistent fruit that is typically red but occasionally orange or yellow.

HEIGHT AND SPREAD: To 15 feet (4.5 m) tall and as wide.

BEST CLIMATE AND SITE: Zones 6–9. Deep, moist, well-drained, humus-rich soil. Full sun to light shade.

CULTIVATION: Transplant container-grown plants in spring. Prune anytime to remove suckers or excessively long shoots.

PROPAGATION: Take cuttings in summer. Sow seed in fall or late winter.

PEST AND DISEASE PREVENTION: Avoid over-fertilizing, which can promote succulent growth that is subject to fire blight. Plant disease-resistant cultivars.

COMMON PROBLEMS: Leaves may be damaged by cold winter temperatures.

LANDSCAPE USE: Specimen shrub; foundation plantings; espalier; hedges; screens.

CULTIVARS: 'Aurea' has yellow fruit. 'Lalandei', somewhat hardier than the species, is an upright grower to 12 feet (3.6 m) tall with orange-red fruit. 'Mohave' produces upright growth and orange-red fruit; it is resistant to scab and fire blight.

RHODODENDRON

The genus Rhododendron *is generally divided into two groups: smaller-leaved and deciduous types often called azaleas, and larger-leaved evergreens referred to as rhododendrons.*

FLOWER COLOR AND SEASON: Hybrids: white, pink, red, lavender, or yellow flowers in early spring to midsummer, varying with cultivar. *R. arborescens:* white fragrant flowers in early summer. *R. calendulaceum:* yellow, orange, or red flowers in late spring. *R. carolinianum:* rosy purple flowers in mid- to late spring. *R. catawbiense:* lavender flowers in mid- to late spring.

HEIGHT AND SPREAD: Hybrids: 1–20 feet (30–600 cm) tall and as wide or slightly wider, varying with cultivar; *R. arborescens:* to 9 feet (2.7 m) tall but not as wide; *R. calendulaceum:* to 10 feet (3 m) tall but not as wide; *R. carolinianum:* to 6 feet (1.8 m) tall and as wide; *R. catawbiense:* to 12 feet (3.6 m) tall and as wide.

BEST CLIMATE AND SITE: Hybrids: Zones 4–9, varying with cultivar. *R. arborescens* and *R. catawbiense:* Zones 4–8; *R. calendulaceum* and *R. carolinianum:* Zones 5–8. Moist, acid soil. Light shade.

CULTIVATION: Transplant container-grown or balled-and-burlapped plants in spring. Prune after flowering to control size if necessary.

PROPAGATION: Take cuttings in midsummer. Layer in summer. Sow seed indoors in late winter.

PEST AND DISEASE PREVENTION: Avoid planting in poorly drained soil. Mulch with compost or aged manure to keep the shallow roots cool and moist.

R. calendulaceum, *flame azalea, is a very showy deciduous plant native to the eastern United States. The flowers bloom just before or as the new leaves emerge in spring.*

COMMON PROBLEMS: Very sensitive to salinity and high pH.

LANDSCAPE USE: Foundation plantings; specimen shrub; massed plantings; containers.

OTHER COMMON NAMES: Azalea.

HYBRIDS: Innumerable. Several groups are listed.

Exbury azaleas are deciduous: 'Berry Rose' has rose pink flowers. 'Firefly' has red flowers. 'Gibraltar' has bright orange flowers. 'Sun Chariot' has yellow flowers. 'White Swan' has white flowers.

Gable hybrid azaleas are small-leaved and evergreen: 'David Gable' has rose pink flowers. 'Girard's Red' has red flowers. 'Purple Splendor' has purple flowers. 'Rose Greeley' has white flowers.

Ghent azaleas are deciduous, with single or double flowers: 'Bouquet de Flore' has bright pink flowers. 'Daviesii' has white flowers.

SPECIES:

R. arborescens, sweet azalea, has bright green deciduous leaves that turn rich red in fall.

R. calendulaceum, flame azalea, has an upright habit and medium-green deciduous leaves.

R. carolinianum, Carolina rhododendron, is an evergreen shrub with 3-inch (7.5 cm) dark green leaves that are brownish on the undersides.

R. catawbiense, Catawba rhododendron, has evergreen leaves. It is the parent of many hybrids.

ROSE

Floribunda roses, such as the red-flowered 'Europeana', bear large clusters of flowers on vigorous plants. The long-lasting blooms add a splash of color to any sunny garden.

Hybrid tea roses have long been prized for their elegant flowers and delightful fragrance. 'Peace' is a classic cultivar with large pale yellow flowers edged in pink.

FLOWER COLOR AND SEASON: White, pink, orange, yellow, red, lavender, or multicolored single or double flowers, often fragrant, from late spring to late summer, depending on the type and cultivar.

HEIGHT AND SPREAD: Depends on type and cultivar.

BEST CLIMATE AND SITE: Zones 4–10, varying with cultivar. Deep, moist, well-drained, humus-rich soil. Full sun.

CULTIVATION: Transplant bareroot plants in fall or winter or container-grown plants in fall or spring. So-called 'climbing' types often attach themselves to their supports by their thorns but still need to be fastened or tied. Fertilize regularly in spring and again in summer to ensure many blooms. Prune hybrid tea and floribunda roses in early spring, and climbers and species roses after flowering.

PROPAGATION: Take softwood cuttings in summer, hardwood cuttings in winter. Layer in spring or fall. Remove seed from its fleshy covering and sow in spring or fall. Bud-graft hybrids in spring.

PEST AND DISEASE PREVENTION: Choose a site with full sun and good air circulation. Plant disease-resistant species and cultivars. Avoid wetting foliage when watering to reduce the incidence of black spot on the leaves. If aphids or spider mites attack, spray with insecticidal soap. Knock Japanese beetles into a bucket of soapy water.

COMMON PROBLEMS: Hardiness varies greatly among species and cultivars. Some plants may be damaged or killed by cold winter temperatures.

LANDSCAPE USE: Shrub or flower borders; containers.

HYBRIDS: Thousands of hybrid cultivars are available, varying in color, size and form of flower, and fragrance. A few of the best are listed here.

Hybrid teas produce large flowers borne singly on long stems. 'Michelle Meilland' bears light pink-and-cream fragrant flowers. 'Mister Lincoln' has deep red very fragrant flowers. 'Pascali' has white lightly fragrant flowers. 'Peace' is very vigorous with pink-and-yellow flowers. 'Queen Elizabeth' is very vigorous with pink lightly fragrant flowers.

Floribundas bear clusters of smaller flowers on shorter stems. 'Angel Face' has very fragrant semi-double lavender flowers. 'Betty Prior' has deep pink flowers. 'Europeana' has rich red flowers. 'Gold Badge' has rich yellow flowers. 'Iceberg' has fragrant white flowers, touched with pink.

SPECIES:

R. rugosa, rugosa rose, has red, pink, or white spring flowers and rough foliage that turns gorgeous orange in fall. It is tolerant of seaside conditions and less subject to pests and diseases than most. 'Albo-plena' bears double white flowers. 'Plena' has double reddish flowers. Zones 3–10.

THUNBERG SPIREA

LACE SHRUB

Thunberg spirea is a small twiggy deciduous shrub that produces masses of small white flowers in spring before the leaves appear. The foliage turns yellowish orange in fall.

FLOWER COLOR AND SEASON: Clusters of small white flowers in midspring.

HEIGHT AND SPREAD: To 5 feet (1.5 m) tall and as wide or slightly wider.

BEST CLIMATE AND SITE: Zones 4–8. Tolerates a wide range of soil conditions. Full sun to partial shade.

CULTIVATION: Plant in spring. Prune after flowering.

PROPAGATION: Sow fresh seed in summer. Take cuttings in midsummer. Divide in spring or fall.

PEST AND DISEASE PREVENTION: Avoid overfeeding, which promotes succulent growth that is attractive to aphids. If these pests become a problem, spray with insecticidal soap.

COMMON PROBLEMS: Will not thrive in poorly drained soils.

LANDSCAPE USE: Informal low hedges; shrub borders; specimen shrub.

OTHER SPECIES:

> *S. japonica,* Japanese spirea, produces small pink flowers in flat clusters in late spring to early summer. 'Atro-sanguinea' has deep red flowers. 'Ruberrima' has deep pink flowers. 'Shirobana' has white, pink, and red flowers borne simultaneously. Zones 5–9.

> *S.* x *vanhouttei,* Vanhoutte spirea, is a hybrid of arching habit with deciduous foliage. Clusters of white flowers bloom in late spring. Zones 4–8.

Lace shrub is a dense, compact deciduous plant native to Japan and Korea. Its leaves are small and very finely cut, and they turn purple or red in fall. It tends to spread by suckering.

FLOWER COLOR AND SEASON: Greenish white flowers in small clusters in late spring; little landscape effect.

HEIGHT AND SPREAD: To 5 feet (1.5 cm) tall and as wide.

BEST CLIMATE AND SITE: Zones 5–9. Widely tolerant of varying soil conditions, but prefers moist, well-drained, acid soil. Full sun to light shade.

CULTIVATION: Transplant container-grown plants in spring. Pruning is unnecessary.

PROPAGATION: Take cuttings in summer. Divide in spring.

PEST AND DISEASE PREVENTION: No serious pests or diseases.

COMMON PROBLEMS: When exposed to winter winds, tips of branches may die back.

LANDSCAPE USE: Fine-textured low hedges that require virtually no trimming.

OTHER COMMON NAMES: Cut-leaved stephanandra.

CULTIVARS: 'Crispa' is a very dwarf, dense form.

Syringa vulgaris   Oleaceae

COMMON LILAC

Common lilac is a deciduous shrub with heart-shaped leaves. The species bears lavender purple spring flowers, but cultivars with white, pink, or blue flowers are also available.

FLOWER COLOR AND SEASON: Very fragrant lavender flowers in long clusters in mid- to late spring.

HEIGHT AND SPREAD: To 20 feet (6 m) tall and 12 feet (3.6 m) wide.

BEST CLIMATE AND SITE: Zones 3–7. Neutral or somewhat alkaline, humus-rich, well-drained soil. Full sun to light shade.

CULTIVATION: Plant in fall or spring. Prune after flowering to remove spent flowers and to prevent seed formation. Also cut a few of the oldest stems to the ground each year.

PROPAGATION: Take cuttings in fall. Layer in spring or summer.

PEST AND DISEASE PREVENTION: Thoroughly clean up dropped leaves to remove overwintering sites for disease spores. Select sites with good air circulation.

COMMON PROBLEMS: Lilacs are sometimes grafted onto privet (*Ligustrum* spp.) rootstocks, which produce suckers. Prune off suckers as they appear.

LANDSCAPE USE: Specimen shrub; shrub borders; screens or hedges.

CULTIVARS: 'Lavender Lady' bears lavender flowers and blooms reliably in areas too warm for other lilacs. 'Miss Ellen Willmott' bears double white flowers. 'President Lincoln' has single blue flowers. 'Sensation' has wine red flowers edged in white.

Taxus baccata   Taxaceae

ENGLISH YEW

English yew is a narrow-leaved evergreen shrub native throughout Europe. Its habit ranges from upright and tree-shaped to prostrate and spreading.

FLOWER COLOR AND SEASON: Inconspicuous white flowers in early summer; followed by red fruit on female plants.

HEIGHT AND SPREAD: To 60 feet (18 m) tall and 40 feet (12 m) wide.

BEST CLIMATE AND SITE: Zones 6–8. Virtually any well-drained soil. Full sun to partial shade.

CULTIVATION: Transplant container-grown or balled-and-burlapped plants in spring. Take cuttings in late summer or fall. Prune to shape in spring and late summer.

PROPAGATION: Sow seed in spring. Take cuttings in late summer or fall. Layer in fall.

PEST AND DISEASE PREVENTION: Subject to scales and black vine weevil. Encourage native biological controls. Weak plants are more vulnerable to attack; avoid planting in water-logged sites.

COMMON PROBLEMS: Foliage, bark, and seeds are toxic when ingested.

LANDSCAPE USE: Foundation plants; hedges; topiaries.

CULTIVARS: 'Adpressa' has a naturally rounded form. 'Fastigiata' has a columnar form.

OTHER SPECIES:

T. x *media,* Anglojapanese yew, usually grows in pyramidal or spreading form up to 30 feet (9 m) tall. Zones 4–8.

| *Viburnum carlesii* | Caprifoliaceae | *Weigela florida* | Caprifoliaceae |

FRAGRANT VIBURNUM

OLD-FASHIONED WEIGELA

Fragrant viburnum is a deciduous shrub with dark green leaves that turn purplish red in fall. The pink flower buds open to sweetly scented white flowers in spring.

FLOWER COLOR AND SEASON: Very fragrant white flowers tinged with pink in midspring; followed by blue-black fruit.

HEIGHT AND SPREAD: To 5 feet (1.5 m) tall and nearly as wide.

BEST CLIMATE AND SITE: Zones 4–9. Virtually any well-drained soil. Full sun to light shade.

CULTIVATION: Plant in fall or spring. If necessary, prune after flowering to shape the plant.

PROPAGATION: Take cuttings in summer. Sow seed when ripe. Layer in fall.

PEST AND DISEASE PREVENTION: Avoid overfeeding, which encourages succulent growth attractive to aphids. If aphids attack, spray with insecticidal soap. Clean up dropped leaves to remove over-wintering sites for mildew spores.

COMMON PROBLEMS: Avoid poorly drained soils.

LANDSCAPE USE: Specimen shrub; shrub borders; screens or hedges.

OTHER SPECIES:

V. opulus, European cranberrybush viburnum, has clusters of white flowers in midspring, yellowish to purplish red fall color, and red fruit that persists into winter. Zones 3–8.

V. plicatum var. *tomentosum,* double file viburnum, has large flower clusters and markedly horizontal branching. Zones 4–9.

Old-fashioned weigela is an opposite-leaved, free-flowering deciduous shrub native to Korea and northern China. It is commonly grown for its pink spring flowers.

FLOWER COLOR AND SEASON: Funnel-shaped, rosy pink flowers in late spring.

HEIGHT AND SPREAD: To 8 feet (2.4 m) tall and nearly as wide.

BEST CLIMATE AND SITE: Zones 4–8. Cool, deep, moist, humus-rich, well-drained soil. Full sun to light shade.

CULTIVATION: Transplant bareroot or container-grown plants in spring or fall. Prune back severely after flowering.

PROPAGATION: Take cuttings in summer.

PEST AND DISEASE PREVENTION: No serious pests or diseases.

COMMON PROBLEMS: Old canes produce few flowers.

LANDSCAPE USE: Shrub borders; mass plantings.

CULTIVARS: 'Bristol Ruby' has ruby red flowers. 'Bristol Snowflake' has white flowers tinged with pink. 'Candida' has pure white flowers. 'Eva Supreme' is very dwarf with deep red flowers. 'Foliis Purpureis' is a dwarf form with purplish foliage. 'Variegata' has leaves edged with pale yellow.

VARIETIES: The variety *venusta* is hardier than the species with purplish pink flowers.

Actinidia kolomikta   Actinidiaceae

HARDY KIWI

Hardy kiwi is a twining deciduous vine with heart-shaped leaves. The foliage is purple at first and later becomes variegated with pink and white, especially on male plants.

FLOWER COLOR AND SEASON: Fragrant white or green flowers in late spring and early summer; followed by edible green fruit on female plants.

HEIGHT: To 20 feet (6 m) with support.

BEST CLIMATE AND SITE: Zones 4–10. Moist, well-drained soil. Full sun to partial shade. Best color when soil is alkaline.

CULTIVATION: Plant in early spring. Prune in winter if necessary. Male and female flowers are borne on separate plants. You'll need to buy one male for every three to four female plants to get fruit on the females.

PROPAGATION: Layer in spring. Take cuttings in midsummer.

PEST AND DISEASE PREVENTION: Keep soil moist in hot weather. No serious pests or diseases.

COMMON PROBLEMS: Intolerant of drought.

LANDSCAPE USE: Excellent foliage vines to use on wire supports.

OTHER COMMON NAMES: Cape gooseberry, kolomikta vine.

OTHER SPECIES:

A. arguta, hardy kiwi or tara vine, has very large shiny leaves and bears edible greenish fruit. 'Issai' can produce fruit without a male vine.

| *Allamanda cathartica* Apocynaceae | *Ampelopsis brevipedunculata* Vitaceae |

COMMON ALLAMANDA

PORCELAIN AMPELOPSIS

Native to South America, common allamanda is a vigorous, evergreen twining vine with opposite or whorled glossy leaves, 4–6 inches (10–15 cm) long.

FLOWER COLOR AND SEASON: 5-inch (12.5 cm) trumpet-shaped bright yellow flowers with paler throats in summer; followed by spiny fruit.

HEIGHT: To 17 feet (5 m) with support.

BEST CLIMATE AND SITE: Zone 10. Humus-rich, well-drained, neutral to acid soil. Partial shade.

CULTIVATION: Plant in spring. Requires frequent feeding. Stake stems to provide support. Water freely when in active growth, less when dormant. Prune in spring.

PROPAGATION: Take softwood cuttings in spring or summer.

PEST AND DISEASE PREVENTION: Mulch with organic matter to keep soil evenly moist. No serious pests or diseases in a garden. Subject to whiteflies and spider mites when grown in a greenhouse. Spray with an organically acceptable insecticide, such as insecticidal soap, to deter pests.

COMMON PROBLEMS: Very frost-sensitive.

LANDSCAPE USE: An excellent vine to grow on fences and walls in warm climates; elsewhere, a good greenhouse plant.

CULTIVARS: 'Hendersonii' has leathery, glossy leaves and buds tinged brown. Very free-flowering.

A deciduous vine native to Asia, porcelain ampelopsis bears three- or occasionally five-lobed leaves and distinctly hairy young shoots. It is a vigorous grower, climbing by tendrils.

FLOWER COLOR AND SEASON: Clusters of small white flowers in late spring; followed by clustered fruits of amethyst-blue in fall.

HEIGHT: To 20 feet (6 m) with support.

BEST CLIMATE AND SITE: Zones 4–9. Humus-rich, moist, well-drained soil. Full sun to partial shade.

CULTIVATION: Plant in winter or spring. Grows quickly. Cut to ground in late winter to produce new fruiting growth.

PROPAGATION: Take cuttings in midsummer.

PEST AND DISEASE PREVENTION: Avoid planting in poorly drained soil.

COMMON PROBLEMS: Japanese beetles may attack and skeletonize the leaves. Shake beetles from plants into a bucket of soapy water in early morning. Deter with an organically acceptable insecticide.

LANDSCAPE USE: Chiefly valued for its striking fruit. Grow on fences, arbors, or trellises.

OTHER COMMON NAMES: Porcelain vine.

CULTIVARS: 'Elegans' has foliage handsomely variegated with white and pink. Less hardy than the species. Zones 5–9.

VARIETIES: *A. brevipedunculata* var. *maximowiczii* has leaves more deeply lobed than the species.

Aristolochia elegans   Aristolochiaceae

CALICO DUTCHMAN'S PIPE

Calico Dutchman's pipe is a twining evergreen vine with heart-shaped alternate leaves. The speckled flowers are curiously twisted and resemble a curved smoking pipe.

FLOWER COLOR AND SEASON: 3-inch (7.5 cm) purple-and-yellow scentless flowers in late spring and early summer.

HEIGHT: 10–15 feet (3.5–5 m) with support.

BEST CLIMATE AND SITE: Zones 9–11. Rich, loamy, moisture-retentive but well-drained soil. Full sun to partial shade.

CULTIVATION: Transplant container-grown plants in spring. Cut back in winter to control size.

PROPAGATION: Take stem cuttings in early summer or root cuttings in late winter. Sow seed in spring.

PEST AND DISEASE PREVENTION: Avoid poorly drained soil.

COMMON PROBLEMS: Occasionally susceptible to spider mites, which cause yellow curled leaves with fine webs on undersides. Deter with an organically acceptable insecticide, such as insecticidal soap.

LANDSCAPE USE: Grow on fences or trellises; excellent for screening.

OTHER SPECIES:
  A. macrophylla (durior), Dutchman's pipe, is deciduous with leaves up to 1 foot (30 cm) long. Green-and-yellow flowers bloom in late spring and early summer on vines that can reach 20–30 feet (6–9 m) tall with support. Zones 4–8.

Bougainvillea glabra   Nyctaginaceae

LESSER BOUGAINVILLEA

Native to Brazil, lesser bougainvillea is a spiny alternate-leaved vine that occasionally grows into a loose shrub. The small summer flowers are surrounded by showy bracts.

FLOWER COLOR AND SEASON: Inconspicuous flowers surrounded by brilliantly colored bracts of red, yellow, purple, white, or magenta all summer.

HEIGHT: To 20–30 feet (6–9 m) with support.

BEST CLIMATE AND SITE: Zone 10. Well-drained, humus-rich soil. Full sun.

CULTIVATION: Plant in spring. Cut back severely after flowering to maintain desired shape and size. Mulch freely in spring with aged cow manure or compost.

PROPAGATION: Take cuttings during active growth.

PEST AND DISEASE PREVENTION: Avoid damaging with pruning tools; these wounds are common entry points for pests and diseases.

COMMON PROBLEMS: Vigorously growing plants often produce ferocious thorns; avoid planting in areas where children play or where passersby will come in contact with the thorns.

LANDSCAPE USE: Where hardy, excellent to cover trellises and porches or to hang over walls and banks. Elsewhere, a lovely hanging basket plant.

OTHER COMMON NAMES: Paper flower.

HYBRIDS: Many hybrid cultivars are available. 'Barbara Karst' has brilliant red bracts. 'California Gold' bears golden yellow bracts. 'Cherry Blossom' has rose pink bracts with a white or light green eye. 'Jamaica White' has white bracts, sometimes tinged with pink. 'Tahitian Maid' has bluish pink bracts.

TRUMPET VINE   CLEMATIS

Trumpet vine is a summer-blooming deciduous climber that supports itself by means of root-like holdfasts. Its leaves are pinnately compound, with 7–11 leaflets.

FLOWER COLOR AND SEASON: Orange or red flowers, borne in pendulous, terminal clusters of 2-inch (5 cm) wide, trumpet-shaped blooms in early to late summer.

HEIGHT: 30–40 feet (9–12 m) with support.

BEST CLIMATE AND SITE: Zones 4–9. Virtually any well-drained soil. Full sun.

CULTIVATION: Plant in early spring. Prune in spring to restrain growth. Often needs additional support because of its weight.

PROPAGATION: Take cuttings in spring to summer; layer in fall to spring; sow seed in spring.

PEST AND DISEASE PREVENTION: Enrich soil with organic matter to promote healthy growth. No serious pests or diseases.

COMMON PROBLEMS: *C. radicans* can become invasive, as it tends to spread by underground runners. Remove unwanted shoots at soil level.

LANDSCAPE USE: Excellent flowering vines for fences, walls, and trellises or to climb up trees.

CULTIVARS: 'Fiava' bears yellow flowers.

OTHER SPECIES:

C. *grandiflora*, Chinese trumpet creeper, native to China, is somewhat less rampant. Its leaves consist of seven to nine leaflets. Zones 7–11.

Clematis are usually deciduous vines with opposite, compound leaves that climb by twining. C. montana 'Rubens' has fragrant lavender-pink flowers in early summer.

FLOWER COLOR AND SEASON: Hybrids: White, pink, red, blue, lavender, or purple blooms, in early summer to midfall—varying with cultivar; *C. x jackmanii*: rich purple flowers in early summer and again in early fall; *C. maximowicziana*: very fragrant white flowers in late summer to early fall; *C. montana*: white or pink flowers in early summer.

HEIGHT: 8–24 feet (2.4–7.2 m) with support, varying with species or cultivar.

BEST CLIMATE AND SITE: Zones 5–9. Moisture-retentive, humus-rich soil. Full sun at the tops, partial shade at the roots.

CULTIVATION: Plant during spring or fall. Spring-blooming types flower on the previous year's growth; prune after flowering to remove dead wood and to shape the plant. Summer and fall bloomers generally flower on the current year's growth; prune these in late winter or early spring. Many clematis tend to die back during winter in the colder parts of their range. Mulch around the root of the climber to keep it cool. Water regularly during hot weather.

PROPAGATION: Take cuttings in spring or early summer. Layer in spring.

PEST AND DISEASE PREVENTION: When planting, set the crown 2–3 inches (5–7.5 cm) below the soil surface to encourage strong, healthy growth.

BLEEDING GLORYBOWER

The hybrid 'Niobe' has rich red flowers in early summer and again in early fall. To keep it vigorous, trim the stems back to just above a set of plump buds by early spring.

COMMON PROBLEMS: Clematis borer may occasionally be a problem. Prune off damaged canes and seal ends with paraffin. Clematis wilt, a disease of unknown origin, can kill vines to the ground; deeply set plants may recover.

LANDSCAPE USE: Outstanding flowering vines to grow on arbors, trellises, or even to intertwine with climbing roses.

SPECIES:

C. x *jackmanii,* Jackman clematis, is a popular summer-flowering hybrid that usually reblooms in fall.

C. maximowicziana, sweet autumn clematis, is a very vigorous plant, with compound leaves of three to five leaflets.

C. montana, anemone clematis, has three leaflets to each leaf. 'Grandiflora' has white flowers, 3–4 inches (7.5–10 cm) across.

HYBRIDS: Many hundreds of hybrids, varying in vigor, color, and flowering period. A few of the most popular are: 'General Sikorski', lavender-blue flowers in early summer and again in fall; 'Henryi', white flowers in early summer and again in early fall; 'Nelly Moser', soft-pink flowers marked with red in early summer.

Native to West Africa, bleeding glorybower is a twining evergreen vine with opposite 5-inch (12.5 cm) leaves. The showy red-and-white flowers bloom from summer into fall.

FLOWER COLOR AND SEASON: Clusters of flowers with red petals, striking white calyces, and long, curving, protruding stamens in summer and fall.

HEIGHT: To 10 feet (3 m) with support.

BEST CLIMATE AND SITE: Zones 9–10. Rich, loamy, moisture-retentive soil. Partial shade.

CULTIVATION: Plant in spring. Prune lightly after flowering if needed to control growth. Never allow to dry out.

PROPAGATION: Sow seed in spring. Take cuttings in spring and summer.

PEST AND DISEASE PREVENTION: Avoid overwatering during winter when plant is not growing as quickly. Mulch with organic matter to keep soil evenly moist during spring and summer.

COMMON PROBLEMS: Drought-sensitive.

LANDSCAPE USE: Where hardy, grow on a fence or trellis. Elsewhere, a fine hanging-basket plant.

OTHER COMMON NAMES: Bag flower, bleeding heart vine, glory tree, tropical bleeding heart.

Gelsemium sempervirens　　　　　Loganiaceae

Yellow Jessamine

Native to the southeastern United States, yellow jessamine is a twining vine with glossy opposite leaves; it is evergreen in the warmer portions of its range.

FLOWER COLOR AND SEASON: Funnel-shaped, fragrant yellow flowers borne in axillary clusters in early to midspring.

HEIGHT: To 20 feet (6 m) with support.

BEST CLIMATE AND SITE: Zones 7–10. Virtually any well-drained soil. Full sun to light shade.

CULTIVATION: Transplant container-grown plants in spring. If necessary, prune after flowering to control growth.

PROPAGATION: Take cuttings in summer. Sow seed in spring.

PEST AND DISEASE PREVENTION: Avoid waterlogged sites. No serious pests or diseases.

COMMON PROBLEMS: Flowers, leaves, and roots are poisonous when eaten. Keep children and animals away from plants.

LANDSCAPE USE: Excellent flowering vine for woodland plantings or as a groundcover for banks. Plant on a fence, trellis, or arch as a screen.

OTHER COMMON NAMES: Carolina jasmine, evening trumpet flower, woodbine.

CULTIVARS: 'Pride of Augusta' ('Plena') is a vigorous and free-flowering double form.

Hedera helix　　　　　　　　　　Araliaceae

English Ivy

English ivy is a vigorous evergreen vine native throughout Europe. It climbs by means of root-like holdfasts. Leaves are lobed, except on mature, fruiting stems.

FLOWER COLOR AND SEASON: Cream-colored flowers on mature plants in fall; followed by inconspicuous black fruit.

HEIGHT: 30–40 feet (9–12 m) with support.

BEST CLIMATE AND SITE: Zones 5–10. Virtually any well-drained soil. Full sun to partial shade.

CULTIVATION: Plant in spring or fall. In colder zones shield from winter sun. Cut back in late winter to promote denser growth.

PROPAGATION: Cuttings root easily in spring or summer. Layer in spring or summer.

PEST AND DISEASE PREVENTION: Choose a site with good air circulation and thoroughly clean up all dropped leaves to remove overwintering sites for disease spores.

COMMON PROBLEMS: In colder areas leaves tend to turn brown if exposed to winter afternoon sun. Subject to attack by scales, mealybugs, and red spider mites; deter with organically acceptable insecticides. Bacterial leaf spot may also be a problem; destroy infected plants.

LANDSCAPE USE: Excellent foliage vines to climb walls and trees or to use as groundcover.

CULTIVARS: *H. helix* has numerous cultivars differing in hardiness, leaf size, and form. '238th St.' is a hardy form resistant to winter burn. 'Baltica' is a hardy form with small leaves.

Humulus lupulus   Cannabaceae

HOP

Hops are hardy, deciduous twining vines with large, three- to five-lobed leaves. The female plants are the source of hops used in the commercial brewing industry.

FLOWER COLOR AND SEASON: Insignificant greenish flowers in late spring; followed, on female plants, by green cone-like pods.

HEIGHT: To 30 feet (9 m) with support.

BEST CLIMATE AND SITE: Zones 3–8. Virtually any well-drained soil. Full sun to light shade. Best where nights are cool and moist.

CULTIVATION: Plant in spring. Prune to the ground after frost.

PROPAGATION: Take cuttings in spring.

PEST AND DISEASE PREVENTION: No serious pests or diseases.

COMMON PROBLEMS: Can be invasive.

LANDSCAPE USE: A fast-growing cover or screen vine for a trellis, arch, or pergola.

CULTIVARS: 'Aureus' has attractive golden yellow leaves.

Hydrangea anomala subsp. *petiolaris* Hydrangeaceae

CLIMBING HYDRANGEA

Climbing hydrangea is a deciduous vine with rounded, glossy dark green leaves, white summer flowers, and peeling brown bark. It climbs by means of root-like holdfasts.

FLOWER COLOR AND SEASON: White flattened clusters with large, sterile flowers on the outside of the clusters and small fertile ones in the center; early summer.

HEIGHT: To 60 feet (18 m) with support.

BEST CLIMATE AND SITE: Zones 4–9. Virtually any moisture-retentive soil. Full sun to nearly full shade.

CULTIVATION: Transplant container-grown plants in spring. Prune only if necessary to maintain shape.

PROPAGATION: Take cuttings in early summer.

PEST AND DISEASE PREVENTION: Mulch with organic matter to keep the soil evenly moist. No serious pests or diseases.

COMMON PROBLEMS: Often very slow to grow until established.

LANDSCAPE USE: A superb flowering vine for walls or to climb on trees or over boulders.

Ipomoea purpurea   Convolvulaceae

COMMON MORNING GLORY

Common morning glory is a twining vine that is grown in many gardens for its colorful flowers. Although perennial in the warmest zones, it is most commonly used as an annual.

FLOWER COLOR AND SEASON: White, pink, red, blue, or variegated, varying with the species and cultivar; summer to early fall.

HEIGHT: To 15 feet (5 m) with support.

BEST CLIMATE AND SITE: Zone 10; grow it as an annual in colder regions. Rather dry, moderately fertile soil. Full sun.

CULTIVATION: Plant in spring. Water freely during spring and summer and less at other times. Thin out or cut back congested growth of perennials in spring.

PROPAGATION: Sow seed in spring. Take cuttings in summer.

PEST AND DISEASE PREVENTION: Avoid overfeeding, which promotes succulent growth that is attractive to pests.

COMMON PROBLEMS: Seedlings slow to develop. Excessive fertility and moisture can promote vegetative growth at the expense of flowers.

LANDSCAPE USE: Use on a trellis or fence or grow in containers.

OTHER SPECIES:

I. alba, moonflower, is also sold as *Calonyction aculeatum*. It bears oval or three-lobed leaves and fragrant white flowers that open at night.

I. nil bears large flowers in a range of colors.

Jasminum officinale   Oleaceae

COMMON WHITE JASMINE

Native to the Near East and China, common white jasmine is a vigorous semi-evergreen vine or loose shrub with compound leaves. The white flowers are delightfully fragrant.

FLOWER COLOR AND SEASON: Very fragrant white flowers in late spring to late summer.

HEIGHT: 30 feet (9 m) with support.

BEST CLIMATE AND SITE: Zones 8–10. Moist, humus-rich, well-drained soil. Full sun to light shade.

CULTIVATION: Plant during spring. Prune after flowering to keep vigorous growth under control.

PROPAGATION: Take cuttings during active growth in spring or fall.

PEST AND DISEASE PREVENTION: Keep soil evenly moist in summer to avoid stressing the plant. No serious pests or diseases.

COMMON PROBLEMS: Needs protection, such as a warm wall, in all but the warmest zones.

LANDSCAPE USE: Where hardy, excellent for growing on trellises or arbors.

OTHER COMMON NAMES: Poet's jessamine.

VARIETIES: *J. officinale* var. *grandiflorum* bears larger flowers, up to 1¾ inches (4.3 cm) across.

Lonicera periclymenum   Caprifoliaceae

WOODBINE HONEYSUCKLE

Woodbine honeysuckle is a scrambling shrub or vine with oval, deciduous leaves. The fragrant late-spring to late-summer flowers are followed by small red berries.

FLOWER COLOR AND SEASON: Fragrant flowers in varying proportions of yellow, white, and red in late spring to late summer.

HEIGHT: To 30 feet (9 m) with support.

BEST CLIMATE AND SITE: Zones 4–9. Moist, humus-rich, well-drained soil. Full sun to partial shade.

CULTIVATION: Plant in spring. Prune after flowering to keep vigorous growth under control.

PROPAGATION: Take cuttings in early spring.

PEST AND DISEASE PREVENTION: Mulch with organic matter to keep soil evenly moist.

COMMON PROBLEMS: Subject to scales which suck the plant sap, weakening plants and causing them to turn yellow. Prune and destroy infested parts; spray remaining stems with organically acceptable insecticide like horticultural oil.

LANDSCAPE USE: Well suited for clambering over bushes and fences.

OTHER SPECIES:
L. x *heckrottii,* goldflame honeysuckle, is a handsome, twining vine with blue-green leaves and reddish flowers with yellow centers.
L. *sempervirens,* trumpet honeysuckle, is a shrubby climber that is evergreen in the warmer portions of its range. It bears nonfragrant orange-scarlet flowers with yellow centers. 'Sulphurea' bears yellow flowers.

Mandevilla suaveolens (syn. *M. laxa*) Apocynaceae

CHILEAN JASMINE

Chilean jasmine is a fast-growing, twining semi-evergreen vine with narrow heart-shaped leaves. Clusters of fragrant white flowers grace the plant in summer.

FLOWER COLOR AND SEASON: Very fragrant white to pinkish trumpet-shaped flowers borne in clusters in late spring to midsummer.

HEIGHT: To 20 feet (6 m) with support.

BEST CLIMATE AND SITE: Zones 9–10. Any well-drained, humus-rich soil. Full sun to light shade.

CULTIVATION: Plant in spring. Water freely when in full growth; sparingly at other times. Thin out and cut back in early spring.

PROPAGATION: Take cuttings or sow seed in spring.

PEST AND DISEASE PREVENTION: No serious pests or diseases when grown outdoors. As a greenhouse plant, whiteflies and spider mites may cause trouble. Spray with insecticidal soap to deter pests.

COMMON PROBLEMS: Very sensitive to frost.

LANDSCAPE USE: Where hardy, an excellent plant for growing on a pillar. Elsewhere, a lovely greenhouse or hanging-basket plant.

Mina lobata (syn. *Quamoclit lobata*) Convolvulaceae

CRIMSON STARGLORY

Crimson starglory is a vigorous, twining herbaceous vine with alternate three-lobed leaves. Clusters of reddish flower buds fade to orange and yellow as the flowers open.

FLOWER COLOR AND SEASON: Long-stalked clusters of fiery scarlet buds and creamy yellow-and-orange flowers all summer.

HEIGHT: To 20 feet (6 m) with support.

BEST CLIMATE AND SITE: Zones 8–10; in colder regions, treat as an annual. Light, well-drained soil. Full sun to light shade.

CULTIVATION: Plant in spring. Mulch with organic matter to keep soil evenly moist.

PROPAGATION: Start seed indoors in pots about 5 weeks before planting outside.

PEST AND DISEASE PREVENTION: No significant pest or disease problems.

COMMON PROBLEMS: Will not thrive in poorly drained soil or in dense shade.

LANDSCAPE USE: Use on a trellis or fence.

Parthenocissus tricuspidata   Vitaceae

BOSTON IVY

Boston ivy is a deciduous vine that climbs by means of root-like holdfasts. The large, maple-like three-lobed leaves turn from lustrous green to brilliant scarlet in fall.

FLOWER COLOR AND SEASON: Inconspicuous creamy white flowers in late spring; followed by purple fruit.

HEIGHT: To 60 feet (18 m) with support.

BEST CLIMATE AND SITE: Zones 4–10. Humus-rich, well-drained soil. Full sun to light shade.

CULTIVATION: Transplant container-grown plants in spring. Prune only to control growth in early spring.

PROPAGATION: Take softwood cuttings in late summer; hardwood cuttings in early spring.

PEST AND DISEASE PREVENTION: Avoid overfeeding, which provides succulent growth that is attractive to pests.

COMMON PROBLEMS: Sometimes slow to become established. Japanese beetles, which skeletonize leaves, may be a major problem. Shake beetles into a bucket of soapy water. Scales, mildew, and leaf spot may also appear. Prune and destroy infested parts.

LANDSCAPE USE: The premier foliage vine to mask a wall.

OTHER COMMON NAMES: Japanese ivy.

CULTIVARS: 'Lowii' has small leaves that are sometimes purple when young. 'Veitchii' bears small purple leaves.

Passiflora caerulea   Passifloraceae

BLUE PASSIONFLOWER

Blue passionflower is a deciduous summer-flowering vine that climbs by means of tendrils. It dies back to the roots each winter in the colder portions of its range.

FLOWER COLOR AND SEASON: Blue or (rarely) white flowers in summer; followed by conspicuous orange fruit.

HEIGHT: To 12 feet (3.6 m) with support.

BEST CLIMATE AND SITE: Zones 7–10. Well-drained, humus-rich soil. Full sun to light shade.

CULTIVATION: Plant in spring near a warm wall for winter protection.

PROPAGATION: Sow seed in spring. Take cuttings in summer.

PEST AND DISEASE PREVENTION: Mulch with organic matter to keep soil evenly moist. No serious pests or diseases.

COMMON PROBLEMS: Dies back to the ground annually in all but the warmest portions of its range.

LANDSCAPE USE: Grow on a trellis for the flowers and foliage.

CULTIVARS: 'Constance Elliott' is a white-flowered form.

OTHER SPECIES:

P. incarnata, wild passionflower or maypop, is native to the southeastern United States and has three-lobed leaves. It bears white flowers with blue stamens in summer; followed by edible fruit.

Stephanotis floribunda   Asclepiadaceae

MADAGASCAR JASMINE

Madagascar jasmine is a twining opposite-leaved vine with rather large round to oval glossy green leaves. Its waxy white summer flowers are highly fragrant.

FLOWER COLOR AND SEASON: Narrowly tubular waxy white flowers borne in clusters in midspring to fall.

HEIGHT: To 12 feet (3.6 m) with support.

BEST CLIMATE AND SITE: Zone 10. Humus-rich, moisture-retentive soil. Full sun to light shade.

CULTIVATION: Plant in spring. Cut back long or crowded stems in fall.

PROPAGATION: Take cuttings in summer.

PEST AND DISEASE PREVENTION: Keep soil moist with organic mulch. Avoid dry or poorly drained soil. Ensure adequate air circulation.

COMMON PROBLEMS: Subject to scales and mealybugs when grown as a greenhouse plant. Treat plants with insecticidal soap.

LANDSCAPE USE: Where hardy, a compact vine to grow on a trellis. Elsewhere a beautiful greenhouse plant. Also grown for its cut flowers, which are used in bridal bouquets and leis.

Thunbergia alata   Acanthaceae

BLACK-EYED SUSAN VINE

Black-eyed Susan vine is a perennial climber that is commonly grown as an annual. The triangular bright green leaves are accented by the colorful summer flowers.

FLOWER COLOR AND SEASON: White, yellow, or orange blooms, often with purple-black centers, in midsummer.

HEIGHT: To 6 feet (1.8 m) with support.

BEST CLIMATE AND SITE: Zone 10; in colder regions, treat as an annual. Moist, humus-rich, well-drained soil. Full sun to partial shade.

CULTIVATION: Plant in spring. Thin crowded stems in early spring. Water during periods of drought.

PROPAGATION: Sow seed in spring. Take cuttings in summer.

PEST AND DISEASE PREVENTION: Avoid dry or poorly drained soil. No serious pests or diseases.

COMMON PROBLEMS: Very sensitive to frost. Protect with mulch.

LANDSCAPE USE: Use on trellises or fences. Also a good hanging-basket plant.

OTHER COMMON NAMES: Clock vine.

CULTIVARS: The 'Susie' series has white, yellow, or orange flowers, with or without black eyes.

Trachelospermum jasminoides   Apocynaceae

STAR JASMINE

Star jasmine is a rapidly growing, evergreen twining vine with glossy green leaves up to 4 inches (10 cm) long. Its fragrant white flowers bloom in late spring to summer.

FLOWER COLOR AND SEASON: Very fragrant 1-inch (2.5 cm) white flowers borne in small clusters in late spring to early summer.

HEIGHT: To 20 feet (6 m) with support.

BEST CLIMATE AND SITE: Zones 8–10. Moisture-retentive, humus-rich soil. Sun to partial shade.

CULTIVATION: Plant in spring. Mulch to keep roots cool. Prune after flowering to control vigorous growth.

PROPAGATION: Take cuttings in late summer or fall. Sow seed in spring. Layer in summer.

PEST AND DISEASE PREVENTION: Take care not to damage plant when pruning; these wounds are common entry points for pests and diseases.

COMMON PROBLEMS: Tends to grow beyond desired bounds. Prune back annually.

LANDSCAPE USE: Excellent for screening or for growing on a trellis, up trees, or as a groundcover.

OTHER COMMON NAMES: Chinese jasmine, confederate jasmine.

CULTIVARS: 'Japonicum' has white-veined leaves that turn bronze in fall. 'Madison' is reputedly an extra-hardy cultivar. 'Variegatum' has leaves variegated with green and white, often tinged with red.

| *Vitis coignetiae* Vitaceae | *Wisteria floribunda* Leguminosae |

CRIMSON GLORY

JAPANESE WISTERIA

Crimson glory climbs by means of tendrils. It is an extremely rapid grower, capable of covering up to 1,000 square feet (300 m) of trellis in 1 year. It displays red fall color.

Japanese wisteria is a deciduous, vigorous twining climber with alternately compound leaves. The vines are covered with long hanging flower clusters in late spring.

FLOWER COLOR AND SEASON: Clusters of small inconspicuous cream flowers in late spring, followed by black fruit in fall.

HEIGHT: To 100 feet (30 m) with support.

BEST CLIMATE AND SITE: Zones 5–9. Well-drained soil of low nutrient content. Full sun.

CULTIVATION: Plant in winter or spring. Prune to desired dimensions in winter. Provide stout wire or trellis support on which to climb.

PROPAGATION: Layer in fall. Take cuttings in fall; graft in late winter or early spring. Sow seed in spring.

PEST AND DISEASE PREVENTION: Take care not to damage plant when pruning. These wounds are common entry points for pests and diseases.

COMMON PROBLEMS: *V. coignetiae,* as a result of its enormous growth rate, can easily exceed its desired limits. Choose a site carefully to avoid problems. Japanese beetles may skeletonize leaves; shake or brush beetles into a bucket of soapy water.

LANDSCAPE USE: Especially valued for its fall foliage color. An excellent cover for trellises or arbors.

SPECIES:

V. amurensis, amur grape, is a vigorous deciduous vine native to Manchuria. Its leaves are large, up to 10 inches (25 cm) across, three- to five-lobed, and turn crimson or purple in fall. Zones 4–7.

FLOWER COLOR AND SEASON: Long clusters of slightly fragrant white, pink, lavender, or violet flowers in late spring.

HEIGHT: To 50 feet (15m) with support.

BEST CLIMATE AND SITE: Zones 4–10. Moist, well-drained soil preferably with low nitrogen content. Lighter, infertile soil reduces vegetative growth and increases flowering. Full sun to light shade.

CULTIVATION: Plant in spring. Prune after flowering.

PROPAGATION: Take cuttings in late winter and spring. Layer in fall. Graft in late winter or early spring. Sow seed in fall or spring.

PEST AND DISEASE PREVENTION: Avoid poorly drained soil. Stress makes plants more prone to pests and diseases.

COMMON PROBLEMS: Requires stout hardwood or wire support. Plants produced from seed may be slow to bloom. Subject to leaf beetles, webworms, scales, crown gall, leaf spot, canker, and mildew. Treat with organically acceptable controls.

LANDSCAPE USE: Fine vines to climb on stout supports like arches or pergolas. May be trained to standard form.

CULTIVARS: 'Ivory Tower' is a very heavy-blooming white form. 'Plena' has double blue flowers. 'Rosea' has rose pink flowers. 'Royal Purple' bears deep violet purple flowers.

USDA
PLANT HARDINESS ZONE MAP

The map that follows shows the United States and Canada divided into 10 zones. Each zone is based on a 10°F (5.6°C) difference in average annual minimum temperature. Some areas are considered too high in elevation for plant cultivation and so are not assigned to any zone. There are also island zones that are warmer or cooler than surrounding areas because of differences in elevation; they have been given a zone different from the surrounding areas. Many large urban areas are in a warmer zone than the surrounding land.

Plants grow best within an optimum range of temperatures. The range may be wide for some species, and narrow for others. Plants also differ in their ability to survive frost and their sun or shade requirements.

The zone ratings indicate conditions where designated plants will grow well, and not merely survive. Refer to the map to find out which zone you are in. In the "Plant by Plant Guide," starting on page 78, you'll find recommendations for the plants that grow best in your zone.

Many plants may survive in zones warmer or colder than their recommended zone range. Remember that other factors, including wind, soil type, soil moisture and drainage capability, humidity, snow, and winter sunshine, may have a great effect on growth.

Average annual minimum temperature (°F/°C)

Zone 1	Below -50°F/-45°C	Zone 6	0° to -10°F/-18° to -23°C
Zone 2	-40° to -50°F/-40° to -45°C	Zone 7	10° to 0°F/-12° to -18°C
Zone 3	-30° to -40°F/-34° to -40°C	Zone 8	20° to 10°F/-7° to -12°C
Zone 4	-20° to -30°F/-29° to -34°C	Zone 9	30° to 20°F/-1° to -7°C
Zone 5	-10° to -20°F/-23° to -29°C	Zone 10	40° to 30°F/4° to -1°C

ACKNOWLEDGMENTS

Photo Credits

Bruce Coleman Ltd: photographer Hans Reinhard: back cover (bottom) and page 69 (bottom); photographer John Shaw: pages 16 (top) and 81 (left); photographer Carl Wallace: page 25 (top right); photographer Jules Cowan: page 30 (top right); photographer Jack Dermid: page 61 (bottom); photographer M. P. L. Fogden: page 62 (top); photographer G. Dore: page 62 (bottom center); photographer Jeff Foott Productions: page 63 (bottom center); photographer Kim Taylor: page 65 (bottom left); photographer Dr. Frieder Sauer: page 65 (bottom center); photographer John Shaw: page 81 (left); photographer Eric Crichton: page 140 (left).

John Callanan: half title page, pages 17 (top), 28, 31 (top), 47, 56 (left), 68 (top left, top center, top right, and bottom left), 72, 74 (bottom left, bottom center, and bottom right), 77, 81 (right), 82 (left), 84 (right), 90 (left and right), 94 (right), 95 (right), 96 (left and right), 99 (right), 104 (left and right), 107 (left), 131 (right), 134 (right), 136 (right), 139 (left), 140 (right), 143 (right), 145 (left), and 153 (right).

Michael Dirr: Back cover, pages 84 (left), 91 (right), 97 (right), 98 (right), 102 (left and right), 108 (left), 111 (right), 114 (right), 117 (left), 131 (left), 132 (right), 133 (left), and 148 (right).

Thomas Eltzroth: pages 11 (left and right), 56 (right), 82 (right), 88 (right), 91 (left), 92 (left), 93 (left), 95 (left), 103 (right), 105 (right), 108 (right), 109 (left), 112 (left), 124 (left and right), 125 (left), 129 (left), 130 (left), 132 (left), 142 (right), 145 (right), 146 (left), 147 (left), 150 (right), 151 (right), and 152 (left and right).

Derek Fell: endpapers, pages 12, 14 (top left, top right, and bottom), 30 (top left), 32, 33, 37, 52 (bottom left, bottom center, and bottom right), 62 (bottom left), 63 (bottom left), 64 (bottom left and bottom center), 65 (bottom right), 68 (bottom right), 87 (right), 92 (right), 112 (right), and 115 (left).

The Garden Picture Library: photographer J. S. Sira: copyright page, pages 50 and 63 (top); photographer Roger Hyam: page 8; photographer Brian Carter: pages 16 (bottom left), 31 (bottom), 48, and 67 (bottom); photographer Steven Wooster: page 17 (bottom); photographer John Baker: page 18 (bottom right); photographer Linda Burgess: page 29; photographer Clive Nichols: pages 52 (top) and 78; photographer Brigitte Thomas: page 55 (bottom); photographer C. Fairweather: page 64 (bottom right); photographer John Glover: pages 66 and 70; photographer Ron Sutherland: page 100 (left).

Robert E. Lyons: pages 86 (right) and 122 (left).

Stirling Macoboy: pages 80, 83 (left), 85 (right), 99 (left), 137 (left and right), and 143 (left).

Pam Peirce: page 89 (left).

Photos Horticultural: opposite title page, title page, contents page, back cover, pages 6, 16 (bottom right), 18 (top and bottom left), 22, 25 (top left), 26, 27 (left and right), 30 (bottom), 34, 36, 42, 44, 45, 49 (top and bottom), 53 (left), 58, 61 (top), 62 (bottom right), 63 (bottom right), 64 (top), 65 (top), 67 (top), 69 (top), 73 (top and bottom), 74 (top), 75 (top and bottom), 83 (right), 85 (left), 87 (left), 88 (left), 93 (right), 94 (left), 97 (left), 98 (left), 100 (right), 107 (right), 109 (right), 111 (left), 114 (left), 115 (right), 118 (left and right), 119 (left), 120 (left and right), 121 (left), 125 (right), 126 (left and right), 127 (right), 134 (left), 135 (right), 136 (left), 138 (right), 141, 144 (left), 146 (right), 147 (right), 148 (left), 149 (left), 150 (left), 151 (left), and 153 (left).

Rodale Stock Images: pages 24, 46, and 121 (right).

Tony Rodd: pages 101 (right), 110, 113 (left and right), 123 (left and right), 128 (left and right), 130 (right), 133 (right), 135 (left), 138 (left), 139 (right), 142 (left), 144 (right), and 149 (right).

Susan Roth: pages 106 (left and right), 116 (right), 117 (right), and 119 (right).

Anita Sabarese: page 122 (right).

John J. Smith: pages 105 (left) and 116 (left).

David Wallace: pages 57 (top right), 86 (left), 89 (right), 101 (left), 103 (left), 127 (left), and 129 (right).

Weldon Russell: front cover, contents page (top left and bottom left), pages 20, 53 (right), 55 (top), and 57 (top left).